DISCARD

Emotional Connections

ZERO TO THREE wishes to thank the Donnell-Kay Foundation, for generously providing funds that enabled the development and production of this important resource, and the Harris Foundation, for supporting its field tests.

Emotional Connections

How Relationships Guide Early Learning

By
Perry McArthur Butterfield
Carole A. Martin
Arleen Pratt Prairie

ZERO TO THREE PRESS
WASHINGTON, DC

ZERO TO THREE
PRESS

Published by
ZERO TO THREE
2000 M St., NW, Suite 200
Washington, DC 20036-3307
(202) 638-1144; Fax: (202) 638-0851
Toll-free orders: (800) 899-4301
Web: http://www.zerotothree.org

The mission of the ZERO TO THREE Press is to publish authoritative research, practical resources, and new ideas for those who work with and care about infants, toddlers, and their families. Books are selected for publication by an independent Editorial Board.

The opinions and views contained in this book are those of the authors and do not necessarily reflect those of ZERO TO THREE: National Center for Infants, Toddlers and Families, Inc.

Cover design by GO! Creative and text design by Betsy Kulamer

Library of Congress Cataloging-in-Publication Data

Butterfield, Perry M., 1932-
    Emotional connections : how relationships guide early learning / by Perry Butterfield, Carole A. Martin, Arleen Pratt Prairie
        p.   cm.
    Includes bibliographical references.
    ISBN 0-943657-64-4
    1. Emotions in infants. 2. Emotions in children. 3. Children and adults. I. Martin, Carole A. II. Prairie, Arleen. III. Title.

    BF720.E45 B879 2003
    649'.1'0248--dc21   2003008724

Photo credits: pp. ii and 2, Stockbyte; pp. 32 and 182, Eyewire; pp. 44 and 164, Comstock; pp. 66, 100, and 124, Florence Sharp; p. 82, Nancy Alexander; p. 144, Frank Wispell.

First Edition First Printing March 2004
Printed in the United States of America

Suggested citation:

Butterfield, P. M., Martin, C. A., & Prairie, A. P. (2003). *Emotional connections: How relationships guide early learning.* Washington, DC: ZERO TO THREE Press.

29.95   8/23/06

Contents

Introduction

Emotional connections: a poignant phrase that we have all experienced and we all value. But do we understand what emotional connections really mean to our lives and to the lives of infants and toddlers? This text is about emotion, emotional connections, and emotional development. At the same time, it is about how emotional connections influence early learning.

This book is addressed to child-care providers. As caregivers and teachers of infants and toddlers, you will be entrusted with children in their most formative years. This means that you will play a significant role in their lives and in our society. Today, children are going to child care at younger ages, sometimes as wee infants of 6 weeks. Child-care providers provide these children with a safe haven and an emotional ground. You will be with them for some of their first experiences, first thoughts, first social interactions, and first problem-solving experiences. You will be their model and their guide through these times. You will be one of their first relationships.

The first three chapters of this book explore a theory of emotional development and introduce you to some specifics about how infants and toddlers learn. In particular, the text explores the effect of relationships on early learning and how the emotional connection between child and adult regulates, focuses, and organizes the mind. Physical and cognitive development have been studied and taught extensively, but we are just beginning to realize the importance of emotion sharing and emotion regulation on our ability to learn and function effectively.

As we watch a typical 6-month-old sitting on his mother's lap and reaching for objects on the table, we are rarely thinking about what this baby is learning or what is happening in the brain. Yet we know that each motion the baby makes is initiating a brain connection. Subsequent actions or experiences will lead to a chain of connections or pathways for learning. Motor skills are expanding; memory is building. Because the baby is sitting on his mother's lap, he feels her support and is confident to reach out to objects close by. The mental chain that is stimulated by the baby's action can be directed and enhanced by his mother's response, particularly her emotional response. For example, she might either interrupt the baby's reach by saying, "Oh, no, hot!" or encourage the action and expand the learning process by saying, "Look, pretty. Listen, ding-ding!" The mother's interaction with the baby and the emotional responses she gives will provide both energy and direction to the baby's learning.

This book begins with the newborn and presents a conceptual view of how the baby's brain is in the process of development and of how emotion guides this developmental process. We consider nature and nurture and explore the competencies of the infant and the contribution of the caregiver. The relationship between the infant and the caregiver fosters learning.

In the first three chapters, you will gain a theoretical view of how emotion sharing and emotion regulation contribute to learning. As you build an understanding of this process, you will be building skills for implementing all of the concrete suggestions about child care that follow.

You will begin to understand how children learn. The text examines how children's nature equips them to learn and how their emotions and anxieties influence the way that they learn. Chapters will discuss your role as a caregiver in providing meaningful learning opportunities and in modulating stimulation. Your relationship with each child in your care will be the most important factor in nurturing strong development.

Chapters will also explore the power of relationships and give you practice in the skills needed to build strong relationships with the children in your care. We will explore all facets of learning, chapter by chapter, defining how emotional connections enhance or degrade learning. We will end with some concrete skill-building and ideas for working within the diversity of child-care centers available today.

Emotional Connections

How Relationships Guide Early Learning

Chapter 1
Relationships Nurture Early Learning

Infants and toddlers are fascinating people. They are wonderfully appealing, intensely motivated, and ever changing. Like spring flowers, we can see these children emerging as we watch. We are awed by the baby's rapid growth and amazed when he or she is suddenly a toddler who runs, climbs, sings songs, and reads books.

You must be interested in these fascinating people if you are reading this book because it covers in detail how infants and toddlers learn and how they develop. In particular, this text will explore the effect that relationships have on learning and how our emotions and the emotional connections between caregiver and child regulate, focus, and organize the child's mind. Emotions and emotional connections drive early learning. Physical and cognitive development have been studied and taught extensively, but we are just beginning to realize the importance of understanding our emotional development and how it affects our ability to learn and function.

Imagine that you are holding a typical 6-month-old on your lap. You watch this baby reaching for objects on the table, but you are probably not thinking about what is happening in this baby's brain. Yet, you know that each motion the baby makes is initiating brain connections and that subsequent actions or experiences will lead to a chain of connections or pathways for learning. Motor skills are expanding; memory is building. Because the baby is sitting on your lap, she feels your support and is confident to reach out to nearby objects. The mental chain, which is stimulated

Goals of Chapter 1

- ▦ Learn introductory information about how nature and nurture are intertwined from birth to initiate and promote learning in the young child.

- ▦ Discover what motivations and abilities babies are born with and how these contribute to their learning.

- ▦ Examine the effect of sensory learning and how all development occurs through interactions with places, objects, and people.

- ▦ Be able to define why connections with people are the most important connections.

- ▦ Understand the salience of emotional cues for communication and learning.

- ▦ Discuss observing and listening to children as the best ways to form an emotional connection with them.

- ▦ Build skills for observing and listening to children's emotional cues.

by the baby's action, can be directed and enhanced by your response—particularly by your emotional response. For example, you might interrupt the baby's reach by saying, "Oh, no. Hot!" or you might encourage the action and expand the learning process by saying, "Look—pretty! Listen—ding-ding!"

Your interaction with this baby and the emotional responses you give will provide both energy and direction to the baby's learning. Interactions with others are always dynamic and unique. Examining the role of how these interactions become relationships between child and caregiver will give us an exciting new look at how early thought processing and first learning are influenced by these relationships.

> *Your interaction with this baby and the emotional responses you give will provide both energy and direction to the baby's learning.*

To understand the magic of relationship, we must understand what both parties contribute. Chapter 1 will consider the contribution of the child, beginning at birth. First we will examine how nature equips infants to participate in their learning, and then we will consider some basic information about how first learning contributes to the development of the brain. Chapter 2 will focus on the caregiver's contribution to learning. We will discover how nurture becomes a necessary partner for strong development. Chapter 3 will put it all together by presenting a theoretical view of emotional development. Throughout the rest of the text (chapters 4–10), this view of emotional development will be applied to all aspects of caregiving.

As caregivers and teachers of infants and toddlers, we play a privileged role in our society. We are entrusted with children in their most formative years. Today, children are coming to child care at younger ages, sometimes as wee infants, just 6 weeks old. Some children spend more awake time at a child-care center than at home. We will be with them for some of their first experiences, first thoughts, first social interactions, and first attempts at problem solving.

Birth to 3 years is a period when first learning occurs. First learning is more about building a structure for thinking than about adding knowledge. It is also about building patterns of behavior, such as relating to others or negotiating a goal. First learning is about discovery—a first ball, first words, first books. It is also about learning self-regulation and about understanding the feelings of others. Our interactions with the children in our care will play a vital role in their futures and in our own.

Key Concept One
Babies Have Amazing Capacities to Learn

Nature has equipped infants to begin learning from the moment of birth, or even before. Much of the infant's or toddler's early physical development is preprogrammed, like that of an embryo evolving. We know from child development research that physical development in the first 3 years unfolds in a preset and predictable pattern, except in extreme cases. Most children around the world are able to stand when they are 1 year old, walk when 2 years old, and communicate with gestures, sounds, and words by the age of 3 years.

Infants are also born with motivations that push them to explore and master new tasks and to communicate and connect with other humans. Their new and limited nervous systems are ready to receive sensory stimulation and to evaluate it as good or bad, pleasure or pain. This evaluation leads to the initiation of an action, forming a new connection within the brain. Learning pathways are established. For example, when you step outside with an infant, the baby's eyes close tight, and the baby turns his or her head into your neck. As you step into the shade, the infant opens his or her eyes and lifts his or her head, eyes exploring the yard.

Nature makes us unique. Although we are similar as humans, we are not the same. Each of us is an original—made of a genetic mix with a specific physical potential, nervous system, and emotional core. Thus, the way we think, the knowledge we seek, and the skills we choose to develop also will be unique.

Throughout this chapter, we will explore each of these natural gifts in more detail, but first, let us explore in general how caregivers support these natural gifts to promote first learning.

Nature and Nurture Are Inextricably Intertwined

Amazingly, our nature also predisposes us to connect with our initial caregiver, someone who will help us survive. We are biologically connected to one another. From the moment of conception, we need nurturance to grow. For example, imagine a semidark hospital room where mother and father are quietly alone with baby Jose immediately after his birth.

> Jose scans the room, wide-eyed, stopping at areas of clear light-dark contrast. His mother's eyes attract the baby. He brightens and his eyes widen. He fixes his gaze on her. She pulls him close and strokes his head, then begins to unwrap and stroke each part of his small, damp body. His pink skin pales, his movements become jerky, and his face

wrinkles into a wizened grimace. His mother cuddles him close to her bare breast and covers them both with a warm blanket. The baby quiets, his face softens, and his eyes again begin searching.

Infant and mother are still an interdependent biological system, baby signaling and mother responding almost automatically, without thought. Jose's mother touches and cuddles him when he looks to her face. Her actions are spontaneous and appropriate. This newborn has connected immediately to his caregiver. This connection begins a relationship that will ensure Jose's survival. This relationship will also guide and interpret his learning.

A 3-day-old infant will alert to her mother's face and will follow it as she moves around nearby. The infant can see her clearly when she is nursing and will concentrate on her eyes. She responds to the mother's voice, which also was heard in the womb, and quiets to the familiar rhythms of her body and heartbeat. As mother touches the infant, she will relax in her arms. The baby is the stimulus for the responsive caregiver, and her responses will, in turn, define the baby's learning.

Newborns elicit a predictable pattern of responses from almost any adult. For example, imagine 6-week-old Sarah.

Anywhere Sarah goes, she quickly becomes the center of attention. People line up to hold her; they raise the pitch of their voices and say silly cooing things, rocking her gently back and forth.

This adult response is part of our biology. We react appropriately to the stimulus of the baby. The baby is the trigger for the actions of the adult. This dynamic enables infants to define their needs, thus shaping schedules to fit their particular biological patterns. Children's ability to help us define their needs for care and for learning will remain during the first 3 years and perhaps beyond.

Everything that happens to us from birth forward is in relationship to something else—the environment, objects around us, and especially other humans. For each of us, these relationships have been unique. Those who nurtured us provided the sustenance and survival that allowed us to develop physically, but they also provided the experiences that shaped our thoughts and memories. Our caregivers defined the environments that we experienced both before and after birth. Our caregivers were the ones to calm our anxieties and focus our attention. Our caregivers modeled ways of processing information and helped us to manage our impulses as we first encountered challenge. Nurture that is combined with our particular nature continues to make us unique.

Nature Motivates Babies to Learn

Nature provides for babies to initiate and sustain learning. Nature has given us motivations that drive us toward learning, sharing, and surviving throughout our lives. When we know about and understand these inborn needs, we will better understand the actions of our colleagues, friends, and families as well as the children in our care.

Babies are born with a biological system that connects them with a caregiver (Box 1.1). They connect through a unique system of cues that are universally understood. In this way, they ensure their survival and their con-

---

Box 1.1
Inborn Motivations

We are internally motivated to do the following things:

▓ **Connect emotionally with other humans**
— We need an attachment relationship.
— We learn from shared experiences.
— We find joy in shared understanding.
— We feel protection and safety from the love of another.
— We find emotional balance through relationship.
— We gain resiliency and self-esteem through positive sharing.

▓ **Seek physical and emotional equilibrium**
— We find comfort in routines, patterns, and rhythms.
— We need regular sleep, nourishment, exercise, and stimulation.
— We can tune in or tune out stimulation to modulate our needs.
— We seek an emotional connection to balance our anxieties.
— We strive to "self-right" in extreme situations.

▓ **Explore and master the new**
— We like to explore the new and novel.
— We like challenge and goals.
— We become absorbed in learning.
— We practice until we gain the skill or knowledge.
— We feel confident and proud when we master our goals.

▓ **Adapt and fit in with others—belong**
— We copy the model of another.
— We seek a guide or structure for learning new skills.
— We are willing to inhibit our impulses and adapt our behaviors to fit in.
— We want to be accepted by the group and belong on the team.

tinued learning. But infants are also motivated, or internally driven, to continue to reach out and connect with others. This inner need for relationship and interaction with others is a lifelong motivation. We will continue to seek friends, mentors, and family, ever expanding our learning and our feelings of stability.

A second and vital internal motivation that nature provides us is a drive to seek physical and emotional balance. This need for equilibrium pushes infants to attach to trusted others for emotional and physical nurturance. In turn, these relationships will help them learn to self-regulate and to modulate the extremes in their lives.

Nature also motivates us in a third way, from infancy onward, to explore and master new things. This urge pushes babies to continue to learn about new objects, places, and people. A fourth inborn motivation is to copy models and adapt behaviors to fit into the patterns and actions of others. Babies will learn more by watching and copying than by what is formally taught. They will also accept limits and correction that enables them to belong and feel accepted by others.

Because babies are born with motivations to connect, explore, seek neurological balance, as well as copy models and adapt to the behaviors of others, they are eager learners who define their interests and their developmental readiness to learn from birth forward.

Babies Direct Their Learning Through States of Awareness

Infants communicate through their states of awareness (Box 1.2). Throughout the day, an infant cycles from sleep to wakefulness, showing hunger, interest, contentment, drowsiness, and again sleep. These conditions are called states of consciousness or mental awareness. The infant is able to tune in to what is interesting and to tune out what is stressful or boring. Because of this ability, newborns have often been referred to as "competent infants."

States of awareness help us interpret the needs of the infant or toddler. Children give us one message when they are blissfully sleeping and another when they are actively moving their feet and squealing. The competent infant shuts out stimulation that is stressful but alerts or cries when he or she needs to interact. For example, imagine 2-month-old Alex, who is on a mat in the child-care center.

The light from the window is bright and sunny. Alex has his eyes closed, but he is not asleep. He hears a sound across the room and turns his head toward it. He opens his eyes and finds that the light in this corner is soft and dim because the wall shades it. Alex opens his eyes wider and can see other children. He studies the colors and the movement of the children. He coos softly and kicks his feet.

Box 1.2
States of Awareness

We all modulate the stimulation around us through states of awareness. We protect our minds and bodies by tuning in or tuning out our environment. Most babies are good at this. They sleep when they need to, fuss when they are uncomfortable, and become alert to learn.

Some babies are good at state modulation, and others are not. These babies need our help to regulate their state from being anxious to being calm, for example, by rocking a fussy baby.

Can you define what state you are in now? Can you define the state of others in the room? Who is alert and who is drowsy?

Deep Sleep
— Nothing bothers the person. The person is unaware of the surrounding environment. With age, periods of deep sleep increase.

Light Sleep
— The person may be restless, moving, and making noises. The person's eyes may be fluttering. This is an important sleep.
— Adults often dream or integrate their thoughts during light sleep.
— Babies are in light sleep about every 15–20 minutes. With age, deep sleep increases.

Drowsy
— This state is the phase between being asleep and awake. The person can go either way.
— Some babies take a long time to wake up completely; others may find it hard to move from a drowsy state into sleep. When babies learn to fall asleep on their own, they have gained an important emotion regulation skill.

Quiet Alert
— The person is receptive to learning in this state.
— Babies focus clearly and with energy.

Active Alert
— The person feels highly energized, excited, and full of adrenaline.
— This is a fun state, but it may be difficult to leave.
— Babies may become overstimulated and need adult help to regain emotional balance.

Fussy
— When the person is overwhelmed, tired, hungry, or cold, he or she may be cranky.
— When the person's needs are met, he or she calms down.
— Responding to the needs of a fussy baby averts problems.

Crying
— This state signals true distress. The person is calling for help and support.
— A caregiver is usually needed to regulate a baby's distress.

Alex was able to find equilibrium, or balance, by shutting out the high stimulation of bright sunlight. When he turned to the sound and opened his eyes (motivation to explore), the light stimulation was less. Alex kept his eyes open and was able to connect and learn. Newborns can control the stimulation around them by changing their state of awareness.

Have you ever seen a baby sleep through a movie or a ball game? Competent infants shut out stimulation by turning away, closing their eyes, fussing, or going to sleep. They let us know when they are hungry, tired, or overstimulated by being fussy. When they are quietly alert, they communicate that they are ready to learn. In this way, Alex was able to change the stimulation around him and provide for his internal needs. For example, a baby can sleep through the family party but be wide awake, kicking and smiling in the middle of the night when he or she is alone with a parent. As infants realize their abilities to modulate states of awareness, they are taking the first important developmental step in emotional self-control. Competent infants can move from one state to the next in a smooth, modulated fashion. As we contemplate our role as their caregivers, we need to understand states of awareness and remain sensitive to a child's state as we participate in his or her learning.

> *Changing the state of awareness is also a way that infants protect their brains from overstimulation.*

Changing the state of awareness is also a way that infants protect their brains from overstimulation. They shut their eyes to intense light, they turn away from intense interactions, and they fuss about changes in temperature or loud sounds. As adults, we have learned to mask our boredom or leave when the sound is too loud or the activity overwhelming. A baby cannot use these strategies. When external stimulation is too much, a baby or toddler may need your help. Caregivers can help modulate state-of-awareness change in the child. They can change the baby's environment, reduce the stimulation, and calm the baby.

As infants mature, a particular state might have a different meaning. As children develop, their signals become more individualized and complex. Toddlers may demonstrate hunger, exhaustion, or overstimulation in ways that are different from infants. Some toddlers become cranky and oppositional. Some become wildly active, running in circles or choosing repetitive actions. Others may retreat to a corner and suck their thumbs. Sensitive caregivers modulate children's states by finding them a snack, a crib, a quiet refuge, or whatever they may need.

States of awareness are a key to understanding what each infant and toddler needs. As a caregiver, you must practice reading a child's state.

Before you offer a new experience, ask yourself, "Is this child alert and ready for new learning?" If the child is not, ask yourself, "How can I help the child modulate his or her state to be ready for learning again?" As a caregiver, when you approach a child, ask yourself, "What state is this child in?" In fact, we all should approach any interaction by asking the same question: What state is this person in? The answer may change how you present your-self to that person. States of awareness allow infants to expand their learn-ing when they are ready to handle the stimulation.

Babies are also born with unique temperaments, which will define their responses to their environment and signal others of their needs. Tempera-ment plays a strong role in what and how babies learn and in how they respond to others. Temperament will be explained in chapter 2.

Babies Learn Through Sensory Stimulation

Newborns began using their sensory learning system when they were fetuses in the womb. At birth, infants are able to hear, see, feel, smell, and taste. In addition, infants perceive another important sensory learning track: They experience and process motion. This sensory system is called the vestibular system. It is important to babies, whose early experience has been rocking gently in amniotic fluid. The fetus has been experiencing the motions and rhythms of mother's heart, breathing patterns, and body fluids. Motion and rhythm are keenly developed sensory guides for the nervous systems of infants. These guides help fulfill the baby's need or motivation to find phys-iologic and emotional balance (Box 1.3).

Every sensory stimulus sends messages to the brain. For infants, this process usually informs muscle groups and leads to motor development. If the stimuli are repeated, then pathways are reinforced. Experiences with light and shadow will school the newborn's eyes to react and adjust to vary-ing levels of light. Muscles in the eye become increasingly efficient. Very soon, the baby is seeing at greater distances and with increased focus. By 1 month, the baby shows pleasure at faces. By 3 months, the baby recognizes specific faces and objects. Memory tracks are built and shaped by stimulus and reflex responses. With repetition, these become purposeful. For exam-ple, the baby might begin to remember, "My arm can move toward what I see." With experience, he or she might then think, "What my arm moves toward, I might touch." And then, "I can make my arm move, reach, and touch."

Infants learn from their sensory environment and the objects in it. Sensory-motor learning is a major component of early physical develop-ment. As infants experience touching and grasping, they will practice and practice the new action. Our internal motivation drives us to connect with others for learning, but our nature also motivates us to master new skills.

Box 1.3
The Senses

Brains are stimulated by the senses. These senses enable us to take in stimulation from outside the body for the brain to process and understand. At birth, we are learning through our six senses.

Sight—Babies can see at birth. They see best at a distance of about 8 inches, which means that a nursing baby can see the mother's face. This face is usually the most familiar vision a baby has early on. Babies watch faces, and they learn from the expressions on the faces they see. Older babies and toddlers refer to their caregivers' faces for signals of approval and disapproval. What does your face say?

Touch—Touching and being touched are other ways babies learn. Babies learn to know people by the way they are picked up, held, and put down. Touch can excite or calm. Touch can regulate behavior extremes. Touch stimulates muscles. Touch stimulates development. Touch is a way to explore and master new skills. Touch is a way babies learn about themselves and about you. What does your touch say?

Hearing—At birth, babies turn to the sound of a human voice. Tones seem to be understood from the womb. By 2 or 3 months of age, babies alert, divert, smile, and relax to rhythmic speech. Beginning in the early months, they also imitate cooing sounds and cry in reaction to loud and harsh sounds. During the first 3 years, imitation of sounds is a major way children learn. Are you talking to the children in your care?

Taste—A newborn can distinguish sweet, sour, and bitter, and salty tastes. By 6 months, babies are beginning to eat some solid foods. Their likes and dislikes will depend on adults' preferences and adults' faces and actions. Babies use taste to learn. They lick or bite almost every new thing they can touch. As a caregiver, you may have the opportunity to expand learning through taste with the variety of foods you serve.

Smell—Newborns can identify their mother's breast milk by smell. They also respond to foul smells by crying. Bodily smells become recognized and comforting for baby. With toddlers, exploring different smells is a fun way to learn.

Motion—Motion and rhythm give balance to babies. This combination is called the vestibular sense, and it is actually perceived through a part of the ear that contains a balancing mechanism. In the womb, babies are moving gently, and their vestibular sense is stimulated. They are learning to gain balance or equilibrium through motion. Many believe that this ability to balance helps organize the baby's brain for further development. Motion and rhythm remain important ways to get babies' attention and to calm babies during the first 3 years. Do you play motion and rhythm games with the children in your care?

Babies become totally focused on repeating an action. This repetition strengthens brain pathways. As the action is repeated, muscle groups learn. When reaching becomes an action that a baby remembers, he practices over and over. When the baby masters it, he can use it at will. In this way, early mental pathways become reinforced until they are part of the baby's permanent mental structure. They become internal working models for his future actions. For example, as adults, we do not have to consciously think about how to reach for and grasp a coffee cup. This early motor learning is resilient, adversely affected only by early neurological damage, physical injury, or adverse relationships.

Caregivers Determine Sensory Experiences for Infants and Toddlers

Caregivers define what babies see, hear, and touch. They select how much fresh air, sunlight, or exercise the baby will have. For example, a 6-month-old's learning will be influenced by how much space and freedom she experiences. The baby who is swaddled in a sling on her mother's hip learns different movements and a different style of communication with her mother than the baby who lies diapered on a blanket on the open floor, watching his mother move about the room.

As caregivers of infants and toddlers, we will be creating the spaces, choosing the objects, and defining the interactions that will provide their learning experiences. The environments in a child-care center will be different from home; nevertheless, we will be the human connection that will be nurturing children, encouraging them, and calming their anxieties for much of their day. We will be promoting their interests or limiting their actions. To do these things well, we must understand the role that a child's state of awareness plays in communication with us. We must also learn how to listen to each child's nature and respond in the appropriate way for each child.

Key Concept Two
Emotion Is Our Inborn Link to Learning

We are born with the ability to read emotions in others. Just as the newborn's brain is able to receive sensory stimulation, it also processes feelings—internal feelings such as hunger and external signals such as a smiling face. Because of this ability, emotional signals are the major communication link between infant and caregiver.

Newborns are able to signal pleasure, contentment, and discomfort. Through their crying, active rooting and sucking, or quiet alerting, infants start an interaction with a caregiver. The infant is signaling a feeling or emotion. "I'm hungry." "I'm anxious." "I'm interested." "I'm tired." Adults understand these feeling states from their own experience, and they respond to their babies' needs.

Babies Communicate Through Emotional Signals

Babies' actions signal their feelings. Babies connect with us through their faces, their movements, and their voice tones. These emotional signals are a baby's only means of communication. They represent the "language of infancy." For example, imagine the following scene.

> A newborn stops sucking during a feeding. The baby looks to mom's face, and mother smiles, strokes the baby's head, and kisses his hands.

Both mother and baby have connected by expressing their feelings. The baby takes a break from sucking and swallowing. He can see mom's face and likes to look at it. The baby has learned through repeated experiences to recognize mom's face and touch. He feels calmed and rested from the effort of sucking. Mom has been reinforced in her love for her new baby. Reciprocal emotional communication has begun.

Our first communications are through emotional cues. Parents are uniquely sensitive to their babies' cues, but more remarkably, babies are able to process and understand emotional cues from parents. They can read the faces, voices, and touches of their caregivers. This "language of infancy" stays with us throughout our lifetimes. We continue to communicate and connect to others through emotional signals. We retain our inborn need to connect at the emotional level.

In our everyday lives, we express and respond to emotions. We can define another's feelings—for example, interest, joy, anger, and sorrow—by looking at his or her facial expressions. We respond to the postures and voice tones of others before we process their words. These nonverbal cues remain our base of communication. The emotional connection is our first and most powerful link to others. It is the foundation of relationships.

Babies can also read our signals of emotion. The competent infant can not only connect to her caregivers but also can respond to their voices, touch, and facial expressions in ways that will help her learn. The infant will signal caregivers when she has an internal or external need. The emotional responses of the caregiver will shape the baby's learning and will modulate or excite the baby's nervous system. The infant is not a solitary competent organism but remains connected to the adult for survival, protection, stimulation, modeling, guidance, and emotional regulation. The baby's attachment relationships are defined by this emotional connection.

As infants leave the cocoon of their first connection with their parents, they will continue to have a need to find emotional connection with others.

Caregivers who can fill this role will continue to organize and focus learning in appropriate ways.

Shared Emotions Focus and Expand Learning

Most of what children learn during the early years of life occurs because of their ability to connect through emotional cues. When caregivers can read the nonverbal cues of infants and toddlers, they can respond with shared understanding and provide meaningful experiences. They can use emotion to energize and motivate learning or to inhibit action. For example, imagine the following scene.

> Shafali, a 12-month-old, is being carried by her caregiver. She reaches out and points to the bulletin board, saying, "Gog." Her caregiver responds to her by saying, "Yes! Dog. That's a dog. Let's go see the dog picture!" As they approach the bulletin board, Shafali reaches to pat the image, saying "Dog, dog." Her learning and her memory have been expanded.

With a different response from a caregiver, Shafali's learning would also be expanded, but in a different direction. For example, suppose that, when Shafali points to the bulletin board, her caregiver takes her hand and says, "Don't point! We don't point." Shafali would learn that she made a mistake with her impulsive show of interest. She might learn with repetition not to point and, perhaps, to be cautious about showing emotions or interest.

Another caregiver might have ignored Shafali's pointing. With no response to her recognition of the image on the bulletin board, Shafali likely would feel satisfied that she saw something she had in memory, but her learning would not have expanded.

The interactions with the first two caregivers expanded Shafali's learning. These caregivers' responses established emotional connections. One was a positive connection and one was negative, but both expanded learning, albeit in different ways. With the caregiver who did not interact, Shafali was on her own. Learning was reinforced, but no new learning occurred.

Emotional Connections Organize and Regulate Our Behavior

For all of us, emotional connection is vital. We rely on parents, partners, and peers to help us gain equilibrium when we become anxious or overstimulated. Our interactions with others help us learn to inhibit impulses and cope with stress. Through these emotional connections, we find models and guides for our behavior. Emotional connection allows us to understand not only the feelings of others but also how our behavior affects them.

From this understanding, we learn the dos and don'ts of staying alive and of living well together.

As adults, we have learned to focus our attention on verbal signals. We rely on words for communicating and learning. Many of us have diminished our ability to notice and understand nonverbal cues. How much do you notice the actions of others as you talk to them? How much do you use their actions to determine their real feelings and needs?

Key Concept Three
Observation Is the First Step in Caregiving

Nature has given infants the ability to communicate and connect with us from the moment of birth. We have learned that infants achieve this interaction through their states of awareness and their emotional cues. In this way, infants and toddlers direct us in their care. They help us know how to plan their environments, their stimulation, and their schedules. They can help us know when to set limits or when to help them regain equilibrium. The first step in becoming a skilled child-care provider is to learn to listen to children. We need to practice becoming skilled baby watchers. What does this skill involve? Imagine the following scenario.

> We have just entered a child-care center. We stop and watch 6-month-old Ashley sitting on the lap of her caregiver, Helen. The room is pleasant, sunny, and calm. Ashley looks comfortable and engaged. She reaches out to the table in front of her and grabs at some plastic keys hooked onto a ring that Helen has put there. Ashley shakes the keys, smiles, and puts them into her mouth.

Let's examine this scenario more carefully and extend our thinking about what Ashley might be learning. Ashley is using new muscles, she is practicing reaching and grabbing, she hears the rattle, she realizes she could increase the noise, and she remembers that she can get the keys to her mouth. She has reinforced some existing knowledge and expanded her learning. Her muscles, her memory, and her understanding all have been enhanced by the experience.

Detailed Observation Has Increased Our Knowledge of Child Development

Some of our earliest information about child development has come from research observations of children like Ashley in the scenario above. People who were interested in behavior and in learning about the origins of behavior wrote about what they saw when they watched and documented the behavior of their own children or the children in their clinical practices. The developmental milestones that were observed in the 1930s, 1940s, and 1950s remain the basis for our understanding of early physical and cognitive development today.

We can expand our observational skills further by examining the previous scenario as though we were professional baby watchers or researchers. We could ask some more detailed research questions such as, "How do we know what Ashley is feeling? How do we know what Ashley is learning? Does the relationship with Helen influence Ashley's learning?"

When we first started watching Ashley, we noted that she seemed content and engaged. Being on Helen's lap seemed to give her a sense of connection and confidence. Ashley felt supported and safe to reach out for the keys that Helen had placed on the table in front of her. How did we know how Ashley felt? We watched her face and her movements, and we listened to her voice sounds. Focusing allowed us to observe Ashley in a different way—to think about her feelings and her actions. Let's continue observing as the scenario resumes.

> Helen kisses Ashley's hand, laughs, and takes the keys. She places a blue plastic cup in front of Ashley and drops the keys inside. Then she tips the cup over and the keys fall out. Helen laughs and repeats the task, then gives the keys back to Ashley, who looks up at her and smiles. "Your turn. You do it," says Helen. Ashley slowly puts the keys inside the blue cup, pushes it over, and grabs the keys again. Helen sets the blue cup upright, and Ashley carefully puts the keys in the cup again. This time, Helen knocks it over. The keys fall out again. Ashley waves her arms excitedly and looks up at Helen. They both laugh. Ashley turns to look at Helen; she reaches up and touches Helen's face.

What might Ashley have learned from sharing the experience of the keys with Helen? Did Helen extend Ashley's learning? How? Was Helen reinforcing any former learning? What did Ashley experience from her caregiver? Was there emotional communication? Did it influence Ashley's learning? As early research observation led to more specific and complex questions such as these, research then moved into the laboratory and became systematic and scientific. Studies began to focus on how relationships affect development. Through detailed observation of parent and child, we have learned about the power of attachment and emotional regulation. We have learned about temperament and how it affects relationships.

To illustrate, imagine the following scenario, similar to the one above but with a different child, whom we will call Jorge.

> When Helen dropped the keys in the cup, they made a cracking sound. Jorge startled and began to cry. His back stiffened against Helen's body, and his arms and legs began to jerk out of his control.

Helen turned Jorge around to face her and held him close. She pulled his legs under him and swayed quietly for a moment or two. Jorge quieted. Helen reached for the keys and handed them to Jorge as she held him. He put them in his mouth and bit with his gums as he put his head down on Helen's shoulder. In a few moments he alerted and held the keys up as if showing them to Helen. He rattled the keys vigorously and smiled.

Helen treated these two babies differently. Why do you think she did? What effect did her change of behavior have on Jorge? What was he feeling? Why do you think he behaved the way he did? Was he learning? As we ask questions, we think of more things to watch for in children. This type of questioning will make us better caregivers because we will develop a deeper understanding of the differences and the needs of each child in our care.

As we examine our observations of Ashley, we realize that, like most babies, she has been able to see, hear, and experience tactile sensation from birth. Her sensory experiences have guided her to expand her motor skills. She has learned to reach and grab in a purposeful, controlled manner. She knew that she could pick up the object she saw on the table.

> *Listening to Jorge through his emotional signals told Helen that, to expand his learning, she must first help Jorge quiet his fear of the sharp noise.*

An even more detailed examination of our observations might lead us to thinking about how Ashley's early sensory experiences made connections in her brain. Each motion Ashley makes is initiating a brain connection. Her interactions with the keys stimulate neurological chains of auditory and tactile activity that send a signal to her muscles and increase her memory.

Jorge showed Helen that he had a different sensitivity to the sound of the keys going into the cup. It frightened him. He also showed Helen that he was not developmentally ready to play the in-and-out game with the keys. He was still focused on learning about them through sight and touch. Listening to Jorge through his emotional signals told Helen that, to expand his learning, she must first help Jorge quiet his fear of the sharp noise. Then she could refocus him on the keys at his individual level of learning.

Eventually, as research in child development expanded within the laboratory setting, it began to focus on the study of heart rate as well as skin and voice-tone responses. Soon, this research included the addition of the biochemical sciences. We now understand more about the interaction of genes and experience. We also have more information about individual differences in children, including how temperament and culture affect development. As child-care providers, you will do better to keep reading, attending conferences, and discussing with colleagues new information within your profession, but your observational skills will remain the most effective way to enhance your ability to work with and enjoy the children in your care.

Key Concept Four
The Brain Is the Processing Center for Learning

Child development researchers have always been intrigued with how the brain develops. However, knowledge was sparse because studies of the brain could be done only with animals and pathology specimens. With new techniques for examining the brain and the central nervous system—techniques such as brain imaging and the ability to measure activity in the brain (Box 1.4)—scientists can learn much more about how we think and how we learn. Research in child development has expanded into the fields of neuroscience and biochemistry. On a regular basis, researchers are reporting new

---

Box 1.4
New Techniques

During the past 15 years, new brain-scanning techniques have produced detailed images of brain structures and meaningful measures of brain activity. These methods include the following techniques:

MRI (magnetic resonance imaging)
This technique produces detailed computerized images of specific areas of the brain. How the brain works when a person moves, speaks, or thinks can also be recorded with an MRI.

PET (positron emission tomography)
This scanning technique records the activity level in different parts of the brain. PET scans of babies at different ages reveal how parts of the brain responsible for various capabilities—movement, vision, language, thinking, and emotions—are turned on in a predictable developmental pattern.

EEG (electroencephalogram)
Using electrodes attached to the head, scientists can record the brain waves of young children as they interact with the world around them. Levels of brain activity change as children move from one state to another (e.g., wakefulness to sleep). EEG patterns also document the child's reactions to comfort, stress, and problem-solving situations.

facts about their understanding of the child's brain and how learning occurs. These reports include bits of information waiting to be pieced together into a meaningful pattern of research knowledge.

As caregivers, learning some basic facts about early brain development will be helpful to our understanding of how children learn. This information will also be meaningful as we study more about the role that emotional connection and relationships play in advancing learning. However, we should remain cautious about overinterpreting what we read about the brain. We must think about and interact with each child as an individual.

The Brain Is the Most Complex System in the World

When we are born, we have approximately 100 billion neurons, or brain cells, fully formed and ready for action. These cells make up our central nervous systems. Each neuron has a specific job description at its core or nucleus. Some neurons are ready to receive stimulation from our sensory experience; others, from our internal feelings and needs. When stimulated, they direct our responses by connecting to other neurons.

Connections among neurons are beginning to be established before we are born, but most of the pathways that connect our thoughts and actions are established after we are born. Thus, each of our brains will develop in a different way because of the caregiving relationships we experience after birth. Nature and nurture combine from the beginnings of life to shape the structure and development of our brains (Box 1.5).

Box 1.5
Amazing Brain Facts

— Seventy-five percent of a child's brain develops after birth.
— Scientists estimate that brain connections can increase from 50 trillion to 1,000 trillion in the first 3 years of life.
— A toddler's brain is twice as active as his or her caregiver's.
— No two brains are the same because brain circuitry depends on experience and nurturance.
— The brain has optimal times when it is ready to "turn on" to different areas of learning.
— Brain connections that are not repeated are eliminated.
— Responsive relationships directly affect how the brain is wired.
— Stressful events produce hormones that can destroy brain cells and connections.

Note. Adapted with permission from Shore. Copyright 1997 by Families and Work Institute.

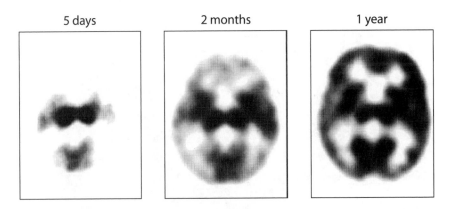

| 5 days | 2 months | 1 year |

Figure 1.1. Rapid early development.
(Reproduced with permission from Shore. Copyright 1997 by Families and Work Institute.)

Most neurons remain in the brain and serve specific areas that will receive stimulation, record feelings, and integrate actions. Different areas of the brain control different functions, such as sight or hearing. The brain work that we call learning—functions such as thinking, planning, and remembering—is handled by cells in the cerebral cortex, which is in the front and top part of the head. It is the largest portion of the brain. At birth, the brain can receive and react to sensory stimulation, but much of the cortex, which is responsible for complex thought, has yet to develop. To understand this concept, consider the eye and the function of sight. At first, the infant eye muscle will simply contract in a reflexive way when light is intense, and it will relax when the room darkens. These reflexes are inborn and remain part of our basic survival mechanisms. With maturation and learning, the baby begins to focus and recognize images, as well as to choose what to look at and for how long. Development in the brain is rapid as infants experience more each day (Figure 1.1).

At birth, infants express and process emotion. Under the cerebral cortex, safely tucked deep inside the brain, are the amygdala and the hippocampus, specific areas that contain our inborn motivations and feelings—our core nature. Emotion is processed in these areas. The feelings signaled from here control our nervous systems. Neurochemicals dispatched by our feelings tell our nerves to be alert and anxious, interested, or calm. From this core, we are also motivated to survive, to connect, to master, and to belong. As you have learned, we are internally motivated to find emotional and neurological balance, and we instinctively reach out or pull back to maintain our comfort range. These feelings and motivations are similar across all ages of human beings. They provide us with an inborn link to learning and to all humankind (Figure 1.2).

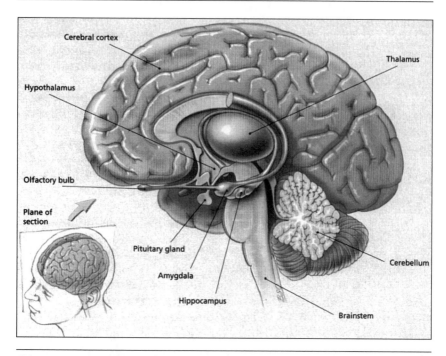

Figure 1.2. The brain in brief.
(Reproduced with permission from Shore. Copyright 1997 Families and Work Institute.)

During the first 3 years, many neurons will migrate to other parts of the body, where they serve specialized functions. For example, neurons in the spinal cord transfer messages from the brain to specific muscles, for example, sending energy to muscles in a hand or foot, whereas other neurons have specific assignments, such as keeping the heart pumping or the liver functioning.

Early Development Is About Building Brain Structures

Every neuron has an axon, or "output fiber," that sends impulses to other neurons. Each neuron also has many hairlike fibers called dendrites, or "input fibers." These are like the root hairs on a young plant. Many dendrites are available to each cell, but not all of them will be used. This over-abundance of dendrites may be our "insurance policy." Regardless of our environment or our experiences, we will have the dendrites we need to develop and learn. The child of the desert needs to adapt differently than does the child of the forest; the child raised in Chicago will have different skills from the child raised in Rio de Janeiro.

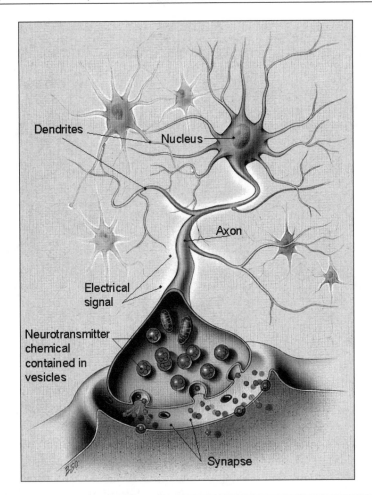

Figure 1.3. Making connections is a neuron's mission.

(Reproduced with permission from Shore. Copyright 1997 Families and Work Institute.)

Cells become connected, or linked, when electrical energy causes a dendrite from one cell to connect with the axon from another. This link happens when the space between them fills with energy and an electrical impulse occurs. This space is called a synapse. When a stimulus sends energy to a synapse and two neurons become connected, a pathway is formed that allows energy to pass from one cell to another (Figure 1.3). As this connecting process is repeated across many cells, pathways of interconnection develop throughout the brain and body, allowing us to think, to remember, and to act.

During the first 3 years, a child's brain forms trillions of connections or synapses. Each neuron may be connected to as many as 15,000 other neu-

At birth   6 years   14 years

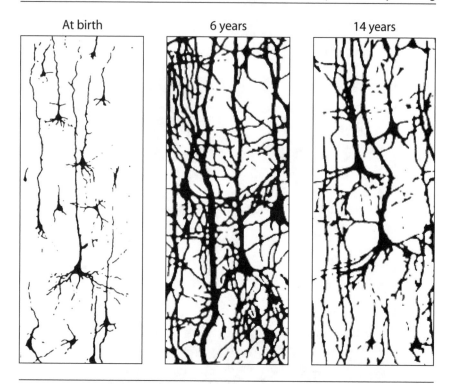

Figure 1.4. Synaptic density.
(Reproduced with permission from Shore. Copyright 1997 by Families and Work Institute.)

rons, establishing the complex circuitry of our brains. First learning is about forming and reinforcing these initial connections throughout the nervous system. This rapid and meaningful structuring of the nervous system is the foundation for the child's future learning. The initial pathways that are established in the first 3 years provide the base for continued development. Layer by layer, experience builds learning (Figure 1.4).

Evidence indicates that some initial pathways are critical to future learning. If the early foundations are not laid, future development may not be able to occur. For example, the child who is born without the ability to hear may learn sign language but struggles to learn to speak and rarely learns to talk with typical speech sounds. In contrast, the infant who has heard language sounds and rhythms for even a few months before losing his or her hearing will be able to learn to talk with typical tones and rhythms.

Chemical Messengers Power and Direct Our Brains

Chemicals in our bodies carry the impulses that will unlock, or fire, our synapses. The quality or type of the chemical messengers will affect how nerve pathways grow. Chemical messengers are called neurotransmitters. Our bodies contain many kinds of neurotransmitters, such as hormones, peptides, and steroids. As research expands in this area, much more will be known about them.

At this point, we know that neurochemicals enhance or inhibit the flow of energy through the brain. Different kinds of messengers alert different parts of the brain. We also know that these chemical messengers are influenced by emotions and emotional connections. Remember Shafali, who recognized the picture of the dog? Different caregivers in the scenario stimulated different kinds of learning: One caregiver stimulated thoughts about words and symbols, and the other stimulated thoughts about behavior regulation and impulse control. Similarly, different neurochemical messengers stimulate different neural pathways.

Neurotransmitters are affected by caregiving. For example, researchers have taken a closer look at one neurotransmitter called cortisol, a stress hormone that can be easily measured in saliva. High cortisol levels reflect anxiety and can immobilize a child. In cases of repeated and persistent anxiety, excess cortisol damages cells. Studies have shown that cortisol levels in children are affected by relationships with caregivers. Children with insecure attachments are more likely to show cortisol elevations when faced with new or challenging situations, whereas children with secure attachments can address challenge without elevated cortisol or stress hormones. When the infant or toddler knows that a caregiver will be available to connect with his or her needs and provide guidance or protection, anxiety is not triggered; rather, pathways for problem solving and self-control are reinforced.

Relationships Regulate the Nervous System

A child's emotional connection with a caregiver can provide moments of calm or can stimulate integrative thought. Caregivers can regulate emotional impulses in the baby by comforting or setting expectations. This regulation, in turn, is regulating the chemistry of the brain. Through the interactions between the caregiver and the baby, the caregiver can guide the baby's thought processing to the executive parts of the baby's brain rather than let the baby's actions be defined directly by impulses of fear, anger, or excitement. Researchers' studies describe how relationships can help children begin to solve problems, learn right from wrong, learn how to use their internal resources for self-regulation, and integrate new skills. With repeated guidance from a caregiver, pathways for problem solving and emotional control will become as accessible to the child as motor skills.

Integrating and modulating neurochemical messengers through relationships is an effective way for all of us to process our anxieties. The more we learn about the brain's chemistry, the more we understand the value of the synergy between nature and nurture. Early interactions directly affect the architecture of the brain.

When the Brain Is Calm or Resting, It Uses Different Neurochemicals

Some neurochemicals help growth, some help memory, and some promote cell integration or healing processes. Much of the brain's activity to integrate cells or to heal occurs when the brain is calm or resting. For this reason, regular sleep cycles are important for all of us, but especially for young children. Quiet or resting brains are doing important work. Like our hearts and other organs, our brains continue to function even when we sleep. Have you ever awakened to realize that you have solved a problem and suddenly know what to do? Much of that problem solving was done during the time you slept. Moments of calm activity or no activity are also integrative times for the brain. Have you noticed a child just staring into space or quietly watching the sky? Children do not always need to be engaged. Allow them these important moments of "open space" or tranquillity.

Synaptic Connections Continue to Be Made and Pruned

Throughout our lifetimes, we will be making new synaptic connections. We are constantly learning. We will continue to expand our memories and our knowledge. However, the things we learned in the first 3 years remain deeply embedded and become our "internal working models." Consequently, the first patterns we learned through watching and sharing with others became our patterns for processing information and managing anxiety. The models we saw around us were internalized. They became our ways of thinking and behaving. The early patterns and routines we experienced became the habits, attitudes, and values by which we may still live.

During the first 3 years, internal working models are also being formed for behavior and social connection. The preschooler will continue to use the early patterns that were successful in child care as he or she approaches new adults or interacts with other children. In the same way, the first models learned for inhibiting behavior or for attaining goals will continue to be used.

In the first 3 years, our brains form many more dendrites than we will need. At about 4 or 5 years of age, excess dendrites begin to disappear (Figure 1.4). The experiences of the first 3 years have established the major structures or "highways" for thinking and behavior. At that point, learning becomes more about amassing information. Children's memories are now able to store knowledge; children are learning words, colors, and numbers. They are expanding and refining the skills that they will use, for example, stacking blocks, turning knobs, and coloring as well as skipping, jumping, kicking balls, and riding tricycles.

Through adolescence, excess dendrites will continue to be pruned. Neural connections that have not been reinforced will be eliminated. The neural pathways that have been used repeatedly will remain and will be refined and extended throughout adulthood. Because of this pruning process, we have a much harder time as adults initiating new fields of learning that require different neural pathways (e.g., consider an adult English speaker who is learning to read Chinese or a writer who is learning to use calculus). Instead, we become knowledgeable or skilled in specific areas such as engineering, teaching, sewing, and basketball.

Each of our magnificent brains is unique and unbelievably complex. Information about the brain in general changes constantly as knowledge expands. We caution you not to let some new finding about stimulating the brain influence your caregiving, and we urge you to think of your interactions with children as part of a complex human relationship (for example, do not allow some rule or new teaching method inhibit your ability to listen to the child and individualize your caregiving). If you would enjoy knowing more about the brain and the nervous system, we encourage you to refer to the resource lists at the ends of the chapters in this book.

Chapter Summary

Early development is an intricate fabric woven from threads of nature and nurture alike. Biology equips infants and toddlers to communicate with us through their states of awareness and their emotional signals. By telling us how they feel and what they need, they affect their early learning. Nature has given infants internal feelings and drives that push them to seek emotional balance, to connect with others, to explore and master the new, and to adapt. Nature has made the infant an individual—a separate and competent person. A skilled caregiver knows how to listen to this individual and to be child directed in his or her caregiving.

Caregivers who work with infants and toddlers know that first learning is about first thoughts, first discoveries, and first experiences. They observe toddlers experimenting with objects, trying ideas, and shaking their heads in agreement or disagreement with their actions. Through a caregiver's nurturance, a child's learning is guided and nourished.

Each day, as caregivers, we provide new learning experiences. We become purposeful about reinforcing meaningful paths of thought, structuring tasks that will lead a specific child to repeat a productive action or solve a problem. The caregiver watches the child, learning the child's interests, understanding what motivates this child, and determining what developmental milestone is emerging. Through the caregiving relationship, we become aware of maturation and know that we must wait for the child's brain to be able to process a new idea before we can present it. As child-care providers, we guide and nurture children, but we also affect the pathways for thought and action that these children will build on in the future. Becoming a skilled baby watcher is your first step in becoming a skilled caregiver.

Resources

Ainsworth, M. D. S. (1973). The development of mother-infant attachment. In M. B. Calwell & H. N. Ricciuti (Eds.), *Review of child development research* (Vol. 3, pp. 1–94). Chicago: University of Chicago Press.

Barr, R. G., Boyce, T., & Zeltzer, L. K. (1994). The stress illness association in children: A perspective from the biobehavioral interface. In R. J. Haggerty, L. R. Sherrod, N. Garmezy, & M. Rutter (Eds.), *Stress, risk and resiliency in children and adolescents* (pp. 182–224). New York: Cambridge University Press.

Bowlby, J. (1969). *Attachment and loss* (Vol. 1). New York: Basic.

Brazelton, T. B. (1974). The origins of reciprocity: The early mother-infant interaction. In M. Lewis & L. Rosenblum (Eds.), *The effect of the infant on its caregiver* (pp. 49–76). New York: Wiley.

Brazelton, T. B. (1984). *Neonatal behavioral assessment scale* (2nd ed.). (Clinics in Developmental Medicine No. 88, Spastics International Medical Publications). Philadelphia: Lippincott.

Campos, J. J., Bertenthal, B. I., & Kermoian, R. (1992). Early experience and emotional development: The emergence of wariness of heights. *Psychological Science* 3(1), 61–64.

Campos, J. J., Emde, R. N., & Caplovitz, K. (1984). Emotional development. In R. Harre & T. Lamb (Eds.), *The encyclopedic dictionary of psychology* (pp. 193–195). Oxford, England: Blackwell.

Chugani, H. T. (1997). Neuroimaging of developmental non-linearity and developmental pathologies. In R. W. Thatcher, G. R. Lyon, J. Rumsey, & N. Krasnegor (Eds.), *Developmental neuroimaging: Mapping the development of brain and behavior* (pp. 187–195). San Diego, CA: Academic Press.

Dawson, G., & Fisher, K. W. (1994). *Human behavior and the developing brain.* New York: Guilford.

Dettling, A. C., & Krueger, W. K. (1999, April). *Physiological activity in relation to the child's age and temperament in center-based and daycare settings and at home.* Paper presented at the biennial meeting of the Society for Research in Child Development, Albuquerque, NM.

Dunn, J. (1988). *The beginnings of social understanding.* Cambridge, MA: Harvard University Press.

Dunn, J. F. (1976). How far do early differences in mother-child relations affect later development? In P. P. Bateson & R. A. Hinde (Eds.), *Growing points in ethology* (pp. 481–496). Cambridge, England: Cambridge University Press.

Eisenberg, L. (1999). Experience, brain, and behavior: The importance of a head start. *Pediatrics, 103*(5, Part 1), 1031–1035.

Eliot, L. (1999). *What's going on in there? How the brain and mind develop in the first five years of life.* New York: Bantam.

Emde, R. N. (1988). Development terminable and interminable: Innate and motivational factors from infancy. *International Journal of Psychoanalysis, 69,* 23–42.

Erikson, E. H. (1950). *Childhood and society.* New York: Norton.

Frieberg, S., Addison, E., & Shapero, V. (1975). Ghosts in the nursery. *Journal of the American Academy of Child Psychiatry, 14,* 387–421.

Greenough, W. T. (1991). Experience as a component of normal development: Evolutionary considerations. *Developmental Psychology, 27,* 14–17.

Gunnar, M. R. (1995). Neonatal stress reactivity: Predictions to later emotional temperament. *Child Development, 66,* 1–13.

Gunnar, M. R. (2000). Early adversity and the development of stress reactivity and regulation. In C. A. Nelson (Ed.), *The effects of adversity on neurobehavioral development: Minnesota symposia on child psychology, Vol. 31* (pp. 163–200). Mahwah, NJ: Erlbaum.

Gunnar, M. R., Tout, K., deHaan, M., Pierce, S., & Stansbury, K. (1997). Temperament, social competence, and adrenocortical activity in preschoolers. *Developmental Psychobiology, 31*(1), 65–85.

Haith, M. M., Hazan, C., & Goodman, G. S. (1988). Expectation and anticipation of dynamic visual events by 3.5 month-old babies. *Child Development, 59,* 467–479.

Harlow, H. F., Harlow, M. K., & Suomi, S. J. (1971). From thought to therapy: Lessons from a primate laboratory. *American Scientist, 59,* 538–549.

Hofer, M. A. (1994). Hidden regulators in attachment, separation, and loss. In N. A. Fox (Ed.), *The development of emotion regulation: Biological and behavioral considerations* (pp. 192–207). *Monographs of the Society for Research in Child Development, 59*(2–3, Serial No. 240).

Kagan, J., Reznick, J. S., & Snidman, N. (1987). The physiology and psychology of behavioral inhibition in children. *Child Development, 58,* 1459–1493.

Klaus, M. H., & Klaus, P. (1985). *The amazing newborn: Discovering and enjoying your baby's natural abilities.* Reading, MA: Addison-Wesley.

LeDoux, J. (1996). *The emotional brain.* New York: Touchstone Books, Simon & Schuster.

National Research Council and Institute of Medicine. (2000). Rethinking nature and nurture. In J. P. Shonkoff & D. A. Phillips (Eds.), *From neurons to neighborhoods: The science of early childhood development* (pp. 39–56). Washington DC: National Academy Press.

Panksepp, J. (2001). Long-term psychobiological consequences of infant emotions: Prescriptions for the twenty-first century. *Infant Mental Health Journal, 22*(1), 132–173.

Piaget, J. (1936). *The origins of intelligence in children* (2nd ed.). New York: International Universities Press.

Sander, L. W. (1962). Issues in early mother-child interaction. *Journal of the American Academy of Child and Adolescent Psychiatry, 1,* 141–166.

Schore, A. N. (2001). Effects of a secure attachment relationship on right brain development, affect regulation, and infant mental health. *Infant Mental Health Journal, 22*(1), 7–66.

Shore, R. (1997). *Rethinking the brain: New insights into early development.* New York: Families and Work Institute.

Siegel, D. J. (2001). Toward interpersonal neurobiology of the developing mind: Attachment, relationship, "mindsight" and neural integration. *Infant Mental Health Journal, 22*(1), 67–94.

Spitz, R. A. (1945). Hospitalism: An inquiry into the genesis of psychiatric conditions in early childhood. *Psychoanalytic Study of the Child, 2*, 133.

Sroufe, L. A., & Fleeson, J. (1986). Attachment and the construction of relationships. In W. W. Hartup & Z. Rubin (Eds.), *Relationships and development* (pp. 51–71). Hillsdale, NJ: Erlbaum.

Stern, D. N. (1985). *The interpersonal world of the infant.* New York: Basic.

Thomas, A., & Chess, S. (1977). *Temperament and development.* New York: Brunner/Mazel.

Trevarthen, C. (2001). Intrinsic motives for companionship in understanding: The origin, development and significance for infant mental health. *Infant Mental Health Journal, 22*(1), 95–131.

Tronick, E. (1980). The primacy of social skills in infancy. In D. B. Sawin, R. B. Hawking, L. O. Walker, & J. H. Penticuff (Eds.), *Exceptional infant* (Vol. 4, pp. 144–158). New York: Brunner/Mazel.

Tronick, E. Z., Cohn, J., & Shea, E. (1986). The transfer of affect between mothers and infants. In T. B. Brazelton & M. W. Yogman (Eds.), *Affective development in infancy* (pp. 11–25). Norwood, NJ: Ablex.

Werner, E. (2000). Protective factors and resilience. In J. P. Shonkoff & S. J. Meisels (Eds.), *Handbook of early childhood intervention* (2nd ed., pp. 115–132). New York: Cambridge University Press.

Winnicott, D. W. (1971). *Playing and reality.* New York: Basic.

Video

A Mind of Their Own. The Brain and Early Childhood Series. Tape 1. (2000). Alexandria, VA: Association for Supervision and Curriculum Development. (35 min.).

Chapter 2

The Caregiver Builds Relationships

In the first chapter, we explored how infants and toddlers communicate and relate to caregivers. These relationships with children stimulate and focus their young minds. Through practice in observing and reading their nonverbal cues, you have discovered how much infants and toddlers can communicate and contribute to their development through states of awareness and emotional signals. When infants tune in with interest and focus their attention, they enlist interaction. When they turn away or doze off, they are usually put down to rest. When infants are excited, interested, sad, tired, or angry, they show it through facial, vocal, and body cues. Learning to listen to the language of infancy is crucial to good caregiving. However, developing this ability is only part of the relationship story.

We must also consider the caregiver's contribution to a relationship. Infants are able to read our emotional signals from birth. Young children understand, react to, and imitate the nonverbal cues that adults give. Our feelings and needs are being expressed through our actions more than our words. It is important to spend time getting in touch with ourselves. Self-awareness goes hand in hand with our ability to be responsive to a child. This chapter will define the roles that temperament and culture play in our communications and behaviors. It will help us explore our personal backgrounds, feelings, and moods as well as how we communicate these to children. Ideally, this chapter will help you gain a new awareness of yourself within your professional and personal life.

Goals of Chapter 2

▦ Observe and analyze nonverbal signals in adults and understand how these affect children.

▦ Become more aware of your own nonverbal cues and how these are affected by your moods and culture.

▦ Understand temperament and how this affects emotional signaling and shared relationships.

▦ Define responsive relationships as interactions that occur across time and that show an understanding of and a response to the emotional signals of another.

▦ Understand how responsive relationships build trust.

▦ Become more aware of your own emotional signals by practicing a variety of emotional signals and experiencing children's reactions to them.

Key Concept One
What the Caregiver Brings to Relationships

As caregivers, we bring our feelings, moods, attitudes, and goals into each interaction with a child. This form of expression is often done through behaviors that may not be conscious to us—a serious frowning face, a rough touch, inattention to a bid by the child. As adults, we are used to expressing our ideas and knowledge with words. We forget to think about what our behaviors are saying for us.

Relationships Are Mutual

A relationship is a link between two people that is made through communication. Biology has made this communication possible for children, even though they may not have full language capacities. Infants and toddlers are keen observers of our emotional signals. A caregiver's face, tone of voice, touch, and eye contact have a powerful effect on a child. From birth, children seem programmed to respond to the emotions and behaviors of adults. They attend to what they see, hear, and feel, and they also retain and copy these models. Just as the cry of a toddler brings a response from an adult, the nonverbal signals of adults define and change behavior in children. A toddler running down the hall will often trip and fall when he or she hears an adult gasp in fear. A cautious 2-year-old in a new situation will be emboldened by a smile from a trusted caregiver. Communication with a child occurs primarily through nonverbal signals. This mutual sharing of emotion-based signals is the foundation of relationships.

Adults' signals play a key role in relationship building, so we need to recognize and identify what emotional signals we are expressing. Our nonverbal cues are the first communications acknowledged by others. Our face, our body language, and our tone of voice set the stage. In most interactions with adults and children, these cues often override the spoken word. For example, let's imagine that we are in a child-care center.

Eight-month-old Tanisha is on Hanna's lap in the rocker. She looks up and smiles at Hanna, then reaches for Hanna's earrings and chirps happily. Her legs begin to move back and forth as she reaches for the shiny bobbles. Hanna is looking away, out the window. "Hey!" Hanna says when she feels the pull of the earring. She takes Tanisha's hand firmly and pulls it down to her side saying, "No, don't! These are new." She then leans forward to get out of her chair and her body pushes Tanisha into a ball, restricting her movement. She puts Tanisha on the floor next to another child and walks away. Tanisha becomes somber, staring at the other child. She tightens her body, pulling legs and hands in and looks down toward her feet. She stays very quiet.

The child in this scenario communicated interest, exploration, and joy toward Hanna's earrings. Hanna was distracted and then annoyed. She had other things on her mind. Her actions and cues were not about Tanisha's needs; they were about her own. However, those actions and cues changed the focus and the learning for Tanisha. Tanisha changed from being interested to being cautious and withdrawn. This caregiver was probably unaware of the cues she was giving or of how her response affected Tanisha. However, her negative feelings and actions influenced the child.

The learning pathways stimulated in Tanisha's brain by Hanna's actions were different than they would have been had Hanna been more responsive to Tanisha's interests. Instead of learning "Look at the pretty bobbles, but don't touch them," Tanisha learned about coping with new and lonely situations. She could experiment with the sound of her kicking feet or crawl over to a familiar toy. She could connect with the other child playing close to her. Many learning experiences are available to Tanisha when she is alone, but for the moment, learning has stopped, and a recovery period is necessary.

Shared emotions carry great power in our communications. The emotions that we express almost always affect others around us. Have you ever watched others laughing and felt happier yourself? When you have felt tired or down, have you ever had someone come in and enthusiastically invite you to go get a soda (or some other treat), pepping up your mood? The emotional component of a communication is what gives it energy and makes learning memorable.

We Must Be Aware of Our Emotional Cues

What we do—our facial expressions, our touch and tone—will be dictated by our inner feelings. As caregivers, we must learn to look inward and be aware of how we are feeling. By becoming self-aware, we will be more in touch with the signals that we might be giving others. Our nonverbal cues reflect the moment of time in which we exist. For example, is an emergency occurring within the room? Are we behind schedule? Will we be expecting visitors or a review today? Hanna might have been preoccupied with thoughts such as these.

Early Experiences Shape Our Ability to Communicate Through Emotional Signals

As caregivers, our ability to be emotionally responsive is directly related to our own relationship experiences. If our emotional sharing with adults was positive during our early years, responding to children in our care with love and nurturing will seem natural. The converse is also true. If we have had difficult experiences with early relationships, we may experience more difficulty being emotionally responsive. However, we can seek positive adult relationships as ways to heal these early wounds. Other ways that adults seek healing include introspection, self-reflection, talking to family members about family events, journaling, and counseling.

Most adults have experienced some negative aspects of relationships. As adults, we have the opportunity to explore the memories of these experiences and to reevaluate our current attitudes in light of what we now know and who we want to be. These efforts will help us become more responsive in all our relationships, but especially as caregivers of young children.

Our upbringing and culture also define the emotional cues we give. All families have certain beliefs and practices that are passed on to their children. For example, in some cultures, eye contact is an important personal connection, whereas in other cultures, this same behavior with anyone outside the family is considered impolite or frightening. Culture also defines how touch, proximity, and expressiveness are used and understood. Some cultural groups greet with hugs, laughter, and much conversation. Others greet with a bow and a step backward. By being aware of our own cultural practices and beliefs, we will better understand our tendency to be either expressive or reserved with our touch, voice tones, or eye contact. In like manner, when we recognize the cultural beliefs of the families we serve, we will have a better understanding of their children's behavior.

Our Emotional Signals Are Affected by Our Temperaments

Human beings have unique personalities. Although nature has equipped us with similar motivations and emotions, our nervous systems are our own. How we respond to stimulation in our environment is individual and specific. A person's style of approaching and reacting to his or her environment is referred to as temperament. When we understand our own temperaments, we can appreciate the temperamental differences of the children in our care. This understanding is a cornerstone in building relationships. Therefore, it is important for us to examine our own temperaments.

Psychologists studying temperament have focused on individual differences in activity level, adaptability, and mood. We all have different thresholds for processing stimulation, change, and ambiguity. For example, some people find a room that is noisy and chaotic to be aversive, whereas others find it exciting. A defined daily routine is welcomed by some adults and causes others to feel constrained and controlled. The ability to focus and stay on task varies from person to person. Similarly, some of us express feelings intensely, whereas others are more subtle about showing emotions.

Because temperament traits are observed soon after birth, child development researchers believe that these traits have a genetic component. Thus, if temperament is inherited, people in the same family would have a higher probability of sharing some of the same traits. Noting this kind of information may help caregivers better understand the families in their programs and some of the parenting decisions that have been made. A child and a specific parent may share similar traits, or they may reflect opposites. When a deliberate, cautious, and exacting parent has a high-energy child who runs fast, climbs high, needs little sleep, and is too busy to eat, you may sense some anxiety in both parent and child. In the same way, you may experience difficulty connecting with some children purely because of differences in temperament. Your colleagues can be helpful in these situations.

Temperament Can Be Regulated by the Environment

Heredity may define temperament, but experience shapes it. Understanding our ability to control how we respond in certain situations allows us to work better with others and choose work settings and tasks that are best suited to us. For example, some teachers may prefer to work with small groups of children or with an individual child in quiet play, whereas others prefer to be outdoors or involved with a larger group in active play. Through self-reflection, we can be aware of our needs and have some control over our environments. We can request or design those activities and settings that suit us.

However, infants and toddlers do not have the ability to choose or control their environments. We must watch and read their cues to be aware of their sensory overload. Over time, infants become more tolerant of sensory stimulation, and their responses are less extreme. For example, a baby may be very sensitive to sound and cry if there is confusion in the room, but as this child grows, he or she may become less bothered by the sound of surrounding activity.

It Is the Caregiver's Role to Mediate Between Environment and Child

How caregivers respond to a child's temperament-driven behaviors can either reinforce or modify elements of a child's sensitivities. For example, a caregiver can calm agitation in a child by sharing his or her own positive mood. Holding and reassuring a child when an unfamiliar person approaches can modify a shy child's fearfulness. Recognizing that the persistent child will need a two-minute warning before it is time to put away the blocks is another way caregivers can help regulate temperament.

Caregivers may discover particular sensitivities, for example, that some children become anxious in certain places, at certain times of the day, or when activities or settings become too loud and confusing. A caregiver who is sensitive to these individual differences can think ahead about how best to respond to an individual child's needs and mediate anxiety for the child. Helping children learn to control how they react to impulses is a necessary part of early development.

Temperaments Can Be Mediated by Relationships

As caregivers become attuned to the individual temperament of each child, their classrooms will function more smoothly. For instance, knowing that Jeremy (22 months old) has difficulty in adapting to change, his caregiver is sure to remind him that Nana will be picking him up today instead of his father. Similarly, knowing that Kendra (30 months old) is easily overstimulated allows her teacher to make sure that she has an inviting private space available for her to play alone. These approaches ensure that neither child will become anxious or fretful.

By individualizing care plans in these ways, caregivers can gently modify a child's responses and, over time, will be modifying the child's expectations and habits of responding. As the baby or child matures, these gradual changes in the environment will become part of an adaptation in the child's brain. Over time, children will begin to internalize ways to regulate their own extremes of temperament. Early relationships with responsive caregivers will have a lasting positive effect.

Goodness of Fit Indicates How Well Different Temperaments Fit Together

When there is a good fit between a child's and caregiver's temperaments, they can more easily develop a mutual understanding and can more quickly establish a relationship. A caregiver's temperament influences the way a child will respond to him or her. Similarly, children come to child care with individual differences in temperament that will affect the way their caregivers respond to them.

Goodness of fit does not mean that the caregiver and child have the same temperament. Rather, a good fit exists when the caregiver's demands and expectations are compatible with the child's temperamental style. Understanding temperament can help a caregiver appreciate his or her own individual needs and how they might mesh or come in conflict with the needs of individual children. Understanding temperament can also help supervisors assign primary caregivers or help teams plan staffing patterns.

Often, staffing decisions can promote goodness of fit. The child with a high activity level may be frustrating for the caregiver who prefers quiet, cognitive activities such as reading, doing puzzles, and playing matching games. However, the same child may bring joy to the high-energy caregiver who likes outdoor activity or spirited gross motor play. In the same way, some caregivers find it easier to care for children with intense emotional reactions because these signals clearly indicate the child's needs. Even so, regardless of the goodness of fit, the caregiver has a responsibility to adapt and respond in ways that help the child.

Key Concept Two
Responsive Relationships

Let's imagine the following early morning at a child-care center as we begin to examine responsive relationships more closely.

> The father of baby Joselyn (2 months old) hands her to Marta, who is standing at the doorway. Joselyn is fussy. "Are you a hungry girl?" Marta asks. She turns to her colleagues, asking, "Does anyone know Joselyn's schedule? Does she need to be fed now? Did her father leave any instructions?" A voice from across the room says, "She usually needs a bottle." Marta takes the baby inside and fixes her bottle. She offers it to Joselyn. The baby tightens her lips and turns her head away. Marta seems frustrated. Marta rocks Joselyn gently and waits a few minutes. Joselyn's wide eyes examine her face. Marta offers her the bottle again. Again, she tightens her eyes and turns away, beginning to fuss. "You're not hungry, are you?" Marta says to the baby. She puts the bottle down and strokes Joselyn's face. The baby brightens. Marta says, "Good morning, Joselyn. You must have had a good breakfast."

Marta was sensitive to Joselyn's cues. Although the baby was too small to talk, she let Marta know with a turn of her head that she was not hungry. Marta was responsive and respected the baby. Although she was frustrated at not knowing this baby or her needs, Marta took time to pay attention to the baby's feelings.

A Responsive Relationship Is One in Which People Respond to One Another's Feelings and Needs

When you can read a child's cues, you begin to understand what that child is feeling. In turn, the child is reading your cues. Each partner is in tune with the other's emotions. A skillful teacher learns to meet the match, or join the emotion that the child has signaled. He knows that his understanding of the child's feelings will in turn allow the child to copy or match the emotion he will then express to the child.

For example, when a child shows interest in an object or event and the caregiver recognizes this interest, then a cooperative feeling is established between them. This connection motivates them both. Imagine a child who alerts to the sound of an airplane and points toward the sky. The teacher lifts the child to the window to see the plane, saying, "Look! Airplane." By sharing in the interest and excitement of an event that the child initiated, the caregiver is meeting the match.

Meeting the Match Requires the Caregiver to Be Emotionally Available

Being emotionally available means that the caregiver is able to suspend her own feelings and listen to the feelings being expressed by the child. When the caregiver is able to be open to the child's cues, she will be available to match them, to respond with understanding and support. The caregiver attunes to the child and, thus, the child becomes engaged with the caregiver. When a 14-month-old excitedly shows off a block tower he has just built and his teacher shares his enthusiasm, they connect with shared feelings. The caregiver might then decide to extend his learning by asking, "Who's inside?" The child puts his head on the floor to look inside the tower and says, "Daddy." A special emotional connection is made that gives both people a sense of positive energy. The caregiver opened a door for the child to process new kinds of thoughts. Learning occurs during this kind of interaction.

Emotional Availability Builds Trust

Newborns are biologically programmed to reach out to others for their survival. When newborns signal hunger and someone comes to feed them, their survival is enhanced. They feel safe with the person who fills their needs.

Our need to survive is a powerful internal motivator that drives us throughout our lives. When we know that a person will respond to our needs and understand our feelings, we say that we can trust them. Trust is based on feelings of safety, survival, nurturance, and support. Trust is the foundation for all relationships.

As caregivers, it is important that we establish a feeling of trust with the children in our care. To establish this trust, we must be emotionally available to connect with the feelings of a child. The process is not always easy. It takes practice and selflessness to be open and ready to connect with the feelings of another, but this ability will make all the difference in how pleasant our days with children will be.

Our emotional availability initiates and establishes our relationship with a child. This relationship, which gives the child a sense of safety, will also give the child a sense of physical and emotional equilibrium, fulfilling another of nature's powerful internal motivations.

The first base of trust for young children is usually their parents, but when their parents are not there, it is vital that they still feel safe, nurtured, and emotionally balanced. A large number of infants and toddlers in the United States spend many of their waking hours in child-care centers. They are building primary learning pathways from experiences that they have there. It is important for their development that the child-care settings provide emotional availability in relationships.

Primary Caregivers Ensure Continuity of Trust

Each child in group care needs a special adult who will provide emotional availability in a relationship. The primary caregiver will be familiar with the child's emotional signals and be able to be a base of trust for that child. This person will become the child's model, the child's guide, and his or her special emotional connection while the child is away from home. If Joselyn, in the previous scenario, had had a primary caregiver, her schedule and needs would not have been in doubt. Both caregiver and baby would have begun the day on a happier note.

Caregivers and teachers are the link that provides continuity for children who are away from their parents. This continuity is not a constancy of place or things but a constancy of trust and connection. Early childhood caregivers and teachers are part of the network that provides first relationships. As such, they are also models for the child's future relationships. The emotional connection that they forge with the child will affect every aspect of development.

Responsive relationships do not imply that the caregiver is anticipating the child's every need. A trust base is not established if the adult meets the child's need before the child signals. A child does not learn to express his or her needs clearly without reciprocal interaction. In addition, the child will not feel a sense of inner control that comes from initiating an interaction with an adult and being understood. Allow the children in your care to define their needs and wants as much as possible and to come to you for help and support. This interaction enhances communication as well as trust and attachment.

Another troubling situation is one in which the child signals a need but is ignored. This situation can occur in child-care settings where a caregiver has too many children to care for. The child whose signals are ignored may give up and withdraw from seeking help or from expecting interaction or communication with you. On the other hand, some children learn to use stronger and more negative signals to get their needed attention; the screamer or the whiner comes to mind. When children are not sure whom they can trust, they feel insecure, often withdrawn, and are chronically anxious and off balance.

Chapter Summary

Adult cues define relationships for children. As adults, we either signal to children that we are positive, welcoming companions who will help them learn or we signal to them to be cautious and on guard. As caregivers, we are the ones who will connect with the children in our care. We can modulate our expressions and our feelings in order to connect with the child. We can signal to children that we are receptive and available to them. When we attune to their needs, we develop a base of trust with them. It is our responsibility to mediate our emotions to meet the match and connect in this way.

Through self-understanding, we will become aware of our nonverbal signals, and we will be able to adapt our actions to interact more responsively with the children in our care. We will be more in tune with what we are communicating to them. Responsive caregiving requires a willingness to work on our nonverbal cues and the internal feelings that preoccupy us. We must be able to adapt our moods and needs to be emotionally available to each child.

Resources

Brazelton, T. B., Koslowski, B., & Main, M. (1974). Origins of reciprocity: The early mother-infant interaction. In M. Lewis & L. Rosenblum (Eds.), *The effect of the infant on its caregiver* (pp. 49–76). New York: Wiley.

Buss, A. H., & Plomin, R. (1984). *Temperament: Early developing personality traits.* Hillsdale, NJ: Erlbaum.

Butterfield, P. M., Dolezal, S., & Knox, R. M. (1995). *Love is layers of sharing.* Denver, CO: How to Read Your Baby.

Chess, S., & Thomas, A. (1984). *Origins and evolution of behavior disorders: From infancy to early adult life.* New York: Brunner/Mazel.

Darwin, C. (1965). *The expression of emotions in man and animals.* Chicago: University of Chicago Press. Original work published in 1872.

Emde, R. N. (1980). Emotional availability: A reciprocal reward system for infants and parents with implications for prevention of psychosocial disorders. In P. M. Taylor (Ed.), *Parent-infant relationships* (pp. 87–115). Orlando, FL: Grune and Stratton.

Erikson, E. H. (1950). *Childhood and society.* New York: Norton.

Garcia Coll, C., & Magnuson, K. (1999). Cultural influences on child development: Are we ready for a paradigm shift? In C. Nelson & A. Masten (Eds.), *Cultural processes in child development: Minnesota symposia on child psychology* (Vol. 29, pp. 1–24). Hillsdale, NJ: Erlbaum.

Howes, C., & Hamilton, C. E. (1992). Children's relationships with caregivers: Mothers and child care teachers. *Child Development, 63,* 859–866.

Kovach, B. E., & Da Ros, D. E. (1998). Respectful, individual, and responsive caregiving for infants: The key to successful care in group settings. *Young Children, 53*(3), 61–64.

Lamb, M. E. (1998). Non-parental childcare: Context, quality, correlates. In E. W. Damon, I. E. Sigel, & K. A. Renninger (Eds.), *Handbook of child psychology: Vol. 4. Child psychology in practice* (5th ed., pp. 73–134). New York: Wiley.

National Research Council and Institute of Medicine. (2000). Growing up in childcare. In J. P. Shonkoff & D. A. Phillips (Eds.), *From neurons to neighborhoods: The science of early childhood development* (p. 313). Washington, DC: National Academy Press.

Papousek, H., & Papousek, M. (1979). Early ontogeny of human social interactions: Its biological roots and social dimensions. In K. Foppa, W. Lepenies, & D. Ploog (Eds.), *Human ethology: Claims and limits of a new discipline* (pp. 456–489). Oxford, England: Cambridge University Press.

Saarni, C. (1990). Emotional competence: How emotions and relationships become integrated. In R. A. Thompson (Ed.), *Socioemotional development: Nebraska symposium on motivation* (Vol. 36, pp. 115–182). Lincoln, NE: University of Nebraska Press.

Sander, L. (1997). Paradox and resolution: From the beginning. In J. Noshpits, S. Greenspan, S. Wieder, & J. Osofsky (Eds.), *Handbook of child and adolescent psychiatry: Vol. 2. Infants and preschoolers: Development and syndromes* (pp. 153–160). New York: Wiley.

Spitz, R. A. (1965). *The first year of life.* New York: International Universities Press.

Sroufe, L. A., & Fleeson, J. (1986). Attachment and the construction of relationships. In W. W. Hartup & Z. Rubin (Eds.), *Relationships and development* (pp. 51–71). Hillsdale, NJ: Erlbaum.

Stern, D. N. (1977). *The first relationship: Mother and infant.* Cambridge, MA: Harvard University Press.

Thomas, A., Chess, S., & Birch, H. G. (1970). The origins of personality. *Scientific American, 223,* 102–109.

Tronick, E. Z., Als, H., & Brazelton, T. B. (1977). Mutuality in mother-infant interaction. *Journal of Communication, 27,* 74–79.

Videos

Flexible, Fearful, or Feisty: The Different Temperaments of Infants and Toddlers. (1993). San Francisco: WestEd. (29 min.).

Getting in Tune: Creating Nurturing Relationships With Infants and Toddlers. (1993). San Francisco: WestEd. (24 min.).

Infant and Toddler Care: Investing in Caring Relationships. (2003). Crystal Lake, IL: Magna Systems. (24 min.).

Life's First Feelings. (1986). Boston: WGBH Educational Foundation. (58 min.).

Seeing Infants With New Eyes. (1984). Washington, DC: National Association for the Education of Young Children. (26 min.).

Relationships
Are Emotional
Connections

This chapter presents the theoretical base for this book. It explains in detail how emotions guide development. By dissecting emotions theory into some of its many parts and graphing some of the dynamics, we hope that these concepts will become easily accessible for you. We will focus on the ways that emotion and emotional communication help young children understand their world and manage their anxieties.

A quick review will be helpful. In chapter 1, we learned that infants are biologically equipped to connect with their caregivers through a system of actions and sounds that signal their feelings. These signals elicit responses from their caregivers that serve as learning experiences for the infants. Amazingly, infants also can read and understand the emotions that adults signal to them. This inborn ability to form emotional communication links with other humans ensures the infant's survival and continued development.

Although all learning from birth forward is in relationship to an environment, an object, or a person, it is the human interactions that instruct the baby's brain in ways that pure sensory stimulation cannot. The caregiver interprets the baby's sensory experiences by expressing emotional responses that will give the baby affective memories of good or bad. For example, a

Goals of Chapter 3

■ Examine the power of emotional signals and their influence on behavior and learning.

■ Demonstrate how shared positive emotions lead to mutual emotional nourishment as well as feelings of confidence and self-worth.

■ Understand the effect of shared negative emotions—how they change brain chemistry and brain function to caution, to alert, or to alter patterns of thinking.

■ Explain how shared emotions connect us in shared goals and in a shared sense of value—a determining factor in fostering self-regulating behavior and resiliency in children.

■ Examine the detrimental effects of negative emotion sharing.

■ Explore the role of empathy and the consequences of a nonresponsive relationship.

■ Discuss how children benefit from several attachment figures, gaining emotional nourishment from both parents and providers.

■ Practice using touch and voice to mutually regulate a child and to observe how shared emotion serves to stabilize and organize the child.

caregiver might say, "Oh, pretty!" or "Yum yum," or "Yuk, no no!" These interactions with caregivers stimulate the creation of neural pathways, giving infants and toddlers increasingly sophisticated ways of processing their feelings and motivations.

In chapter 2, we came to understand the effect of our own beliefs and motivations. Because children are aware of our emotional cues, we must become conscious of our actions and of the feelings that we evoke in others. We examined the influence of early experience, culture, and temperament on the cues that we give. By contemplating how our beliefs and anxieties have evolved, we will be more aware of our responses to the children in our care.

In this chapter, we will discover the power of emotion sharing. This is the mechanism by which nature and nurture become partners. We will learn how emotional communications become shared feelings and how this mutual sharing becomes a regulatory system for both child and adult. In addition, we will examine each emotion separately. We will learn the power of these emotional states to motivate our behavior and our learning in different ways.

Finally, we will discuss the important concept of emotion regulation. The process of emotion sharing between caregiver and child can help the child to find equilibrium and emotional balance, or it can exacerbate anxieties in the child. By understanding our role in the regulation of emotions, we will be influencing development in many ways, including the structure of the child's nervous system, the focus and path of learning, and the ability of the child to become self-confident and self-controlled.

Key Concept One
The Power of Shared Emotions

Our emotional response is our most basic inborn mechanism for evaluating information. Our emotional core is also our first line of human connection. Therefore, studying emotional development is important to understanding how children learn and why they are motivated to learn. To begin, we will examine some ways that our emotions and inner feelings influence children's learning, attitudes, and beliefs.

Emotion Sharing Interprets Sensory Stimulation

At birth, infants' brains are ready to receive information from sensory stimulation and to evaluate this sensation as a feeling. For example, the snow may fall on the baby's face, and this sensation will register as "good" or "bad" in the baby's brain. The baby can also read the caregiver's emotion cues, and this information will also interpret the sensory input the baby is receiving. "Whee! Snow! Cold. Look. Taste. Snow is fun!" The caregiver's emotion cues tell the baby how to feel or how to respond. To explore this idea further, let us imagine the following scenario.

> Eight-month-old Damion crawls up to a dog and touches the fur. His parent says, "Oh-ooo, so soft! Feel the soft fur on doggie. Love the doggie." In contrast, when Helen does the same thing, her parent says, "Oh-ooo! No, no! Doggies bite. Come away. NO Touch. Leave the doggie alone."

Pathways within Damion's and Helen's brains are informed in either of these situations. In both cases, the emotional signals from the caregiver will influence each child's future thinking when the next experience occurs with a dog and, perhaps, with any soft furry object. The sensation of touch was paired with a signal from the parent that expressed an interpretation of the experience and an evaluation of the sensation as positive or negative. Depending on the child's developmental level, this shared emotion between parent and child might also influence Damion's and Helen's attitudes about dogs or even about soft furry things. This emotional learning is much more sophisticated than the mere sensory learning that soft fur feels good.

Because young children are able to read the emotion cues of their caregivers, they understand their caregivers' preferences. Infants and toddlers learn about others' approval or disapproval of the many sounds, sights, tastes, textures, and actions that surround them. As their brains process both the sensory and emotional aspects of experiences, their knowledge expands. Because of children's emotional connection with their caregivers, children are led to more complex ways of thinking about an experience.

Shared Emotions Are Powerful

Our emotions are our internal guides. We have an emotional opinion before we have a cognitive one, and the emotional one probably influences all of our thinking. For example, when a person goes to buy a new coat, do they consider the density of the thread, how well the buttons are sewn on, and the comparative value with other brands? Most will buy the one that feels comfortable or the one that they believe looks good on them. The choice reflects an emotional attachment rather than a rational, intellectual one. Our thinking and learning are also internally guided by our physical condition. If we are hungry, tired, or cold, then our emotions give these internal cues priority.

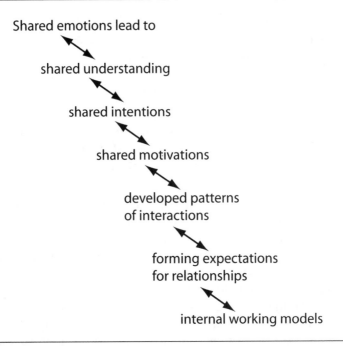

Figure 3.1. The power of sharing emotions.

All of our interactions with others involve shared emotions. We also vicariously experience shared emotions when we cry in a movie or become angry at an item in the newspaper. Emotional learning creates strong memories, especially when the emotion is strong. Years afterward, we still recall a fun party, a winning game, an incident where someone was angry at us, or a time when we shared a fearful experience. These affective memories are some of the first remembrances an infant forms. From early in life, pleasure and pain initiate memories that shape behavior thereafter.

Because emotional connections are so powerful, our relationships with the children in our care are powerful. As we connect emotionally with these children, they begin to define themselves and their own feelings, in part, because of their relationship with us. Our relationships with them will shape their learning and define their social, emotional, and cognitive development.

How do shared emotions define and guide us? It is helpful to consider a theoretical view of emotion sharing and to visualize the process of how shared emotions affect us (Figure 3.1). When people share their feelings, they also experience a shared understanding. This shared understanding is sometimes called a "shared space" or a "moment of meeting." The bond that is created between two people through shared understanding focuses them toward a shared motivation and a shared goal. These shared feelings, shared motivations, and shared goals underlie team spirit. They fuel the cooperation that characterizes cultural unity and the collaboration that supports traditions. When we feel this sharing, we feel accepted by another, and we feel valued. This feeling of belonging is also a feeling of safety. We strive to form relationships with trusted others who connect with us on an emotional level. These people become our attachment figures, our base of emotional stability.

When emotion sharing happens repeatedly between two people, it creates a pattern of interaction and an expectation for future interactions. For children, these patterns become patterns of behavior in their brains, which we call an "internal working model." Children will use these models as they encounter other relationships. When first relationships are formed from positive experiences, they will influence children to interact in positive ways when they meet someone new. If relationship encounters have involved negative affective memories, children may withdraw from meeting new people or may be slow to trust.

When caregivers share an understanding of a child's needs and interests, they gain the child's trust. When trust is established between two people, then a mutual sharing will follow. A responsive relationship can develop. The child will accept the caregiver as a model and guide, sharing the caregiver's feelings and internalizing the behaviors and attitudes of the caregiver. Internalized models of behavior that are defined through emotion sharing form our opinions, perceptions, and values.

Key Concept Two
Different Emotions Affect Us in Different Ways

Positive and negative emotions are processed in different parts of our brains. They elicit different neurotransmitters, which stimulate neural pathways in different ways. Caregivers and teachers need to understand these processes so that they will understand the impact of their emotional communications on others. By examining each emotion separately, we come to understand how each feeling we express can affect the behaviors and the personalities of the children in our care.

Shared Positive Emotions (SPE) Open Pathways to Learning

Shared positive emotions (SPE) can be powerful. Consider the difference between the following three approaches to the same situation:

— "Hey! Listen. We're going to eat lunch outside!!" This caregiver is excited and, in turn, excites the children.

— "Hurry, come now! We have to eat outside today." This caregiver is angry; thus, her group will become more oppositional.

— "Lunch is outside today. See you out there." This caregiver is bland and detached; the children may wander and dawdle getting to lunch.

The caregiver's affect can define in how children will respond. Let us imagine the following scenario:

> A group of 2-year-olds wander independently around the room. Steve, their teacher, says, "Hey, everybody, let's play bend and stretch." He puts on a jolly CD, and familiar music fills the room. Steve stretches his arms up over his head and then out to the sides, motioning with his hands for the children to come to him. Most of the children eagerly run over. In an excited voice he says, "Dance, everyone. Dance around." The children begin to weave and turn to the music. "Now, reach up high. Reach for the stars." Steve reaches high, and the children imitate. "Now, down, down, touch your toes." Steve bends to touch his toes, and the group follows. "Now, reach up high. Then bend to your toes. Now, all fall down!" The children drop to the floor, laughing and rolling around.

The teacher used excitement to collect the group. His emotion and the jolly sound of the music focused them on the game. The children became available to his suggestions. He then organized their thinking in a patterned way, using the bend and stretch activity. Steve was also teaching them about shared activity, connecting with one another through group activity and emotional sharing. The emotion fueled a succession of organized thoughts and actions. Steve had his group actively using their muscles and their minds while they were sharing fun together.

In the scene above, most, but not all, of the children joined in. Let us continue the scene to see how Steve responds to the other children.

> Steve looks toward the two children who are still involved with other toys. He calls to them by name. They do not respond. He starts the music again, and reaches up high, "Remember? Everybody up! Let's go again." He starts singing, and some of the children join in, saying, "Bend" and "Stars."
>
> The two lone toddlers have come closer and are standing by the group, watching. "Hey!" says Steve. "Join the circle. Here, stand by me. Now, reach, reach up high!" Soon, the two children are joining in, reaching, bending, and falling to the ground. They are also laughing.

The emotions, the music, the laughter, and the group activity were all contagious and attracted the two who were initially uninterested. They came of their own choosing because of the desire to belong, to join in, and to share

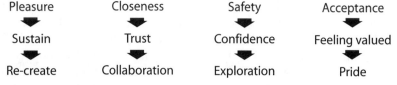

Figure 3.2. Shared positive emotions.

the fun. A sense of collaboration comes from having fun together or having ideas approved.

The children also learn many things from this fun experience. The emotion of excitement ignited their interest. The teacher then organized this focus into an integrated learning experience. Many senses were used, but the activity also incorporated social actions such as following the leader, starting on cue, and stopping together. The children were emboldened to try new things. Complex thoughts were involved, for example, remembering the words and anticipating the next action. The children gained a sense of self-confidence by keeping "in tune" with the team (Figure 3.2).

When the shared emotion is positive, both people feel pleasure. The child wants to sustain this feeling or to re-create it. Children remember what signals or actions led them to a period of positive emotion sharing. Smiling, laughing, reaching up, clapping, dancing, or hugging become standard action patterns for the child who wants more SPE from a caregiver. A child soon learns that these actions also bring positive responses from other adults and children, so these positive behavior patterns become tactics and then habits for relating with others. This process leads to successful social learning and internalized strategies for forming positive relationships.

Calm, quiet emotions represent a different kind of SPE. These shared emotions give us a sense of safety and equilibrium. If the shared emotional signals from the adult are calming, they convey feelings of protection. "I'm okay." "I'm safe." "I'm loved." This sense of protection is a feeling of your emotional stability. An experience of sharing that reduces anxiety leads to feelings of contentment and collaboration.

This sense of shared calm is transferred through touch, hugs, motion, rhythm, gentle sounds, and close body contact. This kind of SPE usually alters the emotional state of the fearful or injured child. It can also alter feelings of anger, frustration, or distress. The older child who has established a responsive relationship with you may need only a smile, a nod of approval, or a hand on the shoulder to feel this sense of safety.

SPE is a force in establishing resilience within a child. In this context, resilience means the ability to find solutions within ourselves. When children feel safe within their relationships and routines, they gain confidence in their own abilities to access resources when they need them. They develop a self-trust, which leads to resiliency. When an attachment relationship has been established with a caregiver, the child seeks guidance and emotion regulation from that person. It is the emotional connectedness that serves to quiet the child's anxieties and guide the child's thoughts toward soltuions. Because of the attachment relationships, the child develops resources within herself for coping and for regaining stability.

When emotion sharing and emotional communication have been predominantly positive, children are more equipped to endure periods of negativity. They are able to see anger in others as a momentary event. They may respond by attempting to alter the adult emotion, or they may adapt their behavior in some way. They are more likely to laugh at mistakes, to ask for help, or to learn alternatives for coping with problems. Their internal working models are positive. They become optimistic, positive people.

Shared Negative Emotions (SNE) Refocus Learning

Negative emotional displays serve a different function. They elicit different chemical messengers within the brain and stimulate different pathways for action. Shared negative emotions (SNE) are extremely powerful because they trigger our survival instincts. They tell us to be on guard for danger. Adrenaline fuels the brain, and prior learning stops (Figure 3.3).

When we share negative emotions, we feel displeasure. We seek to change this feeling or escape from it. We interrupt our current thought processes to evaluate the source of the negative emotion and possible danger. This biological response is functional when danger is present. Shared negative emotions alert us, caution us, and redirect our thinking so that we can protect ourselves. For example, if we are in a movie and a frantic voice yells, "Help! Look out!" we stop concentrating on the show and evaluate

**Controlled negative emotions
(clear, calm, and consistent)**

Alert us	Caution us	Displease us
⬇	⬇	⬇
Uncertainty,	Distrust,	Re-evaluate

Figure 3.3. Controlled shared negative emotions.

the situation around us. Our minds begin thinking about our personal safety. We will not remember the scene in the show or what happened next to the actors.

Shared negative emotions do not lead to shared goals or feelings of connectedness, but instead, they signal us to withdraw. When we share the negative emotions of another, we feel insecure. We distrust what we are doing or the person with whom we are interacting. We feel defensive and seek to repair the situation.

When negative emotions are expressed by others, children are especially quick to become alert. Their nervous system reacts and they become anxious. The negative emotion does not need to be directed toward them to be contagious. It will affect the entire group. For example, imagine the following scenario.

> On the playground for 2-year-olds, Jeffrey falls, skins a knee, and cries. Everyone stops. All eyes are watching until someone comes to help. Eileen picks up Jeffrey and takes him inside. After this event, most of the children change their behavior. Some children go to their caregiver and want to be close or hold the caregiver's hand. Some switch to a quieter game. Some amble around in a disorganized way. They are all influenced by the tears and hurt that Jeffrey experienced. They have all shared his sadness.

Extreme negative emotion or pervasive negativity can damage learning abilities. When shared negative emotions are too strong or if they occur too often, they are detrimental to the development of the children. When pervasive negativity or the memory of it keeps children always on alert, always unsure, then their behaviors are reactive and self-protective. Learning takes a different path. When children are raised with continual negative emotion, they feel devalued, rejected, and ashamed. This shame can become an internal working model that stays with these individuals into adulthood (Figure 3.4).

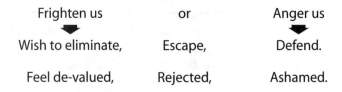

Extreme negative emotions
(angry, fearful, sad)

Frighten us	or	Anger us
Wish to eliminate,	Escape,	Defend.
Feel de-valued,	Rejected,	Ashamed.

Figure 3.4. Extreme shared negative emotions.

Different Negative Emotions Have Different Effects

Anger, fear, and sadness are the main negative emotions. Each of these emotions has different effects on behavior and on the child's capacity to learn and develop.

Anger. Anger is a common negative emotion. Anger is often used as an attempt to change or shape behavior. Most parents and caregivers become angry when they believe that a child has not responded to their needs or when they are tired or feel embarrassed by the child's behavior. Children often evoke our frustration. They are spontaneous and goal directed, and they may not listen to our words. In many instances, adults think that being angry will help the child focus and learn. However, this thinking is actually not correct.

When trusted adults are angry, children are frightened, not only because of what may happen to them but also because of what they see in the person they love. Anger triggers a fear response in a child; thus, that child must think about how best to protect herself. She changes her focus; her goal is now to escape or to defend herself. Because she has forgotten what caused the anger, she will not learn to change the behavior that made her caregiver angry. This fact explains why teaching with anger does not work. Pervasive anger produces anxious and disorganized children. These children are often pessimistic or depressed and have difficulty organizing or focusing their thoughts.

Anger must be tempered to be effective. Because negative emotions transfer quickly from person to person, especially adult to child, they are extremely disorganizing. Like fire, they must be used carefully. To be effective as a discipline tool, anger must be tempered. Caregivers must remain calm, clear, and consistent. If adult displeasure is focused on the problem behavior and if the reason is explained calmly, then you will have success in helping the child learn. Firm, clear limits with neutral emotions do teach, especially if followed by positive action and modeling. For example, imagine the following scenario:

> A caregiver is concerned about Arnie, 30 months old, who is running round and round the playground. She says, "No more running, Arnie. Stay here." She stops Arnie gently with both hands. Her face is neutral. Her voice is calm but firm. She holds Arnie for a moment until his breathing slows. "Arnie, stop," she says. "Stop running. It's story time. We need to get ready for story time now. Hold my hand. We'll go together."

This caregiver followed her verbal message with action and nonverbal cues. The negative message was clear. Short, simple, firm words—"Arnie, stop running"—but not much emotion. Her action gave the real message to Arnie: The jig was up; running was over. When this kind of negative message is given, the child remains in a thoughtful mode and is able to focus on what the adult is saying without becoming angry or fearful. Arnie processes the caregiver's message and alters his behavior rather than reacting and wrenching away from her. The caregiver was able to communicate to Arnie that running was the problem, not that Arnie was a bad person. By going hand in hand with Arnie to story time, she reinforced her caring for him. They joined to accomplish a shared goal. She regulated his emotions and refocused his behavior.

> *Teasing is indirect anger. Teasing, taunting, and persistent tickling are forms of anger displayed by an adult toward a child.*

Teasing is indirect anger. Teasing, taunting, and persistent tickling are forms of anger displayed by an adult toward a child. Teasing is a way for the adult to show power over the child. Under the guise of fun, the adult causes the child to feel helpless, overpowered, or ashamed. Teasing confuses the child and produces an emotional mismatch. No shared goals are involved. If you suspect that a parent believes teasing is fun, consider ways that you or the staff at the center might redirect that parent's belief.

Extreme or persistent anger is detrimental. If anger is too pervasive, the child withdraws from the adult or tries to defend herself. She strikes out in any way possible, learning a behavior pattern in the process. When adults are too powerful against her defenses, she transfers her angry feelings to other children, toys, or animals. She acts out her inner rage or models the actions of those who were angry toward her.

If shared anger is the child's predominant experience, then negative patterns will become the child's internal working models. Learning for these children will be different. They may have difficulty with relationships throughout their lives.

Extreme anger causes fear within the child. In an effort to repair this feeling of fear, children will eagerly seek someone else to make them feel happy again. The child-care setting can represent a place where these children can find positive relationships—where they can explore and learn without inciting angry responses. In the center, you can be an agent of repair; you can effectively redirect behaviors and define limits without anger. By helping children learn what behavior is expected of them, you will be giving these children some resources for self-management in other situations. Repairing and returning to SPE will mediate the effects of anger. Repair gives children resources for solving problems and managing their own behavior successfully. Repair allows children to keep anger in perspective and to adapt their behavior while reinforcing a positive identity.

Intriguingly, in persistent anger situations, children begin to learn what behaviors stop anger, what people or situations to avoid, and how to defuse anger with a hug, a cute antic, an exaggerated display of obedience, or even a lie. In some cases, these coping strategies can save children from harm. However, some children may go too far in conforming or in trying to please, and they become more vulnerable to abusive relationships.

Anger does not have to be directed at a child to be shared. Even if the negative emotion is not directed at the child, it still transfers quickly. For example, when a caregiver expresses anger at the cupboard latch, kicking and pounding on it, the child may begin kicking his toys because he has absorbed the caregiver's anger and then models the related behavior. In the child-care setting, you may have children who come to you with internalized anger or who react quickly to those around them with aggressive responses. Positive relationships will be the means through which these children will learn to act with more thoughtful responses to others. You can help repair some of the withdrawal or aggression in these children through responsive relationships with them.

Fear. Fear is our reaction to perceived danger. Fear motivates us to freeze or to escape, but as adults, we have learned to examine the meaning behind our fear and to look for solutions. We direct the emotion into a cognitive pathway. A fear signal from an adult to a child is perhaps the most powerful emotional signal for alerting the child to withdraw. Fear produces high cortisol levels, leading to high anxiety. For this reason, shared fear must be tempered and repaired by the adult. Let us imagine the following scenario:

> An adult gasps in fear as a toddler is running for the stairs. The toddler, hearing the gasp, stops and falls in place. The adult goes to the child, picks her up, and hugs her. Then the adult takes the child to the stairs, squats down, and says, "Stairs. You could fall. Boom. Boom. Boom. Here, take my hand. We go together."

The fear signal from the adult sent immediate fear to the child, who stopped and fell. The gasp alerted the child and disorganized the child's thinking and motivation. This reaction allowed the adult time to get to the child and redirect or correct the action, thereby protecting the child. However, it also caused the child to fall. When negative emotion is followed by corrective teaching and then by positive emotion, shared goals are accomplished. In the scenario, the caregiver defused the feeling of fear in the child by sharing reassurance and a solution. The caregiver hugged the child, showed her the danger, and then demonstrated that they should go together on the stairs. As we establish relationships with each child in our care, we will become more able to temper and repair our emotional signals.

A word of caution: Memory traces from fear can be strong and lasting. Shared fear serves a vital role for the safety of children, for example, protecting them from the street, medicines, cleaning products, knives, and matches. However, the child may become more fearful than the adult and remain fearful of similar situations in the future. Expressions of fear need to be defused by examining the reasons for the fear. The adult helps the child examine the emotion by asking, "Why is it frightening?" and "What can be done about it?" Without this guidance, children's actions remain impulsive and often troublesome. It can sometimes be difficult for the caregiver to distinguish between fear and anger. When children become obstinate or angry about doing something, they may really be afraid.

If the fears of the adult are irrational, then children's fear memories can be misguided. For many children, the shared fear memories that they have internalized extend to fears of things such as bugs, certain foods, escalators, and new or different people. Child-care relationships can mediate some of the irrational fears that children have assumed from others in their lives. As infants and toddlers develop and expand their knowledge through experiences, they often temper these fears on their own.

Sadness. Shared sadness plays an important role. Sharing sadness with an attachment figure teaches a child to consider the feelings of others. When children experience another's sadness, they are sad, but they also are motivated to fix the problem. The 6-month-old will quickly join the crying of another child, but the 3-year-old usually tries to comfort a sobbing child or adult. Our ability to share in the emotions of another leads to our understanding of the pain behind their sadness. We call this shared sadness empathy.

Empathy is our ability to respond compassionately to the feelings of others. Children who have shared sadness with someone they trust will develop an ability to connect with another's pain. Empathy is developed during the first 3 years of life. Because of the intense emotion sharing and modeling that marks early relationships, toddlers begin to gain an appreciation of the feelings of another. They realize through shared emotion how their actions affect others. Many believe that empathy develops only within the context of a trusted relationship involving someone with whom the child also shares positive emotions and that emotion sharing is what forms a conscience within us. Without strong primary relationships that share joy and sadness, toddlers may not learn to interpret the feelings of others. Evidence suggests that a sense of conscience may never develop in children who lack responsive relationships, especially in cases of neglect, parental depression, or psychological abuse. These children will not learn to share or connect with others through emotions. They do not realize or care how their actions might affect others.

Caregivers need to advance an appreciation for the feelings of others within the child-care center by talking about, sharing, and repairing the sadness, pain, fear, and anger that may occur during everyday experiences. Trusted caregivers help toddlers to internalize a sense of right and wrong when they interpret the toddlers' experiences. The following scenario provides an illustration.

> In the toddler room, Gretchen has pushed Tommy off the trike. Tommy screams and is caught under the wheel. Gretchen is watching. Dayna, the caregiver, approaches. "Oh, Gretchen," says Dayna, "Poor Tommy is hurting. Let's help him. The trike is on his leg. Gretchen, help me pull the trike off of Tommy." Gretchen helps, and Dayna says, "There! See? We made it better." Dayna picks up Tommy and gives him a hug, saying, "You're okay." He wiggles out of her arms and stands, staring at Gretchen. Dayna says, "Gretchen, when you pushed Tommy, that hurt him. That makes me sad." Tommy gets back on the trike and rides off. Dayna takes Gretchen's hand, and they go to find the other trike.

The importance of developing empathy speaks to the need for establishing primary caregivers in child-care programs. A caregiver who will be a consistent guide for interpreting the child's experiences and repairing negative feelings will maintain a continuity of trust between home and child care. In some instances, the child-care provider may be the child's only guide to understanding and managing his feelings.

When the internalization of empathy does not occur, the child turns inward. If the child does not have the opportunity to share the feelings of someone they trust or if the shared emotions that the child experiences are overwhelmingly sad or frightening, the child withdraws to invent safer models of relationship. These children may engage in solitary play and invent strategies that wall off relationships. Some others may develop their own aggressive strategies for obtaining their goals. Strategies that are initially effective for a child might include overpowering another child by pushing, hitting, or biting. Other children might use devious tactics such as hiding things or lying to get what they want. These strategies for gaining a goal can be internalized as working models of behavior within the first 3 years of life. Without guidance, these strategies continue to be used by the child, and thus, they may continue to be reinforced. The child believes that they are okay. These children are often lonely, solitary children. As they become older, they experience more difficulty in sharing emotional relationships or in finding friends, mentors, or social acceptance.

Pervasive sadness or the absence of shared emotions is devastating. When infants and toddlers have primary caregivers who are too busy to connect with them or who are depressed, these children have no expectation that their attempts to communicate with others will be honored. These children may also withdraw into an internal protective shell, often using a fantasy world to create an emotional connection. They do not have adults who share their joys and interests or who interpret and repair their negative experiences. Because their interpretations of experiences and events in their lives must come primarily from inside themselves, these children often plateau or decline developmentally.

Key Concept Three
Shared Emotions Regulate Behavior

Shared emotions change behavior for both child and adult. We not only respond to the emotional signals of another but also tend to absorb them or join in the feeling of another. Through sharing emotional signals, each person is changed by the other. This mutual regulation happens in marriages, with close friends, and with family members. It is important to separate mutual regulation from coregulation. When one person purposefully uses affect to change another, such as quieting a frightened toddler, this is coregulation. This is particularly salient between adults and children. We know that we can share our pain with a loved one; we expect to be comforted by a hug from an attachment figure. Evidence suggests that this ability for one person to temper or excite the emotions of another is a major influence in early brain growth. Coregulation of anxieties in the young child is a major influence in shaping the child's ability to self-organize and self-regulate later in life.

As adults, our emotions are influenced by children. The crying of an infant or the shrill squeals and intense activity of an overstimulated toddler can provoke anxiety within us. We often react with spontaneous responses, not taking the time to temper the extreme emotions we are feeling. As adults, we have the cognitive ability to consider both our feelings and theirs, we must be the ones in control. We must adapt our feelings to find the best solutions for all of us.

Young children cannot control their feelings in this conscious way. Their emotions lead them to reactive responses. They need our guidance to organize their thinking into problem-solving ideas. When emotions zoom out of control for the child, the caregiver can calm and guide the child. This process establishes neural pathways for thoughtful action to replace the impulsive responses.

Mutual Regulation Gives Children Feelings of Continuity

If we have a responsive relationship with a child, then we are likely to be the first to hear his cry or may become more agitated than other adults in the room by the extremes in his behavior. Because of this dynamic, we will have the greatest effect on teaching self-regulation to this child. He will be aware of our special sensitivity for his needs. He will be aware of our responsiveness. When we hold or rock this anxious child, we both will become calmed and relaxed, and we will both return to equilibrium. In a responsive relationship, your understanding signals the child that he is okay. Your emotional connection tempers the child's anxiety levels.

Mutual regulation sets a model of social behavior for young children. Infants and toddlers watch and follow the patterns set by their attachment figures. Children will interact with others in the same way that their trusted adults do. When caregivers are warm and inclusive toward the children in their care, children learn to value others. They also learn the words and the actions that make others feel accepted.

When we hold or rock this anxious child, we both will become calmed and relaxed, and we will both return to equilibrium.

Mutual regulation establishes attitudes, interests, and persistence. Caregivers impart their attitudes and preferences through emotional signals. For example, a child's feelings about animals or plants will be influenced by the likes and dislikes of the people he trusts. When we are excited about a book or a song, the children around us will also become interested. When we keep a child engaged in learning the song or finishing the book, the child will feel the shared accomplishment and will want to do the activity again independently. Books will become one of his interests. When we share joy at completing a task, children will begin to value accomplishment, and they will begin to persist at the tasks they begin. In other words, because of the mutual sharing relationship you have developed, you are extremely influential as a caregiver of young children.

In the child-care setting, your relationships must be individualized. All children enter early childhood programs with a history of shared emotion, but their past experiences will be varied. Expectations within each child will differ. Their age, developmental level, and breadth of experience will influence your ability to establish an attachment relationship. As a caregiver, you will need to respond differently to each child.

Although most children will come to you with a history of positive shared relationships, some children may be emotionally needy. Caregivers will have children coming into their programs who expect adults to be angry or who do not expect to connect at all. These children may signal their feelings to you, but they do not expect to have their signals matched with an empathetic response. Because of this mindset, they may be slow to join into a relationship and may fail to pick up on the excitement or joy of those around them. Recall the two children who did not want to join into the "bend and stretch" game. Connecting with shy or angry children in a shared-understanding, shared-goal relationship will take time and effort. However, not connecting may leave these children with no counter-force to support their development and learning. The extra effort you expend on relationship building at this time may open a door to their future success.

Having too many caregivers can negate emotional connectedness for a child. When the infant or toddler in child care does not have a primary attachment figure, even though many competent caregivers are around, the child feels adrift without a compass. Relationship experiences can seem random. This feeling may also be true for children who have changed providers repeatedly or for children who spend long hours in centers where staff turnover is heavy.

A young child can connect with only a few attachment figures. Most children have more than one caregiver at home. Their relationship network beyond the family should be extended slowly. As they move into child care, assigning only one or two primary caregivers is important. If a child can establish an attachment relationship with a caregiver and maintain this contact throughout her stay, her early learning will be enriched.

The 2-year-old who has received emotional nourishment, continuity, and confidence from earlier relationships will be able to relate to several different caregivers and adapt to different social and emotional situations. However, he will probably choose one person to be his primary relationship. This person is the one the child will seek for comfort when he is anxious and for information about attitudes and actions when he is unsure. Even as adults, we need a responsive relationship within our lives—someone whom we trust and who will provide us with a positive model and an emotion-sharing experience.

Chapter Summary

Shared emotions are powerful. Shared emotions motivate and direct us. In addition, they can calm us and help us regain balance and feelings of equilibrium. Similarly, shared emotions also can agitate us and alert us. We are always influencing those around us with the emotional signals that we express. We call this dynamic mutual regulation or coregulation.

Mutual regulation is important for child-care providers to understand. The emotional signals that infants and toddlers express can change our feelings and our behaviors, but the signals that we express to these children will teach them, balance them, and inspire them. We must be aware of our signals and temper them appropriately so that they are helpful and instructive rather than anxiety producing.

When emotional connections between children and caregivers have been positive and consistent, caregivers become models and guides for toddlers. The caregiver will influence the habits a child learns as well as the child's interests and ability to focus. The behaviors that caregivers use and teach will become internal working models for the child and a basis for his or her future learning.

By examining the functions of shared emotions as communicators, motivators, and inhibitors, we can comprehend their power. Emotions influence our thought processes and define our actions as well as our health. When emotion sharing is positive, emotional and cognitive growth occurs. When emotion sharing is negative, learning is focused on survival and protection.

We are just beginning to comprehend the importance of sharing positive emotion and forming consistent responsive relationships with infants and toddlers. This positive emotional connection seems to be the bedrock of strong neural structure, emotional balance, self-image, resilience, cognitive focus, and socialization. It is vital that the child-care center place priority on developing a system that allows primary relationships of this kind to evolve and to endure.

References

Ainsworth, M. D. S., Blehar, M., Waters, E., & Wall, S. (1978). *Patterns of attachment.* Hillsdale, NJ: Erlbaum.

Beckwith, L. (1990). Adaptive and maladaptive parenting: Implications for intervention. In S. J. Meisels & J. P Shonkoff (Eds.), *The handbook of early childhood intervention* (1st ed., pp. 53–77). Cambridge, England: Cambridge University Press.

Belsky, J. (1986). Infant day care: A cause for concern? *Zero to Three, 6,* 1–7.

Brazelton, T. B., & Cramer, B. G. (1990). *The earliest relationship.* Reading, MA: Addison-Wesley.

Bronson, M. B. (2000). *Self-regulation in early childhood: Nature and nurture.* New York: Guilford Press.

Butterfield, P. M., Dolezal, S., & Knox, R. M. (1995). *Love is layers of sharing.* Denver, CO: How to Read Your Baby.

Cicchetti, D., & Toth, S. L. (1998). Perspectives on research and practice in developmental psychopathology. In W. Damon (Ed.), *The handbook of child psychology: Vol. 4. Child psychology in practice* (5th ed., pp. 479–583). New York: Wiley.

Eisenberg, N. (1998). *Empathy and related emotional responses: New directions for child development.* San Francisco: Jossey-Bass.

Eisenberg, N., & Fabes, R. A. (1992). *Emotion and its regulation in early development.* San Francisco: Jossey-Bass.

Emde, R. N. (1983). The prerepresentational self and its affective core. *The Psychoanalytic Study of the Child, 83*, 165–192.

Emde, R. N., Biringen, Z., Clyman, R. B., & Oppenheim, D. (1991). The moral self of infancy: Affective core and procedural knowledge. *Developmental Review, 11*, 251–271.

Field, T. (1994). The effects of mother's physical and emotional availability on emotion regulation. In N. Fox (Ed.), *The development of emotion regulation: Biological and behavioral considerations* (pp. 208–227). *Monographs of the Society for Research in Child Development, 59*(2–3, Serial No. 240).

Fox, N. A. (1991). If it's not left, it's right: Electroencephalogram asymmetry and the development of emotions. *American Psychologist, 46*, 863–872.

Fox, N. A. (Ed.). (1994). The development of emotion regulation: Biological and behavioral considerations. *Monographs of the Society for Research in Child Development, 59*(2–3, Serial No. 240).

Fraiberg, S. (1966). *The magic years.* New York: Simon and Schuster.

Gunnar, M. R., Brodersen, L., Nachmias, M., Buss, K., & Rigatuso, J. (1996). Stress reactivity and attachment security. *Developmental Psychobiology, 29*(3), 191–204.

Gunnar, M. R., Mangelsdorf, S., Larson, M., & Hertsgaard, L. (1989). Attachment, temperament and adrenocortical activity in infancy: A study of psychoendocrine regulation. *Developmental Psychology, 25*, 355–363.

Gunnar, M. R., & Stone, C. (1984). The effects of positive maternal affect on infant responses to pleasant, ambiguous, and fear-provoking toys. *Child Development, 55*, 1231–1236.

Hofer, M. A. (1994). Hidden regulators in attachment, separation, and loss. In N. A. Fox (Ed.), *The development of emotion regulation: Biological and behavioral considerations* (pp. 192–207). *Monographs of the Society for Research in Child Development, 59*(2–3, Serial No. 240).

Izzard, C., & Malatesta, C. (1987). Perspectives on emotional development: Differential emotions theory of early emotional development. In J. Osofsky (Ed.), *Handbook of infant development* (2nd ed., pp. 494–554). New York: Wiley Interscience.

Kopp, C. B. (1992). Emotional distress and control in young children. In N. Eisenberg & R. A. Fabes (Eds.), *Emotion and its regulation in early development* (pp. 41–56). San Francisco: Jossey-Bass.

LeDoux, J. (1996). *The emotional brain.* New York: Touchstone Books, Simon & Schuster.

Lewis, M., & Rosenblum, L. (Eds.). (1974). *The origins of fear. Vol. 2: The origins of behavior.* New York: Wiley.

Lieberman, A. F. (1990). Early day care from an infant mental health perspective. In S. S. Chehrazi (Ed.), *Psychosocial issues in day care* (pp. 69–81). Washington, DC: American Psychiatric Press.

Panksepp, J. (2001). Long-term psychobiological consequences of infant emotions: Perceptions for the twenty-first century. *Infant Mental Health Journal, 22*(1), 132–173.

Saarni, C. (1990). Emotional competence: How emotions and relationships become integrated. In R. A. Thomson (Ed.), *Socioemotional development: Nebraska symposium on motivation* (Vol. 36, pp. 115–182). Lincoln: University of Nebraska Press.

Sameroff, A. J., & Emde, R. N. (Eds.). (1989). *Relationship disturbances in early childhood: A developmental approach.* New York: Basic.

Sander, L. (1975). Infant and caretaking environment: Investigation and conceptualization of adaptive behavior in a system of increasing complexity. In E. J. Anthony (Ed.), *Explorations in child psychiatry* (pp. 129–166). New York: Plenum.

Schore, A. N. (2001). Effects of a secure attachment relationship on right brain development, affect regulation, and infant mental health. *Infant Mental Health Journal, 22*(1), 7–66.

Sroufe, L. A. (1996). *Emotional development: The organization of emotional life in the early years.* Cambridge, England: Cambridge University Press.

Stern, D. N. (1990). *Diary of a baby: What your child sees, feels and experiences.* New York: Basic.

Stuss, D. T. (1992). Biological and psychological development of executive functions. *Brain and Cognition, 20,* 8–23.

Trevarthen, C. (2001). Intrinsic motives for companionship in understanding: The origin, development and significance for infant mental health. *Infant Mental Health Journal, 22*(1), 95–131.

Tronick, E. A., Als, H., Adamson, L., Wise, S., & Brazelton, T. B. (1978). The infant's response to entrapment between contradictory messages in face-to-face interactions. *Journal of the American Academy of Child and Adolescent Psychiatry, 26,* 166–172.

Tronick, E. A., Cohen, J. F., & Shea, E. (1986). The transfer of affect between mothers and infants. In T. B. Brazelton & M. W. Yogman (Eds.), *Affective development in infancy* (pp. 11–25). Norwood, NJ: Ablex.

Tronick, E. A., & Gianino, A. (1986). Interactive mismatch and repair: Challenges to the coping infant. *Zero to Three, 6,* 1–6.

Werner, E. E. (2000). Protective factors and individual resilience. In J. P. Shonkoff & S. J. Meisels (Eds.), *Handbook of early intervention: Childhood intervention* (2nd ed., pp. 115–135). Cambridge, England: Cambridge University Press.

Zahn-Waxler, C., Radke-Yarrow, M., Wagner, E., & Chapman, M. (1992). Development of concern for others. *Developmental Psychology, 28,* 126–136.

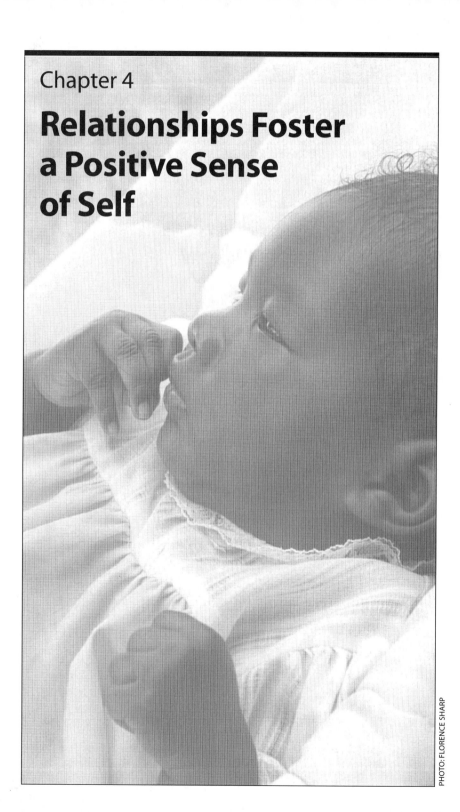

Chapter 4

Relationships Foster
a Positive Sense
of Self

The first three chapters underscored the power and importance of responsive relationships. We learned how relationships are formed through shared emotions and how positive emotion sharing gives us stability and resiliency.

This chapter will expand our understanding of the value of responsive relationships by explaining how they foster feelings of self-worth in children. It will explain how caregiving relationships can help or hinder young children's understanding of who they are and what they can do. The chapter will relate many of the concepts we have learned thus far to the child's emerging sense of identity. In addition, it will examine how the child's motivation toward autonomy and mastery contribute to self-worth. Responsive relationships must support mastery and autonomy in the child. Within this context, we will gain an understanding of the necessity to focus and regulate a child's mastery motivation and learn techniques for doing so. Finally, the chapter will describe scaffolding and will discuss the importance of both emotional scaffolding and cognitive scaffolding.

Key Concept One
Positive Relationships Build Self-Worth

Building a child's positive sense of self is perhaps the most important contribution that we as child-care providers can offer to those in our care. It is important because a child's sense of identity or self-awareness has a major effect on what that child will learn and accomplish. We know that people who believe they have the ability within themselves to do well will tackle complex challenges. People who have experienced a shared positive rela-

Goals of Chapter 4

▥ Examine how responsive relationships help children create a positive sense of self.

▥ Introduce the concept of mastery motivation and autonomy.

▥ Explore how responsive relationships can foster autonomy.

▥ Discuss how mastery motivation needs regulation.

▥ Explore the effect of temperament and culture on mastery motivation.

▥ Understand scaffolding and the importance of self-directed activity in children.

▥ Explore scaffolding strategies and skills.

tionship will have the confidence to reach out to others. People who trust themselves have a resiliency that allows them to endure or manage difficult situations. Our positive sense of self provides a stable context in which to balance the negatives that befall all of us.

Confidence Can Be Transferred From Adult to Child

For infants and toddlers, knowledge of who they are, what they can do, and how others perceive them is just beginning to develop. Infants and toddlers learn about themselves as separate persons by experiencing other people, places, and things. They are gaining new information about themselves with each encounter. They realize that their behavior has an effect on others, and from this realization, they begin to construct a beginning sense of identity. Each positive experience contributes to their internal feelings of self-worth. Each negative experience raises questions about their abilities and their value.

When a child is unsure, she needs a trusting relationship figure to guide her and to model for her. She relies on this person to help interpret her experiences and understand her role. When mutual sharing happens, children learn which behaviors are valued. They will repeat actions that bring them approval. They will develop a repertoire of behaviors that have brought them feelings of competence. For example, consider the following scenario.

> Yee-Jin (18 months old) and her mother enter the child-care center hesitantly. Today is their first day at the center. The director greets them and introduces them to Helen, who will be Yee-Jin's primary caregiver. Yee-Jin's mother says, "Look, Yee-Jin. There is a doll's house with a kitchen inside." Yee-Jin runs over to the dollhouse, then looks back at her mother, who smiles and says, "Yes, go see." Yee-Jin begins to explore the dollhouse while her mother talks to Helen. "She is very confident," says Helen. "Yes," says her mother, "she knows that I would bring her no harm. She knows that I would bring her to a nice, safe place."

The confidence of this child is built on the trust she has in her mother. Helen knows from the child's willingness to separate and be independent on the first day of child care that a strong attachment exists between mother and child. The child feels safe, as her mother said, because she trusts her mother to do the right things for her. She can explore new worlds and learn new things because she is not anxious. She is beginning to trust herself. Yee-Jin has already begun to develop a sense of positive self-worth. To sustain her confidence, she will need to find in Helen the same sense of trust and safety that she has experienced with her mother.

Relationships Foster Self-Worth

Let us review some of the relationship-building strategies we have been learning. Each of these strategies is also a way to foster self-worth.

Watching, waiting, and listening. Children know that they are important to us when we watch them, wait for them to connect with us, and then listen to them. Children feel understood when we read their nonverbal cues and respond to their needs. They feel a sense of control when we take interest in what they are doing. Even small babies gain a sense of power when they feel that their caregivers have listened and have understood their needs. The following scenario provides an example.

> Kalan (20 months old) is wandering around, whimpering. His caregiver, Ella Mae, stoops down, looks into his face, and says, "Kalan, what is wrong?" Kalan comes into her arms, and she hugs him. Kalan points to the giant blocks where two other boys are playing. Ella Mae says, "Would you like to play with the big blocks?" Kalan nods and points again. Ella Mae takes him to the blocks where the other boys are playing. She sits down and hands Kalan a block. Kalan has stopped whimpering and is smiling. He selects some more blocks and begins to create his own tower. Ella Mae says, "Yes, Kalan. You're building a tower!"

Meeting the match. Responding to the child on his level about his goals is what we call "meeting the match." By tuning into Kalan's goals and reading his nonverbal cues, Ella Mae gave Kalan a small sense of power. Kalan's inner voice might have said, "She understands my problem. She is joining me. She thinks I'm okay. She will help me to have the blocks I like and to be here with these other guys."

When we imitate a child's actions or ask the child to show us how to do something, we reinforce that child's positive sense of self. A quick response to a child's needs does not indulge the child. Rather, it can serve to make the child more independent, more confident of success, and more focused on the task because he knows that you will be there to help if he falters.

Sharing positive emotions. We have learned about the power of sharing positive emotions to focus or sustain a child's interest. We have learned that modeling positive emotions will motivate children to try new things, to seek help, and to master skills—activities that give them internal feelings of pride. The sense of "we" or of working together toward a goal that is instilled by shared positive emotion will give children feelings of inclusion and competence.

Ella Mae went with Kalan to the giant blocks and made sure that he got involved. She used the sense of "we" and positive emotions to encourage Kalan. She would not have been as successful if she had just sent Kalan over to join the group. When the feeling of "shared space" or connection comes from someone outside the family, someone such as a child-care provider, children feel an added sense of value. They may be thinking, "I can make friendships with others. I'm okay, even without Mom."

A responsive day-care situation can be a powerful force for shaping children's sense of competence. Relationships with caregivers offer young children human connections that extend their resources and enhance their sense of identity (Box 4.1).

Positive, Specific Feedback Strengthens Self-Worth

Quiet praise is sometimes more valuable for internalizing feelings of accomplishment than cheers or external rewards. Within a responsive relationship, your goal is to have the child continue to work for himself toward successive accomplishments rather than for stars on the bulletin board or the momentary adulation of others. Positive feedback should be quiet, interpersonal recognition. Although global praise, exaggerated cheers, and clapping might be considered examples of shared positive emotions and social rewards, these practices validate the child's ability to please others rather than instilling inner pride. Feelings of self-worth are externalized when the primary goal is making others proud. Our more important goal is to support the development of internalized feelings of self-worth. Specific feedback promotes this internalization.

> *Quiet praise is sometimes more valuable for internalizing feelings of accomplishment than cheers or external rewards.*

Specific feedback uses words that are tied to the child's specific accomplishment. "You didn't spill a drop." "You put the pegs in the holes." "You made it all by yourself." "You must feel proud." This kind of feedback focuses the child on his own actions toward his goal. The focus of the praise is on the child's mastery, bit by bit. The child will be motivated by his feelings of pride. If the child is able to develop this internal system of self-praise—"I did that" "I can do more"—he will continue to accomplish and enjoy learning.

Computerized toys that ring bells or flash lights provide an instant feedback reward to the child. Talking dolls and trucks with sirens or flashing lights also give immediate feedback, but because this feedback is mechanical, it quickly becomes boring. Without relationships, a toddler does little exploration, experimentation, or creative problem solving. One does not experience the same feelings of self-worth as when a special person shares your goals and your pride.

Box 4.1
Entering the Child's World

Approach the child. Watch and listen.
— Approach quietly.
— Watch with approval.
— Assess the child's mood and attention.
— What actions are absorbing the child?

Connect with the child.
— Move close to the child.
— Establish eye contact.
— Ask if you may join the child.
— Sit at the child's level.

Watch and listen.
— Remain quiet and watch at first.
— Watch the child experience the toy or activity.
— Let the child experiment.
— Don't correct or scold. Ignore mistakes.
— Let the child solve problems.
— Help when the child is frustrated.

Follow the child's lead.
— Respond to what the child seems to enjoy.
— Share interest, excitement, and joy.
— Ask the child if you can join in the play.
— Let the child lead you. Do what the child suggests.
— Imitate and take turns.

Experience the shared understanding.
— You will sense when the child has connected with you.
— You will be aware that the child has joined in shared motivation.
— You will know when to extend and expand the play.
— Wait until the child looks to you to share pride.

Reflective Self-Awareness Promotes Self-Worth

Giving specific verbal feedback internalizes feelings of pride, but highlighting the child's accomplishment in the midst of others is especially potent. Reflective self-awareness occurs when a caregiver tells others what the child has done while the child is there to absorb the affirmation. Reflecting a child's good deeds to others has been shown to be a powerful tool for reinforcing that child's positive sense of self and for informing others that you value the child. As we return to our scenario, we find an example of reflective self-awareness.

> As Ella Mae continues to observe the three boys building their blocks, she says, "Look, Kalan, how Martin and Chris have helped you. They gave you some of their blocks to use. They shared with you." Chris looks at Ella Mae and smiles. Chris and Kalan go together to get more blocks from the shelf.

By validating these acts of sharing, the two boys gain more positive feelings about themselves. Because Ella Mae highlighted their actions of including Kalan, these two boys are more likely to repeat this kind of sharing.

Caregivers Foster Autonomy and Self-Worth by Asking Children to Help

Even 1- and 2-year-olds can help by imitating adult tasks and feeling part of a team effort. Carrying the sand toys, helping another child fill buckets, bringing their cups to the kitchen, or finding their socks are all activities that make toddlers feel important. These activities also focus toddlers on the feelings and needs of others. When they see that their efforts help others, they feel good about themselves. Helping is a way of sharing what you know with someone else. This sharing also enhances self-worth. When children teach one another, they feel a sense of pride in themselves.

Key Concept Two
Mastery Is an Inborn Motivation

Our biology pushes us toward learning. We are predisposed to explore, to practice new skills, and to master new knowledge. In previous chapters, we have described our inborn motivation to connect with other humans. Now, we will examine another of the inborn motivations—the mastery motivation. Children are constantly exploring their environments and finding new things to learn. They practice until they understand about an object or gain a new skill. Then they move on to find the next learning adventure. Human beings derive joy from seeking out and mastering challenge. Consider the following scenario.

> We are in a darkened birthing room. A mom and newborn baby are in the bed. The new baby is exploring with his eyes. Wide open, scanning eyes are exercising new muscles. The baby will continue to practice using his eyes and refining his ability to focus on things further and

further away. By practicing, the baby will experience new sensations that will create new learning pathways in his brain. He will soon be adding the ability to see color and detail. In this way, his knowledge will be increased.

The baby described above was refining his ability to see by practicing. When he feels confident in his new ability to use his eyes, he will move on to the next learning level. As new skills develop, this baby will experience feelings of pride. He will build memory pathways to remember what he has seen. The people within his world will explain what he is seeing and connect his visual experiences to emotional meaning. "Hi! I'm your Mommy." "See? See Daddy." His abilities will increase and, through them, so will his confidence in himself.

This motivation to explore, to find new things to learn, and to master new skills is powerful. The crawling baby will be obsessed with crawling. She will squirm out of your arms and take off when put on the floor. She explores the corners of the room, touching and tasting almost everything she encounters. Over and over, she returns to objects and places to reinforce her learning and understanding. If we try to contain or stop this child from mastering this developmental step, we find that it is almost impossible without a cage. Often, this baby will climb out of the high chair or the crib, screaming herself into exhaustion if these efforts at exploration are thwarted. Attempts to restrict the child's physical movement can thwart her learning and frustrate the developing sense of accomplishment and autonomy (Box 4.2).

Mastery Motivation Needs Focus

Although mastery motivation is not driven by relationships, it can be focused by them. When an adult works with a child on a task, the adult can guide the child and keep the child focused. By watching others around them, children are stimulated to try the same thing, to be like the others. Their desire to copy and master what others are doing spurs them on. As you can imagine, this motivation can lead to good things like going to the potty or washing hands for lunch—or not-so-good things like food fights or mud wars. Caregivers will be the ones to focus the child on good models and positive mastery.

Playing alone can also build feelings of self-worth in children. Caregivers should provide opportunity and space where children can be in charge of their own learning. When they look at picture books or create block structures, they are in charge. For most of us, accomplishment is a natural reward. When a toddler finishes a puzzle, he often sits quietly and contemplates the finished project. He is thinking, "I made that! I like it!" He is internalizing feelings of self-worth. Then, the child may turn to look toward

---

Box 4.2
The Mastery Cycle

Mastery: An internal feeling of control and confidence that drives learning and leads to feelings of pride.

Curiosity—Exploration	What's in there? What is it? How does it work?
Discovery—Challenge	Let's see if I can do it.
Learning	I'll find help—a model, a coach.
Practice	Over and over and over again!
Mastery—Competence	I've got it! I'm in control. I'm good at it.
Confidence	I can join the team. I can get the job done.
Pride	I'm okay. I like me. I'm worthy.

---

another person to share his feelings. A nod, a smile, or a touch from a special person may be the only acknowledgment needed. This quiet recognition from the adult brings an important moment of shared pride.

Many toys are designed to give ongoing positive feedback to children. Accomplishment is readily apparent when the child engages in sorting tasks, painting, puzzles, and block building. As these tasks progress, the child feels mastery and the pride of independent accomplishments. With these activities, the child may not look to the caregiver for approval or support; however, adult monitoring is still important. A teacher can make specific statements about the child's progress such as "Look, Mary! You built a wall!" or "Hey, Giorgio, you can jump." Quietly being there supports and focuses children in their ongoing pursuit of mastery and in their feelings of accomplishment.

Temperament Affects Mastery Motivation

In chapter 2, we introduced the concepts of temperament and goodness of fit. Here, we will consider how these factors affect the child's motivation to master. Temperament influences what activities children will choose or enjoy. For example, the highly active child will be drawn to high-energy activities. A caregiver will need to anticipate this tendency and plan to balance this child's development by providing opportunities and guidance for the child's mastery of quieter, more cognitive activities. The responsive caregiver knows that special attention and support will be needed when the active child is asked to do tasks requiring focus and concentration. For example, the caregiver might sit with an active child to work a puzzle, keeping her interested and involved in discovering where the next piece goes. By so doing, this caregiver will be bolstering the child's ability to stay focused. The caregiver is providing an opportunity for new abilities to develop in the active child who might not choose these activities by herself. As this child finds success at fine motor learning, she may choose those kinds of activities more often, thus balancing her development and increasing her self-confidence.

In the same way, an inhibited child may shy away from group activities or novel tasks. This child will need extra support and encouragement to participate with the group. His caregiver will be helping this child reach out and explore different new skills and will then need to support the hesitant child with quiet praise and mutual regulation during the new activity, joining in to help this child toward initial success.

The persistent child may have trouble moving from one activity to another. This child might refuse to join in the bubble game because she is obsessed with mastering the puzzle. The teacher will need to regulate these temperament-driven tendencies by offering advance warnings and enough information about a new activity to pique the persistent child's curiosity. Responsive caregivers know the temperament of the children in their care and are mindful of the need to balance and regulate their learning.

Key Concept Three
Scaffolding Supports Learning

Scaffolding opens doors to a world of possibilities for mastery. In this context, we define scaffolding as structuring and facilitating a learning situation so that it becomes easier to master. To provide this scaffolding, a caregiver must be able to enter the world of the child. Then, the caregiver can structure the environment, simplify the task, extend or add to the possibilities, and give encouragement without interrupting the child's mastery motivation or feelings of accomplishment.

Scaffolding involves being there as a support to the child's development. The caregiver provides a structure around the child's interest that will allow the child to be successful. She observes the child's work, quietly watching until the child encounters difficulty and then offering the exact support the child needs to successfully complete the task himself. For example, if a child is riding a trike and is about to get blocked by a maze of toys, the teacher clears the path saying, "These toys are in your way." By scaffolding the task for the child, you are allowing the child to find success and feel

Box 4.3
The Scaffolding Technique

Scaffolding Fosters Learning

▥ Watch, wait, and listen.

▥ Allow the child to experiment.

▥ Give specific feedback.

▥ Avoid, regulate, or repair frustrations.

▥ Demonstrate (model) a new skill.

▥ Break a task into small, doable steps.

▥ Support the child in mastering each step.

▥ Never scold! Ignore mistakes.

▥ Fix problems quietly, without pointing them out.

▥ If the child tunes out, stop or change.

▥ Do not finish the task for the child.

▥ Reward the child for effort. ("Look at all you did.")

▥ Highlight the child's internalized pride. ("You must feel good.")

self-pride. This process is different from responding to the child's signals for help when he asks for it (Box 4.3).

Caregivers focus the mastery process by structuring activities for success. A responsive relationship helps us to be in touch with a child's developmental status and with the driving motivation for each child. By watching and listening to cues, we know when a developmental skill is attained and when the child is ready to move toward the next challenge. We are able to guide this child toward mastery. Individually or in a group, we will work with this child and structure his environment for learning. We can plan to provide access to the toys for which he is developmentally ready. We will plan one-on-one time to work with him in skill building. In child care, children can experience many successes every day.

Scaffolding does not involve doing the task for someone; rather, it involves providing relevant support. For example, if you are absorbed in learning about Italian cooking and a friend supports your interest by saying, "I have a wonderful book about Italian cooking. I will lend it to you," then that person has added another resource for your learning. He has given you an opportunity to expand your skill. The person has not said, "Let me cook you my favorite Italian supper," which, although generous, does not allow you to develop your own cooking skills.

Adults often think that they are teaching when they tell a child what to do or when they finish a task for a frustrated child. Many adults enjoy playing with toys, building structures, working puzzles, or creating clay dragons for themselves. In contrast, modeling a task is helpful when a child is faced with new learning or when you want to entice a child. Real learning comes when the child experiences actually doing the task. An old fashioned saying reminds us, "The learning is in the doing." For example, the caregiver who says, "You are holding the blue circle. Where will it fit?" will have a different effect on learning and feelings of self-worth than the caregiver who says, "Put the circle here" or, "I'll put it in for you." Expanding a skill is best accomplished through scaffolding. When a caregiver wishes to move the child toward new learning, she uses scaffolding. Consider Gerald's scaffolding technique in the following scenario.

> Emma is successfully putting round blocks in the shape sorter. Gerald watches her, then picks up a square block and demonstrates how the square shape will not go into the round hole but, instead, will fit into the square hole. "Look, Emma." He points to the corners on the block. "This block will go in here, in the square hole." Emma watches and then begins to look for square blocks to put into the box, following Gerald's modeling. She grabs a square block in her fist and begins to push and jam the block at the hole. Gerald holds her hand and gently turns the block. In it plops. "There!" he says. Emma eagerly finds another square block and turns it until it plops in successfully.

Gerald has expanded Emma's learning and her skill. He has taught her to look at the shape of the block and the shape of the hole. He has also helped her realize that the skill is not in pushing the block through but in turning it to fit. Very subtly, Gerald scaffolds Emma's knowledge.

Providing toys that meet the match for a certain developmental stage of learning also fosters mastery motivation. If pounding is the child's obsession, then provide pounding toys. A teacher who knows the children in her care is sensitive to the fact that, for example, Jeremy learns spatial relations using trucks, Hector learns the same concept with construction toys, and Kyle develops this understanding by playing with dishes. When a caregiver allows each child to learn in this individualized way, she is maximizing each child's motivation to learn.

Art experiences within the center are wonderful ways to promote mastery and creativity—as long as they are child-directed. In other words, a planned activity should allow children to "do their own thing," to experiment, and to choose the direction and pace of the task. For example, caregivers sometimes need to help parents appreciate the fact that allowing their child to paste fall leaves in disarray on the page instead of in prescribed places on a tree trunk enhances learning for the child because the decisions about the leaves are his own. He was making choices and defining actions that opened new learning pathways. This independence gave him feelings of creativity and feelings of pride.

Providing a safe area for each child to master developmental tasks can be tricky in a child-care center. For example, if space is limited and not divided into activity areas, the child who wants to concentrate on a puzzle may be thwarted by another child who is practicing beanbag tosses. If children of different ages must be together in a small area, a baby who needs to crawl may be held back by a protective caregiver who recognizes the potential dangers of older children running and jumping in the same space. Part of being a responsive caregiver or teacher is to be able to structure the environment for children so that they can successfully pursue their current stage of learning.

> *Part of being a responsive caregiver or teacher is to be able to structure the environment for children so that they can successfully pursue their current stage of learning.*

Responsive relationships allow for autonomy. Promoting autonomy in the child, that is, allowing the child to be self-directed, is one of the most important ways to promote development. When an adult allows the child to explore the environment, watching and waiting for the child to choose an interest, that adult is supporting autonomy and choice. After the child has selected a toy with which to play, the caregiver asks to join the child and then acknowledges the child's efforts. The child will feel motivated by the adult's interest. The caregiver offers minimal assistance, allowing the child to work on her own. The caregiver makes adjustments to the environment so that the child continues to be successful. When the caregiver quietly rewards the child's mastery, the child internalizes a sense of accomplishment. The adult is fostering the child's self-worth at her level of understanding. The caregiver is not designing the task or needing to have it finished or done "correctly;" instead, he is allowing the child autonomy. Because the child is in charge of what and how this task will progress, she will be learning what she is developmentally ready to absorb.

The ability to approach a child, watch to see where the child's concentration is focused, and then quietly ask to join the child is an art. When an adult learns how to connect with the child who is engrossed in his own activity without disturbing the child's concentration, then that caregiver will be able to gently expand the child's learning by sustaining his motivation to master. The child will love learning because he has chosen the learning track and has been supported in his chosen endeavor. Because the child feels in charge, he is able to say, "I did that!"

Scaffolding Is Also About Emotions

When a child is having difficulty with the task that she has chosen, the responsive caregiver notices the frustration and helps the child. The caregiver does not correct or override the child's actions but simply says, "Here, try this." Then, he rewards the child with a smile or says, "Yes, you put it in." With a voice that expresses excitement, the caregiver can then move the child toward the next step in the task. The responsive caregiver is using positive emotions to maintain the child's interest, to focus the child, and to expand her learning experience. The caregiver is emotionally regulating the child. If the child becomes frustrated with the new idea, the caregiver can lead her back to the earlier play, where she felt confident, by helping the child adjust her mood. The caregiver is subtly teaching the child not only how to concentrate and enjoy learning but also how to mediate her frustrations. Consider Gerald and Emma as we return to the earlier scenario.

> Emma is now frustrated by the shape sorter box. She has picked up the triangle block and is smashing it at the round space. As Gerald approaches, she throws the triangle down and starts to leave. Gerald lifts the top of the box and says, "Emma, look at all you have done!" Emma smiles. Then Gerald takes out a round block and offers it to Emma. He knows that she is good with round shapes. He runs his finger around the edge of the block. "Look, it's round and smooth." Emma puts it through the round hole. Gerald waits until she turns to look at him with a big smile. Then he says, "Hey! See? You can put these round blocks in really well!" He takes more round ones out and sets them next to her.

Gerald reinvests Emma's interest in the task by taking her to her level of comfort. He diverts her from her feelings of frustration to feelings of accomplishment. He helps her realize how effective she has been and gently steers her toward success in the future. In this way, he has extended Emma's learning by refocusing her emotionally and cognitively. She will leave the task with feelings of self-worth.

Redirecting Learning Is a Form of Emotional Scaffolding

If the teacher feels that she needs to redirect a child's focus, then the teacher may present a new challenge for the child to explore independently. In this case, the teacher may demonstrate the new challenge or new toy and then hand it back to the child to explore. After the child has had some time with the toy on his own, then the teacher can enter the child's play again to maintain focus. This process is sometimes called "mentoring." Like coaching, it is supportive and instructive without being demanding or threatening. The following scenario provides an example.

> Gerald is taking Sam by the hand. "Sam, I think that you are ready for Legos®. Come with me. Look what I have here." Gerald sits down with Sam in his lap and pulls a tub of Legos toward them. He takes off the top and reaches inside. He gives two Legos to Sam, one in each hand. Then he takes two and puts them together so that Sam can see. Then he gets two more and adds them to his structure. "Look how they go together. You try it, Sam." He takes Sam's hands and pushes his Legos together. Sam looks pleased. Gerald pours some Legos out onto the floor and sits Sam in front of them. "You pick another one, Sam." Sam snaps it together as Gerald watches.

Redirecting can be used to balance individual and group needs. For example, the child who is intrigued by opening and shutting drawers might be the child who is asked to get the crayons from a drawer when an art activity is being introduced. This request feeds and extends the child's current passion. He will have an opportunity to practice a skill that he wants to show off but, because the teacher has embedded it in another activity, the skill becomes a more complex means-to-an-end task. He feels the pride of helping the group and pride in his ability to open drawers.

Chapter Summary

Responsive relationships build feelings of self-worth through tuning in to the child's goals, sharing positive emotions, meeting the match, and scaffolding to foster the child's learning.

Caregivers also give children feelings of pride when they structure the environment for exploration, provide developmentally appropriate toys, and allow autonomy. Whenever possible, let the children in your care try to do tasks by themselves. Let them struggle a bit to get pegs into the pegboard or shoes on their feet. Allow children to work together and help one another.

Caregivers foster self-esteem when they structure for success. De-emphasize the negatives, and ignore spills or mistakes. Use specific praise and reflective praise to emphasize the positive steps in a child's behavior.

Watching, waiting, and listening are key to entering the child's world and interest area. These efforts allow you to be responsive to the child's goals. Only then can you scaffold emotions and support mastery—a process that enables you to promote the positive identities of the children in your care.

Resources

Berk, L. E., & Winsler, A. (1995). *Scaffolding children's learning: Vygotsky and early childhood education.* Washington, DC: National Association for the Education of Young Children.

Bodrova, E., & Leong, D. J. (1996). *Tools of the mind: The Vygotskian approach to early childhood education.* Columbus, OH: Merrill.

Bronson, M. B. (1995). *The right stuff for children birth to eight: Selecting play materials to support development.* Washington DC: National Association for the Education of Young Children.

Curry, N. E., & Johnson, C. N. (1990). *Beyond self-esteem: Developing a genuine sense of human value.* Washington, DC: National Association for the Education of Young Children.

Elicker, J., & Fortner-Wood, C. (1995). Adult–child relationships in early childhood programs. *Young Children, 51*(1), 69–78.

Greenspan, S., & Greenspan, N. T. (1988). *First feelings: Milestones in the emotional development of your baby and child.* New York: Penguin.

Hauser-Cram, P. (1998). I think I can, I think I can: Understanding and encouraging mastery motivation in young children. *Young Children, 53*(4), 67–71.

Lally, J. R. (1995). The impact of child care policies and practices on infant/toddler identity formation. *Young Children, 51*(1), 58–67.

Morgan, G., & Harmon, R. J. (1984). Developmental transformations in mastery motivation. In R. N. Emde & R. J. Harmon (Eds.), *Continuities and discontinuities in development* (pp. 263–291). New York: Plenum.

Rodgers, D. B. (1998). Supporting autonomy in young children. *Young Children, 53*(3), 75–80.

Schwartz, S., & Heller Miller, J. E. (1996). *The new language of toys: Teaching communication skills to children with special needs. A guide for parents and teachers.* Bethesda, MD: Woodbine House.

Chapter 5

Responsive Relationships Model and Promote Social Skills

Social learning means developing skills for meeting, enjoying, and working with others. Our interactions with others contribute to our self-esteem and influence the life choices we make. They also expand our ideas and our use of language. Social learning allows us to join in the energy and motivation of a group, share positive emotions, and find those people who give us confidence and whom we can trust. Our social skills affect our life course and influence our successes.

To realize the potential of our inborn motivation to connect, we must learn the best ways to initiate and sustain relationships. In the first 2 years, children learn how to adapt their behavior to fit with others. In addition, children learn how to assert their own needs while also being sensitive to the needs of others. This complex task is called socialization. To make friendships, the toddler will have to be able to make an emotional connection with others beyond his or her family. The child will need to be able to share in the joys of others and feel their hurt when they are sad or angry.

Certain social expectations or social rules of behavior help sustain social relationships. These are patterns of behavior that become expected in adult interactions—for example, shaking hands or saying "Please," "Thank you," "Hello," or "How are you?" Toddlers begin to learn these patterns at a young age through the shared experiences they have with those around

Goals of Chapter 5

▦ Understand the development of social skills during the first 3 years of life.

▦ Consider how social expectations are set through consistent relationships.

▦ Become sensitive to different cultural and family patterns of social interaction.

▦ Use and teach social patterns and rules that enhance positive social skills.

▦ Develop an awareness of how modeling is a base for learning social skills.

▦ Develop an awareness of how other children serve as models.

▦ Learn strategies for maximizing positive opportunities for child-to-child learning.

▦ Contemplate how to provide time for social networks to develop.

▦ Plan ways for connection and collegiality to develop among children of different ages and cultures.

them. They are watching, modeling, and experimenting with social encounters. When initial connections with others are positive, toddlers will seek to connect again. They will remember some of the actions that led to this positive experience. A smile, a reach, or a special greeting become learned behaviors for connecting.

When interactions are not positive, children may feel discouraged and avoid new faces or withdraw from shared experiences. They are not learning patterns of connection; rather, they are learning patterns of avoidance. We have all known adults who struggle with meeting or communicating with others. Many of these people did not have the benefit of early guidance in social learning. Their inability to connect with others and form meaningful relationships may also have been a handicap to their academic progress, their feelings of self-esteem, and their life choices.

When toddlers have opportunities to interact with others beyond their families and to experience positive relationships, they will enhance their abilities to connect. This ability will enable a broader range of learning and experiencing to begin. For this reason, caregivers need to understand how to support and promote social skills that give children feelings of self-confidence and expand their circle of learning.

Key Concept One
Social Skills Develop During the First 3 Years of Life

In the first 3 years of life, social development and emotional development are intertwined. The baby in utero is able to hear and attune to his mother's voice, odors, and rhythms. As a newborn, this baby will alert to mother's voice and quiet to her rhythms. The child learns that mother enables his survival. By 3 months of age, he has begun to smile and coo. He quickly learns that this behavior brings positive responses from his mother. This interaction feels pleasurable. It is motivating. Social learning begins.

The emotional responses that a baby receives to his actions will determine what he continues to do. If the 5-month-old shows you his prize rattle and is rewarded when you smile and hold your hand out, he will give up his prize to you in the expectation that you will give it back. If you do, a social reciprocal exchange begins. With each of these positive experiences comes learning. Responding to an infant's initiations with positive emotions and with reciprocal patterns of interaction is one of the most powerful ways to promote social interaction.

By 9 months old, babies begin to understand that there is some consistency in people's behavior. If infants have been comforted in distress, if they have experienced adults as having smiling faces, if their interests have been acknowledged, then their expectations about social interactions will be open and loving.

On the other hand, some infants have been left to cry when they are in distress. If they have been ignored in their bids for interaction and scolded for their experimental squeals and coos, their expectations for interaction with others will be different. This different interaction can be seen in infants as young as 4 months old who do not brighten when a parent comes to them. These children do not look around for faces with which to connect, and they do not expect you to respond to their bids for attention. Infants raised without many expectations of positive interaction create their own private worlds. Their social development is slowed.

Between 2 and 3 years of age, socialization is a primary developmental focus for children.

Normal physical development leads babies toward expanding their social worlds. One-year-olds are beginning to walk and have learned a few gestures to express their wants. They will naturally come in contact with more people because of their mobility. These experiences will increase their interactive skills. Consider the baby in the checkout line at the grocery store who shows you what he is holding. If you give him a slow wink, he will flash you a broad smile. This exchange is a subtle but confirming social interaction, initiated by the child to a stranger. He is experimenting with social bids and learning from the reactions of others. If children have experienced positive attachments and consistency in relationships during their first year, then they will have the self-confidence to enlist and enjoy new social connections.

Between 2 and 3 years of age, socialization is a primary developmental focus for children. Negotiating wants, taking turns, realizing the power of words, and acquiring patterns of behavior that signal social intent are important parts of learning. Children's contact with others will mutually regulate emotions. This contact can give them energy, calm them, or agitate them. Their experiences will define their expectations and will answer their internal questions about their identity, questions such as "Am I liked?" "Do I belong?" "May I join in?" "May I ask for help?" or "Can I help someone else?"

Each of us is socialized differently. Some babies are born into large extended families. As infants, they see many faces, hear many voices, and are rocked and diapered by different people. These children will be more comfortable meeting others in new or strange environments. Other children may be cared for primarily by their parents. They have experienced only a few new relationships, usually within the security of their parents' presence or familiar surroundings. These children may find a new environment and new caregivers upsetting. They may remain aloof and withdrawn unless they can establish a primary attachment figure at the center who gives them the security they need.

Toddlers between 9 and 18 months old are strongly identified by their attachments to people, places, and things. At this age, toddlers may struggle with separation from home, yet this age is when many children are first brought to child care. Caregivers may ask parents who are separating from their child for the first time to remain through the early part of the day or to leave the child at the center for only a short time in the beginning.

> *Toddlers between 9 and 18 months old are strongly identified by their attachments to people, places, and things.*

Social skills develop through observation and experimentation. Social skills do not unfold from a genetic maturational plan in the same way that early motor skills do. Signals and patterns of social interaction are learned through observation and experimentation.

In all species, we find standard behavior patterns that signal greeting or caution to others. Think of an animal wagging its tail or showing its incisors. These are two different but clear signals of expectation to another approaching animal. These behaviors send messages about whether the interaction might be positive or negative.

As people, we do the same thing. We project our expectations for interaction through emotion signals. We have standard social patterns for sustaining interactions or for closing interactions. These patterns develop within a societal group. For example, handshakes, smiles, and verbal greetings are positive signals for social interaction in this country. Learning these patterns is an important key to our success in finding positive interactions.

Infants watch and copy us as they stay safely in our arms. From an early age, they are learning the social signals of approach or caution. By the end of the first year, children learn to wave good-bye or reach up for a hello hug. They will then offer these signals to almost everyone whom their parents seem to accept. Children are schooled by their parents to use the parents' standard greeting patterns, and they also watch Mom and Dad to know when to use these signals.

Toddlers experiment with social patterns. Just as they explore the power of their voices by screeching and making gargling sounds, they will now test the reactions of others as they stamp their feet, throw things, or shake their heads or say "no." Sometimes toddlers will begin to turn away, hide, or run when they are asked to greet a new person. Social experimentation is part of social mastery. It is part of a child's understanding of his or her actions and choices. The responses of the other person will inform the toddler about the best signals for him or her to use.

Culture and Family Beliefs Shape Social Signals

Some cultures greet one another with a bow, others with a kiss on each cheek, and some with a punch on the arm. A person may encounter marked cultural differences in social greetings, but the social expectations to connect, and share are the same. Consider different greeting behaviors such as using eye contact, touching, and hugging. One toddler may have been taught to greet others with a hug, whereas another toddler may have been taught that a reserved smile or head nod is an appropriate initial greeting. The expectation to connect is the same, but the way of going about it is different. Obtaining a history of parents' cultural practices and beliefs when the child enters child care will help you respect the child's cultural expectations.

Eye contact is a social custom that carries many different cultural overtones. U.S. culture values eye contact; other cultures avoid eye contact because it is considered to be disrespectful or, in some cases, evil. Caregivers should be aware when a belief such as *"mal ojo,"* or *"evil eye,"* exists in a family. As caregivers, we must know what social behaviors the child expects from you and what the parents prefer that you teach. Caregivers may need to explore with parents the customs of the child-care center. Does your center prefer to teach social norms that are common in the United States, or does your center try to adapt to each child's expectations? Confusion about social values at this age can be detrimental to the child's developing identity. When caregivers and parents become allies in helping their children adapt to the patterns of both cultures, the child has a more positive experience. Even toddlers are able to learn that different behaviors are used in different places and with different people.

All cultures have standard verbal phrases that represent social patterns. Toddlers learn some of these phrases even before they understand the meaning of the words. For example, "Bye-bye," "See you later," and "Hi there!" are patterned phrases for the 15-month-old. They learn them as if they were a single word, and they understand the social meaning that someone is going away or someone is arriving. All cultures have standard verbal phrases that indicate positive or negative social expectations. Greetings, such as "Good morning. How are you?" "Hey, Bro. What's in it?" and "Shalom" (Peace be with you) contain different words, but they carry similar social meaning. Each phrase sets expectations for positive interaction.

Many toddlers may come to you knowing phrases from a different language that express the child's expectations to interact with you. Caregivers should be aware of this so that they can respond appropriately. "Ooeno-dee" from a toddler may be his way of saying, *"Buenos dias"* (Good morning) in his family's language of Spanish. Being aware of the standard social phrases of his language is helpful in advancing social competence in the multilingual child.

Family environments also shape social behaviors. Some children are raised to be cautious of strangers because their environmental situations demand it. Others may have been raised in communities where parents feel safe letting toddlers run to the neighbors' houses or wander around a store, greeting shopkeepers who give them hugs and offer treats. Some toddlers are the focal point for the family. They are allowed to command the attention of an adult almost all the time. In contrast, other families expect their toddlers to be quiet and listen when others are talking. These expectations become unspoken customs that evolve and define the way families interact. Children will come to child care with these varied expectations and behaviors.

> *Manners are revered in most social cultures as thoughtful, knowledgeable, and honorable ways to behave.*

Larger groups and societies also define social norms—expectations of behavior. These expectations are usually based on respect for others and are called "manners." Manners usually begin within the family. Almost all families expect children to play quietly when others are sleeping, to be gentle with elders, to run and jump only outside, and so on. Children learn these social norms very early. Do we talk with others during meals, or do we eat quickly and quietly? Do we say thanks for support, or do we assume it? Do we go first, or do we let someone older precede us?

Manners are revered in most social cultures as thoughtful, knowledgeable, and honorable ways to behave. The specific actions that are used may be different for different societies or social groups; however, the respectful intent is universal. Phrases such as "a real gentleman" or "a gracious woman" often refer to someone who knows the social rules or manners of the community in which they are living. Patterned expressions such as "Please," "Thank you," "Excuse me," or "May I?" are useful in most groups, and the child quickly internalizes these as habits. A toddler who learns manners will enhance his or her ability to connect positively with others throughout life. The child-care center is a place where manners can be learned and social patterns can be reinforced.

Many social expectations will have been established before a child comes into child care. However, these expectations may vary widely. Some children will be learning manners for the first time. If possible, a provider should have discussed the expectations of the center with parents. Problems occur when social patterns that parents are modeling conflict with what the center teaches. Keep in mind that, if the center's social norms are in conflict with skills that the child needs to survive socially in his or her life outside the center, then the behaviors that relate more to the child's survival may take precedence over manners. For example, in some environments, children are taught to avoid windows. In others, it may be adaptive to learn to fight to protect oneself and one's possessions.

Key Concept Two
Caregivers Support Social Learning

Within the child-care setting, children will be learning behaviors that help them find acceptance within a group. Your relationship with them will represent a model for making new connections easily and for adapting to group needs. As their child-care provider, you will be supporting their first social learning experiences.

Socialization in Child Care Will Be Different From Socialization at Home

Interactions within the child-care setting are different from most home environments. Part of the children's socialization experience will be learning to interact with other children without an adult model. Their socialization experience may also involve learning to interact with several adults or with strangers.

Within the child-care setting, children will be learning behaviors that help them find acceptance within a group. Your relationship with them will represent a model for making new connections easily and for adapting to group needs.

For some children, child care may represent more personal freedom than they have ever known. For others, child care can be the first place where they will experience limitations. The child-care center will be advancing social rules for negotiation and collaboration, including taking turns, waiting for others to finish, or asking to join an activity with others.

Caregivers must help children make the transition. Children cannot be expected to integrate well into the complex social milieu of the center without a guide. Thus, a caregiver at the center must become a child's emotional base, a substitute for his or her parents, and a model for interactive skills. For example, consider the following scenario:

Four children from the 2–3-year-old group are sitting in a circle, rolling a ball back and forth. Their teacher watches and scaffolds their cooperation, helping to keep the ball moving to others, with each child taking a turn. Kevin stands in the corner, kicking another ball at the wall. The teacher asks him to join them, and he hangs his head, shaking it to mean no. She urges him again and comes toward him as if to take his hand. Kevin cries out, "No!" and kicks his ball hard at the circle of children.

Alice, Kevin's primary caregiver, notices this exchange. She comes over and picks him up. She walks away from the group, talking softly to Kevin in her arms. They walk around the room together, and then they approach the circle and greet the group. "Hi! This looks like fun," says Alice. Then she asks the group, "Can we play with you?" The group teacher says, "Sure!" and helps the group open a place in the circle. Alice and Kevin sit down together. She keeps Kevin on her lap as they join the circle. She laughs as another child catches the ball and then says, "Roll it here. We're ready." Kevin reaches for the ball and pushes it back into the circle. As each child has a turn, the group responds, saying, "Zoom!" and soon Kevin is smiling and joining the cheers. He is ready to be put down in his own space in the circle.

Alice asks Kevin if he would like to stay in the circle while she leaves to check on Jenny. He nods. He is absorbed in the game. When she gets up to leave, she tells Kevin where she will be if he needs her. She leaves him to enjoy the group activity.

Kevin may not have had much experience with group play, or he may have had some negative interactions with other children. Kevin's primary caregiver understood this situation. She also noticed that he had chosen to play with a ball, and she believed that he wanted to be part of the ball game. However, he did not know how to join in and was feeling sad and angry. She connected to these feelings because of their bond or "shared space" relationship. She came to him and counteracted his negative feelings when she picked him up and showed her empathy. Together, they entered the group of strangers. She served as Kevin's model and base of confidence. Through her actions and the words she used, Kevin began to learn the dos and don'ts of entering a group. He is gaining a pattern for connecting successfully.

If a child has been in the center for a while, the child may be confident to join the group play and relate to other caregivers, but his first caregiver will remain the one to whom the child looks for support when he is anxious. The child will continue to reference this caregiver when social interactions seem different or when activities are new.

In the scenario, Alice was not supervising the play activity of the group, but she was aware of Kevin's anxious feeling about joining a new group of children. She remained available and saw that he was feeling alone. She noticed that he rejected the other teacher's attempts to include him in the group. She tuned in to his needs from afar and came to his aid. It took a short time for her to integrate Kevin into the activity.

As children grow older, many centers move them into larger groups. Continuity of caregivers is important. If children who have been in child care as infants can retain contact with their original caregivers as they begin to expand their social horizons, they will make the transition more success-fully. During their time in the center, children will have established some expectations about relating to other caregivers. They have been exchanging eye contact and observing others in the center. Often these children are con-fident and even assertive about moving into the larger group and meeting new people.

On the other hand, for children who have experienced feelings of dis-connection and loss in their lives, each change of caregiver will compound these feelings. If these children remain unsupported, they can develop a social withdrawal pattern and become loners, losing the advantage of the expanded learning and emotional balance of group interaction.

When the early walker is moved to a toddler group with a new care-giver, the loss of a secure relationship can disorient the child. As these children begin to move toward greater independence, they seek and need security. Maintaining continuity of relationship through this period will be a major advantage.

Providing a consistent support system for the child will support the staff, too. Children will maintain more emotional balance and will demand less one-on-one interaction. Centers that can schedule personnel to follow chil-dren across transitions will be maintaining relationship continuity during critical developmental periods. Like Alice did with Kevin, primary caregivers will sense "their" children's needs. With dual caregivers in a larger group, children can gradually expand their trust base to "new" adults. These children will then accept both caregivers as guides. As they mature, they will also begin establishing relationships with other children who serve as social models.

Social Learning Experiences Differ for Each Child

In the child-care setting, toddlers will be exposed to many new relation-ships, different cultures, and unfamiliar customs. New acquaintances may not respond as expected. These toddlers will be asking themselves, "How do I fit in with these people? Are other children like me? Are they safe for me? How do I manage my fear and anger? What if I don't want to become a friend?" Some experiences will be comfortable for them, but others will not. As a responsive caregiver, you will be able to observe when a child is being rejected. You will be able to help this child to understand the other person's need for privacy and to find another friend to be with or other toys to use. Imagine yourself as the caregiver in the next scenario.

> At the center, you notice a child you have seen before, sitting in the corner sucking her thumb. You greet her and ask whether you can sit next to her. You introduce yourself and ask her name. You offer her the toy in your pocket. She takes it and then climbs into your lap. You begin to talk to her about what the others are doing. She says, "I'm Nedra." You smile and say, "Nedra." You take her in your arms to walk around the room, naming the other children and talking about their activities.
>
> As you walk, Nedra clings to you. She watches some activities but turns away and clings when you suggest that she join in. Then, she points and reaches toward a girl stringing beads. You stop and say to the girl, "Hi! May we join you?" Nedra smiles as you sit down with her in your arms. The girl hands Nedra some beads and a string. You say, "Thank you. What is your name?" Nedra says, "Janeen." "Oh!" you say, "so you are friends." The two girls smile. You string a bead. Nedra reaches out to Janeen. You put her on the floor. Then you ask Janeen for a red bead. Janeen gives it to Nedra. You give her your string, and she seems to know what to do with the red bead. Then you get up and tell the girls that you will be close by. Nedra seems comfortable, but you keep eye contact with her as you walk away. Nedra soon begins to laugh and show her bead string to Janeen.

Even though you did not know Nedra before, your sensitivity to cues told you that she was feeling lonely and isolated. If you were Nedra's primary caregiver, you would probably know why and could begin to repair the situation immediately. However, even though you were not her primary attachment relationship, you could divert Nedra and replace her sad feelings with good feelings. As you moved with Nedra around the room, you allowed her to pick the activity or friend she wanted to join. You gave her choices. She seemed to want to play with Janeen. She showed you that she recognized a friend.

By 3 years, children who have experienced good interactions have the ability to make good social choices. They evaluate others, connect with friends, limit or leave problem interactions, and use adults as resources. These are skills that will influence their lifelong learning and their identities.

Shared Positive Emotions (SPEs) Help Children to Feel Collaborative and Creative

As we have discussed in previous chapters, sharing positive emotions stimulates the brain to be open to learning. In a similar manner, it opens the door to social interaction and social acceptance. When a greeting is positive, the interaction that follows begins on a positive note.

The face is the most prominent marker of your feelings. Are you smiling? Do you ask the children in your care to smile? We sometimes need to think about putting on our "happy faces"; this action alone can change social patterns.

Tone of voice is an immediate indicator of expectation for interaction. "John, come here," "Yes, may I help you?" or "We need to talk" can be standard phrases to begin either negative or positive interactions. Tone of voice will determine the result. Children tune in to and learn from the tone of the conversations around them as much as from interactions directed to them.

Teaching children to have a "smile in their voices" when they say "Hi" is a valuable exercise. Kids enjoy practicing happy voice tones together and playing games with happy sounds. By teaching emotion sounds along with simple phrases such as "Great job!" or "You're done," children will be armed with habits of positive signaling to others. Model and practice using a "smiling voice" for phrases such as "Hi, my name is _____," or "May I play too?" This smiling voice is a learned skill. Children will copy you and use your voice tones to signal their expectations for positive sharing.

Children will copy you and use your voice tones to signal their expectations for positive sharing.

Touch is also part of many social interactions. Greetings that involve both touch and voice can extend feelings of connectedness. "High fives" are superb greetings to be used in child-care centers. Toddlers love to greet adults and one another in this way. However, note this word of caution: Touch is interpreted differently by different families. For some, social touch is considered taboo, whereas other families feel that touch expresses a strong positive message. Be aware that family values about touch differ; therefore, it is important to check with parents when teaching games and greetings that incorporate touching, especially hugs. These games also open the door for discussing, even with a 2-year-old, when hugs and other touch are not good and why. Children can learn about respect for personal space and can learn to ask, "May I hug you?"

The language of positive social interaction—greetings, requests, words for sharing, and words for separation—can be guided. This language will be learned at appropriate times within the center and will become part of a child's standard vocabulary. Patterned phrases such as "Hi, may I play too?" or "Bye—see you later," become habits of speaking.

Social learning includes learning about respect. As you teach social patterns, talk about others' feelings, both positive and negative. "Susan feels good when we smile with her." "Adam feels bad when we push him out." Learning to identify personal feelings and to express them in words will help children regulate their own emotions in future negotiations and social interactions. Using the word "respect" and defining it for children will also help them to understand what it means. "Let's leave Jodi alone. Let's respect her wishes."

Talking with children about the feelings of others will increase social competence. It is important to learn to congratulate the accomplishments of others as well as to recognize the sadness or anger another child might feel. Child-care providers are often the first people who help children learn the words that describe their feelings. Many households do not talk about feelings or focus on positive social skills. However, we know that defining and sharing feelings with young children increases emotional balance and fosters emotion regulation. These are important functions of the child-care center.

Key Concept Three
Children Serve as Models for One Another

Group free play helps children experiment with and practice social skills. Children watch and copy one another. They want to be alike, look alike, and act alike. They like books about babies and enjoy playing with baby dolls. Children who are 2–3 years old may develop attachments to one another, wanting to walk with or sit with a special person. Even though toddlers seem engrossed in their own individual tasks, they like to be close to someone else. This kind of behavior is called "parallel play." When engaged in parallel play, toddlers may be interested in others or in playing with the same kinds of toys, but they do not interact or share toys.

Free play is not a time for the caregivers to sit back and relax. Free play with toddlers needs to be monitored and regulated to keep social interaction successful. Keep in mind that most toddlers are self-centered, and their goals are intense. They are not mature enough to engage in cooperation without supervision and direction. Children who are playing happily in the same area may suddenly decide that they want the same toy, and they will use power to get it. Your awareness will allow you to intercede appropriately.

The shy child may need your help to negotiate access to the sandbox. The confident, athletic child may be endangering others as he powers his way up the jungle gym. The two children in the playhouse may be pulling the teddy bear apart in a raucous game. Particular patterned actions and words can be used to teach dispute resolution. These patterns can be learned just as "Hi" and "Good-bye" were learned. Expressions such as "I'm sorry" and "Pardon me" are powerful for healing hurt feelings. Also, social acts of kindness such as offering another toy or giving a gift can avoid disputes.

The ability to solicit help when disputes arise is a valuable social skill for all of us to have developed. A third party can reflect the feelings of everyone involved. Teaching children how to ask for help when they are feeling shy or imposed on gives them a valuable resource. Children should learn to use words such as "I need you," "I'm sad," and "Will you help me?" to gain their goals rather than feeling powerless or resorting to impulsive actions. Socialization includes learning to ask for support from others.

Teaching children how to ask for help when they are feeling shy or imposed on gives them a valuable resource.

As children mature, they begin to play in more integrated ways. Between 2 and 3 years of age, two children might share the same intent, the same space, and some toys, even though they are engaged in separate activities. This behavior is called "associative play." Caregivers need to guide associative play because children have not yet developed skills for cooperation. For example, each of two children in the playhouse wants to "cook" something for her own teddy bear. They may start fussing over the kitchen space. Their caregiver suggests that they each cook separately and then share the table and dishes. They might even enjoy a final pretend party together. If they accept the caregiver's idea, he can leave them alone for a while to play. The developmental ability for this shared social play and cooperative behavior is just emerging, and it is fragile. Children will need to be guided by your examples, your social rules, and your monitoring.

Mixing age groups in play increases social learning. When older and younger children play together, some become teachers and others are especially motivated to perform beyond their skill levels. The younger child follows the model of the older. They observe carefully and try hard. The older child increases his empathy by helping, protecting, and demonstrating for the younger. Much of this behavior happens naturally, but it is also helpful for a caregiver to guide and scaffold these social interactions.

Safety is a vital concern. Children who have siblings are more skilled at interacting with others, but they may also know tricks for prevailing or dominating others. Older children may pursue activities that are developmentally beyond the younger ones, but the younger children will follow and try to imitate. Multiple caregivers will need to be involved in mixed-aged play groups to monitor for dangerous, hurtful, or aggressive situations.

You will notice children helping children—getting a ball that is out of reach, passing a cookie to a friend, or explaining to another child how a toy works. Helping one another is a natural human inclination that deserves commendation and spotlighting. When caregivers discuss with children the acts of thoughtfulness they have observed, children see these as mastery tasks that are valued. Promoting this kind of helping behavior not only improves relationships but also increases feelings of positive identity for the child.

> *Promoting helping behavior not only improves relationships but also increases feelings of positive identity for the child.*

Your knowledge of child development is crucial. Children from birth through 3 years vary widely in skills and abilities. Some children may try to use toys or playground equipment that is beyond their ability. Some children may invite their friends to jump from a height that is beyond their skill. Social pressure is a strong force, influencing less-skilled children to try something dangerous. As the caregiver, you will be responsible for knowing the abilities of each child and for managing children's safety in group play. As caregiver, you will know which children are wise about safety when helping younger or newer participants.

Group activities are fun ways to teach social skills. Much of your day in the child-care center is spent in planned activities. Group games that promote SPE also promote social learning. For example song circles with fingerplay actions lead children to learn from and help one another. Group clapping games bring forth giggles and great concentration. Most group activities involve social rules and structured social interactions. These activities continue to expand social learning as children form voluntary social groups and try to re-create this game during free play.

Exercise activities that include songs, voice, or dance lead to wonderful spontaneous social connections. Another way to use SPE to connect children to one another is playing foot exercise games, such as stamping feet in a particular rhythm. During this time, promote the use of fun words that can express lots of emotion, such as "Whee!" "Oh, boy!" or "Zing! Zing!" Laugh about mistakes in a general way when someone misses a prescribed cue. (Be sure that the class is not embarrassing a particular child.)

Respect for differences is promoted through group activities. Respect involves being able to consider the feelings and beliefs of someone else. This ability does not come innately to toddlers. It needs to be taught and felt. One way to teach this ability is by creating something together, for example, making a giant play dough cookie. Each child can shape his or her own play dough but also can add it to the group project. Each addition will be different and individual, but the final product will belong to the group. This project allows the caregiver to make teaching statements about how "we will use everyone's idea." In this way, the caregiver can show children that the opinions and contributions of each person in the group are valuable.

Social rules are learned while the class makes the cookie. Each child gets a turn to add to the cookie. Watching and waiting while other children place their play dough creations on the cookie involves using manners and self-control for the good of the group. Social distances are defined so that each child has personal freedom to add a piece but not to hurt another's work. The activity provides opportunities for children to help one another work and to admire the other person's creation. These toddlers will be learning about social sharing, social distance, and respect for others.

Working side by side on a group project often creates changes in perception and thinking patterns. Children watch one another and copy something that they see; or they may be inspired to try a new idea. This kind of socialization leads to creativity and expands horizons in thinking.

Plan time to admire the completed cookie. Appreciate each child's contribution. This process will give you an opportunity to teach the social words that reflect pride. Again, "high fives" are fun when you want to thank someone or compliment them. Words and actions for showing positive social approval of another child's mastery can include expressions such as "Look what we made. Do you like it?" or "Take a bow."

Remember that toddlers have limited ability. What you see on the cookies will not be what the toddler sees. The cookie may be a funny-looking product to you, but beauty is in the eye of the beholder. The toddlers will think it is wonderful. The goal of this activity is to share effort, feelings of belonging, and group pride.

Other group activities, such as playing in a pool, catching bubbles, or even holding hands while on walks, promote social opportunities for empathy and sharing. These opportunities for social sharing may be one of the most important functions of child care.

Routines are social learning tools that also teach values. Some routines, such as putting a coat on a hook and shoes in a cubby, teach children to value their possessions and keep their things out of one another's way. Social learning includes learning habits of cleanliness and order.

Working side by side on a group project often creates changes in perception and thinking patterns.

Washing hands, using a napkin, putting toys away, taking care of property, and being modest are ways we respect others and live together successfully.

For some children, child care may be the first exposure to some of these social behaviors.

Routines often become rules for group living, for example, "We always line up to go to the bus," "We sit quietly when lunch is being served," and "We don't talk during nap time." These rules are similar to more general social patterns such as letting folks out of the elevator before others enter or not talking in movie theatres. They are social rules that benefit the group, and they become social norms.

Chapter Summary

Gaining skills and confidence in social interaction is one of the major developmental tasks of the first 3 years. Without models and instruction, the rules of interaction may be learned through confrontation and defined by using or experiencing power behaviors. Teaching social skills is important. You are setting habits for future interactions and future successes. The social values of the child-care center should be agreed on by the staff and should become a matter of policy so that they can be easily defined and discussed with parents.

The interactive experiences children have during the first 3 years of life form the basis for their capacities to connect with others intellectually and socially. These experiences will influence their moral sense, their creativity, and their life choices. As children come into your care, the teaching of social skills will be a complex and interesting issue for you and your center to face.

Resources

Asher, S. R. (1985). An evolving paradigm in social skills training research with children. In B. H. Schneider, K. H. Rubin, & J. E. Ledingham (Eds.), *Children's peer relations: Issues in assessment and intervention* (pp. 157–174). New York: Springer-Verlag.

Dunn, J. (1994). Changing minds and changing relationships. In C. Lewis & P. Mitchell (Eds.), *Children's early understanding of mind* (pp. 297–310). Hove, England: Erlbaum.

Garcia Coll, C., & Magnuson, K. (1999). Cultural influences on child development: Are we ready for a paradigm shift? In C. Nelson & A. Masten (Eds.), *Cultural processes in child development: Minnesota symposia on child psychology* (Vol. 29, pp. 1–24). Hillsdale, NJ: Erlbaum.

Howes, C. (1990). Can age of entry into child care and the quality of child care predict adjustment to kindergarten? *Developmental Psychology, 26,* 292–303.

Howes, C. (2000). Social-emotional classroom climate in childcare: Child-teacher relationships and children's second grade peer relations. *Social Development,*

9(2), 191–205.

Howes, C., & Hamilton, C. E. (1992). Children's relationships with caregivers: Mother and childcare teachers. *Child Development, 63,* 859–866.

Howes, C., & Matheson, C. C. (1992). Sequences in the development of competent play with peers: Social and social-pretend play. *Developmental Psychology, 28,* 961–974.

Jervis, K. (1984). *Separation: Strategies for helping two to four year olds.* Washington, DC: National Association for the Education of Young Children.

Katz, L., & McClellan, D. E. (1997). Fostering children's social competence. Washington, DC: National Association for the Education of Young Children.

Nahum, J. P. (2000). An overview of Louis Sander's contribution to the field of mental health. *Infant Mental Health Journal, 21*(1–2), 29–41.

Pratt, M. W. (1999). The importance of infant/toddler interactions. *Young Children, 54*(4), 26–29.

Rubin, K. H., Bukowski, W., & Parker, J. G. (1998). Peer interactions, relationships, and groups. In W. Damon (Ed.), *Handbook of child psychology: Vol. 3. Social, emotional and personality development* (5th ed., pp. 619–700). New York: Wiley.

Rubin, K. H., Coplan, R. J., Fox, N. A., & Calkins, S. (1995). Emotionality, emotion regulation, and preschooler's social adaptation. *Development and Psychopathology, 7,* 49–62.

Sameroff, A. J. (1993). Models of development and developmental risk. In C. H. Zeanah (Ed.), *Handbook of infant mental health* (pp. 3–13). New York: Guilford.

Sroufe, L. A., Schork, E., Motti, F., Lawroske, N., & LaFrenier, P. (1984). The role of affect in social competence. In C. Izard, J. Kagan, & R. Zajonic (Eds.), *Emotions, cognition and behavior* (pp. 289–319). New York: Oxford University Press.

Wertch, J. (1976). From social interaction to higher psychological processes: A clarification of Vygotsky's theory. *Human Development, 22,* 1–22.

Video

First Moves: Welcoming a Child to a New Caregiving Setting. Program for Infant Toddler Caregivers. (1986). Sacramento, CA: Far West Laboratory. (27 min.).

Relationships Guide and Regulate Behavior

Discipline is a subject of major concern for parents and child-care providers. Toddlers are incredibly appealing, energetic, inquisitive, and loving. Yet these same children have been described as willful, oppositional, and defiant. All too quickly, the wonderful baby, who was well adapted to a family routine, is pulling out the light plugs, pounding on the knickknacks, and refusing to get into a car seat. This often occurs around 9–12 months of age, when many parents are choosing to send their children to child care. How should these behaviors be managed? How do we balance our instinct to nurture with the frustrations that are ever present in child rearing? How does the toddler learn right from wrong? Whose needs should be foremost?

When we are confronted with behaviors that need to change, the word *discipline* comes to mind. When many parents think of managing extreme behaviors, they think of punishment. Discipline and punishment are often used as synonyms. For the most part, punishments are not effective teachers for toddlers. They also provide negative models and promote extreme emotional responses in children.

Angry discipline methods can inflict lifelong scars. We have learned about the detrimental effects of the shared negative emotions (SNEs) that often accompany discipline. Frightening emotional displays by an adult will temporarily change behavior; however, children usually resolve these experiences by internalizing the anger and unleashing it on someone else. The child who experiences angry discipline may lash out and overpower smaller children or may withdraw from participation with others. These patterns of interaction are enduring and continue to distort social and emotional

---

Goals of Chapter 6

▥ Explore the reasons for misbehavior in young children.

▥ Understand how physical, emotional, and mastery needs can lead to states of disequilibrium and extreme behaviors.

▥ Describe how our inborn motivation to belong triggers the brain to copy human models and allows us to be regulated by relationships with others.

▥ Examine how mutual regulation organizes and manages behavior.

▥ Discuss the use of daily rituals and routines to regulate behavior and promote feelings of belonging.

▥ Understand that behavior regulation also involves setting limits and controlling extreme behaviors.

▥ Practice mutual regulation techniques in a child-care setting.

connections in the future. Relationships that are formed at the child-care center can mediate this cycle.

This chapter will help you understand why children behave as they do. Your relationship with each child helps you anticipate problems and also helps a child look to you for guidance and regulation. The various sections that follow also will present strategies for intervening when behavior problems occur.

Key Concept One
Understanding Behavior Is the First Step to Managing It

Discipline involves emotional and behavioral regulation. A helpful fact to remember is that the word *discipline* comes from the word *disciple,* meaning one who is learning from a teacher or guide. As the caregiver, you are the child's teacher. Discipline should be about guiding the child toward self-control through mutual regulation of emotions. To successfully guide children in this way, we need to understand the volatility of young emotions and the forces that drive extreme behavior. As we analyze the following scenario in the next few sections, we will discover some helpful insights.

> Rosalie is on an adventure with five 2-year-olds to look for bugs in the garden behind the center. It has taken some time to get ready, but at 11:15 a.m., they are on the path to the garden. Everyone seems excited and active as the group begins the walk. Suddenly, Eloise sits down and whimpers that she is too tired to walk. As Rosalie is talking with her, Henry pushes Hans down and then rushes toward the swings. Sarah begins to run wildly toward the garden saying, "Bug. See bug. Me, bug." Jose is clinging to Rosalie's pant leg and making it difficult for her to move.

Why is the walk becoming disorganized? Are these children naughty? Should they be scolded?

Early Behavior Is Driven by Internal Feelings

Why do children misbehave? Child behavior in the first 3 years is primarily driven by internal feelings. We know that children's internal and external needs register as feelings and are expressed by them as emotional cues. These feelings define children's actions. When these feelings are positive and brain activity is focused, children feel in balance. Behaviors are usually organized toward an activity. However, when internal feelings are uncomfortable and children feel off balance, they will become disorganized, clumsy, and unfocused. Behaviors may be impulsive and are often extreme.

In the previous scenario, all of these children are showing disorganization in their behavior. Rosalie is close to losing control. What would you do? Who would you tend to first? Is there a possible solution for everyone? Which of these options would you use?

a. Blow a whistle and scream, "Stop! Get back in line."
b. Run after Sarah.
c. Scold Henry.
d. Hug Hans.
e. Stand Eloise up and say, "You are okay."
f. Call out, "Snack time, come sit down here and see what I have."

Children's behavior becomes disorganized for three main reasons. These include physical needs (a child is hungry, tired, sick, or cold), emotional needs (a child is frightened, angry, sad, or overexcited), and mastery motivation (a child is totally absorbed in a project or blocked from a goal). Although many factors influence our behavior, for the child, these three reasons are primary. The following sections explore each in more detail.

Physical Needs. Physical needs dictate feelings and set in motion strong behavioral displays. If a child is exhausted, hungry, or sick, then these feelings take precedence. However, physical feelings often develop slowly. For example, at 11:00 a.m., you might say to yourself, "I wonder what's for lunch today?" At 11:30 a.m., you ask, "Can I take the early lunch group?" By noon, you are barking, "Hurry, hurry, let's go. I'm starving!" By 12:15 p.m., you quietly say to your colleague, "Do you have any chocolate?" In the same way, children cannot identify why they are feeling "off." They cannot tell you that they are hungry, so they act out or collapse to show their rising discomfort. Hungry children may become disorganized, irritable, or highly active and attention seeking. When a child who is usually easy to motivate seems bothersome or naughty, think food!

Typically, children who are in physical disequilibrium because of sickness or fatigue experience "meltdowns," or lethargic, weepy periods. When this kind of behavior happens, remember that infants and toddlers typically do not have much endurance and are vulnerable to contagious diseases. Consider getting the child to a quiet space to rest or putting your wrist on the child's forehead for a quick temperature check.

In our previous scenario, the caregiver asked herself, "Why? Why are these children off task and going berserk?" As a wise caregiver, she knows that all of the children could be displaying signs of hunger. She knows that toddlers are grazers and need lots of food energy. Many toddlers cannot wait until the assigned lunch hour. Physical needs are first on the caregiver's solution list. She has brought snacks in her backpack.

Were Hans and Eloise hungry? Or were they coming down with a cold? The caregiver must consider many options; perhaps several reasons are shaping the children's behavior. Other possible explanations may become apparent as we consider emotional needs.

Emotional Needs. Emotional needs also cause children to feel off balance. In contrast to the feelings associated with physical needs, the feelings connected to emotional needs are more defined, and the behaviors that follow are often extreme. Consider the behaviors that accompany the emotion of fear. Children confronting a novel situation will be controlled by their anxiety and will behave in ways that feel safe or protective for them. Their behaviors may involve withdrawal, thumb sucking, refusal to participate, or an urge to cling to someone they trust. Shyness is really minimal fear, an anxiety about the unknown. Do these children need to be disciplined? Their primary need is reassurance. Anxious children need mutual regulation. A responsive caregiver will read the anxiety in their cues and will help them reestablish feelings of safety.

In the scenario above, Jose was probably feeling anxiety about the group excitement and newness of the excursion. He was not confident within the group and wanted to be connected to his caregiver. He clung to her for safety. His behaviors were probably driven more by emotional extremes than by hunger, exhaustion, or sickness.

> *Children confronting a novel situation will be controlled by their anxiety and will behave in ways that feel safe or protective for them.*

Feelings of anger may ignite extreme or dangerous behaviors. Children will act out their feelings. They may destroy a toy, color on someone else's paper, or push another child to release the tensions of overt or pent-up anger. For an angry child, limits must be set quickly and clearly for the safety of others, but the angry feelings within the child will need to be repaired and then regulated. The angry child will benefit enormously from a primary caregiver who will have the understanding and compassion to modulate and repair this child's emotional extremes and monitor his or her activity. That child will trust the caregiver's guidance. In the scenario, who might be an angry child?

Often, sad children retreat to play alone, or they refuse to try a task or connect with a story or song. By listening quietly to these children, by making time for one-on-one interactions, and by empathizing with their sadness, you can repair some of their sad feelings and redirect their attention. Slowly, you will help these children get beyond their sad feelings when they are in the child-care setting. In the scenario, Hans, who was pushed and then fell, will need an adult to regulate his sadness.

Shared excitement leads to overstimulation. Children can become so "wound up" that they cannot stop. The familiar phrase, "Didn't you hear me?" is usually answered, "No!" because children become so absorbed in the excitement or interest connected with a task that all else is shut out of their minds.

Think of Sarah in the scenario. She was delighted with the idea of finding a bug. She may have remembered the bugs that live in the garden from going on this kind of excursion before, so she was motivated. She was oblivious to the fact that the others were not with her or that she had broken from the line of toddlers. She was bug hunting!

Mastery Motivation. Mastery motivation is a powerful influence on early behavior. The drive expressed in the phrase, "I want to!" is a strong feeling within all of us at some time or another. For the child, this drive often ignites immediate actions. As with Sarah, the motivation to attain a goal can consume the child. Sarah was oblivious to the needs of others; she was obsessed with her own task. Children often become angry or sad when their goals are thwarted. Tears, tantrums, and lashing out are common ways for children to show others that their goals have been blocked. As a caregiver, you could show Sarah how she could meet her goal and also stay with the group. You could redirect her feelings toward a delayed goal.

Learning to negotiate goals or to delay desires to meet the needs of the group is a hard lesson for toddlers. Nevertheless, it is one that the toddler and young child can grasp. If children feel emotionally connected to a caregiver, then one of their goals will be to please that person. Because of this dynamic, the caregiver can regulate the "But I want to" motivation more successfully.

Another type of mastery is the mastery of interactions with others. As babies develop and gain new skills, they realize that they have power. At about 4 months old, infants begin to learn that their smiles and cries attract the attention of adults. This realization brings a feeling of mastery. When the adult responds, the child will signal again, and a reciprocal exchange begins. These reciprocal exchanges initiate patterns of communication and interaction, but they also set expectations for behavior regulation. The responses of the adult influence the behavior of the child.

Although this process has been happening since birth, adults may not have been focused on their role in behavior management. Eventually, however, at about 1 year old—when the crawling baby chooses to hurry away from mom or the child in a high chair pushes his or her lunch off the tray—caregivers are challenged to contemplate their responses. Each caregiver may react to the child's actions in a different way. Each reaction will be an intriguing area of exploration for the child. In the same way that children explore their environments, they also explore their effects on others. Their actions now take on new meaning. Learning expands. They begin to realize, "I am a separate person. I can make choices. I can change the behavior of others by what I do."

When a baby realizes that a fake cough can get mom out of her chair or a giggle can keep dad's attention, then interacting with people becomes a mastery skill. Toddlers explore the domain of emotional communication using gestures, facial expressions, and the few words they know, including *more*, *up*, or *no*. The behaviors that are successful will become deliberate, planned, and sometimes contrary. Their communications may become demanding, repetitious, and persistent. Tantrums, wild giggles, whines, singing, dancing, and clapping hands, which once were spontaneous emotional displays, are now frequently initiated by the toddler to gain the attentions of another.

> *Toddlers explore the domain of emotional communication using gestures, facial expressions, and the few words they know.*

As toddlers expand their interactive skills, they continue to experiment with their actions. They are exploring ways to get our attention or negotiate their wants through behavior. When they realize that they can achieve these goals, the sense of power they feel is exhilarating. Toddlers will try selected behaviors with all the caregivers—for example, saying "no" or defying a request—and they will learn from the responses of the adults where their power lies.

In the scenario, Eloise may have been whining to see whether her caregiver would carry her to the garden. If her prior experience has been that grandmother always carries her when she whines, she will expect the same response of this caregiver. She is exploring the reactions of others to her behavior.

Learning that different caregivers react differently to their signals is a major developmental step for toddlers. Toddlers experiment with patterns of interaction, and remarkably, they are able to select and use the signals and behaviors that are successful for them with each caregiver. These patterns of interaction become working models in their brains that guide future interactions. The period between 18 and 36 months is a crucial time for the development of social learning. The toddler is struggling with two conflicting motivations: "I want my way" and "I want to belong and be valued by others." The experiences children have with others during this period will shape their style of interaction and their social competence.

If it has worked well in the past for a child to hit someone and then take what he or she wants, this behavior becomes the child's internal model of success. The act of overpowering becomes this child's idea of interaction. If whining and pestering are strategies that have worked, they become habits. Do you know adults who have maintained these models well into adulthood? Children who have experienced a responsive relationship with a caregiver who guides them in negotiating their wants will internalize social patterns that continue to benefit and expand their pleasure, their learning, and their social network.

The child-care center is a place where some negative behavior patterns can be changed. Primary caregivers become the guide to behavior choices for the toddler. As caregivers, you can affect the internal working models that are being formed within the children. You can explain alternatives, build empathy for others, and guide children toward adaptive strategies to obtain their goals and feel mastery. Your responses to these children contribute to their understanding of themselves. In general, by age 3 children will begin to know that they choose their behavior. They can choose to comply or they can choose to be contrary. This realization is an important developmental step. It is the beginning of an inner sense of self-control. As toddlers experience the responses of others to their actions, they will find answers to questions such as, "How can I get to my goals? Who will help me? Am I okay? Do I belong? Am I liked? Am I safe?"

For the most part, toddlers do not have the ability or the inclination to be subversive or malicious. Their "naughty" actions are most often driven by physical discomfort, high emotion, or mastery motivation. Deciding how to regulate behavior is an easy task if you remember always to ask why. Why has this child's behavior changed? What is the disequilibrium? The need for discipline becomes rare when we assess the root problem, regulate emotions, and reduce physical discomfort.

Key Concept Two
Adults Regulate and Focus Behavior

How can caregivers regulate rather than punish problem behaviors? How we respond to a child's action gives that action meaning for the child. If a behavior brings results for the child, he or she will repeat it and try it with other people. If a behavior is ignored, it will be forgotten. One way we, as caregivers, can regulate behavior is to monitor our responses to children's actions.

In child care, children have the opportunity to try their behavioral patterns on many people. They will get varied reactions. Some caregivers will bow to the power of tears or tantrums, and some will become angry. Others will understand and repair. With a primary caregiver, the child will develop a stable expectation of response and will learn faster how to modulate his behavior and adapt his goals to fit with the patterns and rules.

Behavior management must be thoughtful and responsive to the child's developmental needs. As the child develops new motor skills and cognitive skills, her behaviors change. With each developmental step, the child will be searching again for guidance in behavior management. For example, the toddler who has just learned to run will be euphoric. She will run at every occasion—running around the room, running toward the stairs, running into others. Caregivers must regulate this new behavior without defeating the toddler's feelings of autonomy and pride.

Toddlers can discriminate among caregivers. Because your responses will be different than those of their parents, toddlers will quickly learn who will carry them and who will ask them to walk, who will feed them and who will help them feed themselves. Their expectations and their behaviors change as they change environments and caregivers. When there are too many caregivers or when expectations are too conflicting, children internalize a disorganized complexity of models. They develop problem behavior patterns as well as problems with interactions and with their ability to focus on cognitive tasks.

Each child will respond to limits and sanctions in a different way. This variety may be a challenge for staff members because they will be required to deal with this diversity of child expectations as well as with the diversity of parent beliefs and practices about discipline. A child-care center will benefit from a unified philosophy about behavior management. In addition, parents will benefit from having some written material to read that details the center's philosophy.

> *Behavior management must be thoughtful and responsive to the child's developmental needs.*

Adults manage and focus child behavior through emotion regulation. As we learned in chapter 3, mutual regulation of emotion is central to helping the child process emotional information in a cognitive way rather than an impulsive way. Emotional signals such as "I want to" or "more, more, more" lead to impulsive actions. Children may hit, grab, or push to get what they want. The responsive adult can intercept these impulses and guide children toward alternative ways to think. By using emotion regulation, the caregiver tempers the child's strong feelings and then guides the child by processing with him alternative ways to meet the child's goals (for example, "Ask Clarissa whether she will share," "Look, there is another truck over there," and "Show Clarissa your ball and see whether she will trade"). By sharing problem-solving ideas, children learn to control their impulses and to consider positive alternatives.

Through the mutual regulation of emotions, children gain skills for making choices, defining fears, and assessing dangers. When a responsive relationship with another person is available, children will want to please this person. They become sensitive to their caregiver's reactions to unsafe, unkind, or unhealthy actions. Through the relationship experience, children expand their thinking. They become more aware that they have choices for their behavior. In this way, new behaviors are learned that are primarily productive and appropriate.

Through the mutual regulation of emotions, children gain skills for making choices, defining fears, and assessing dangers.

New behavioral models are internalized slowly. When a consistent caregiver is there to share positive actions, repair fears, and give children control over their frustrations, they begin to feel success with a new behavioral pattern. With consistent guidance and repeated successes, children will become more confident and will internalize the new behavioral model. They will know that, if needed, "their" caregiver is there but that they also have some problem-solving skills of their own. They will be confident of their inner resources, sometimes seeking new challenges, testing behavior choices, and expanding their initiative.

Shared positive emotions (SPEs) are a key to behavior management. As you share the positive emotions of interest, surprise, and joy with children, you will be directing their focus of attention. Looking at picture books, making a clay ball, or blowing bubbles become exciting mastery tasks initiated and sustained by SPE. Your enthusiasm motivates a child to repeat an action. Your positive response emboldens the child. Her behavioral energy will become directed toward positive activity. Behavioral problems will be at a minimum.

When a special emotional connection is present between caregiver and child, the child is especially receptive to regulation by the adult. Because they share a trust base, the child responds to the caregiver's efforts to change his disequilibrium. The child welcomes the positive focus that the caregiver offers. "Look at what I have! Come try this new thing." "Let's finish." "Look, I'll help you." These words and their accompanying actions enable a caregiver to refocus and regulate the child's anxieties. When a child has a consistent positive relationship with an adult, he is more resilient to the negative emotions in others. He tolerates the rules and is willing to delay gratification because he trusts his caregiver to also keep his interests in mind.

Scaffolding is another way to reorganize behavior or avoid problems. When a caregiver scaffolds the toddler's attention toward mental skills, that caregiver is strengthening mental pathways but also avoiding behavior problems. When the caregiver is able to keep the child's attention focused until the child feels a sense of discovery or accomplishment, then the mastery cycle will take over. The skilled caregiver will plan to move a child to the next activity before that child becomes bored, possessive, or tired. Misbehavior and extreme emotions are absent. When you scaffold emotions to focus and maintain concentration, you are helping a child not only to learn from the task but also to learn some self-control. The child will become internally motivated to continue mastering these new skills. The child will begin to scaffold her learning independently. Her attention will be internally focused, and she will not be seeking attention from others.

> *Scaffolding is another way to reorganize behavior or avoid problems.*

Reward the behaviors that the child initiates. Responding to child initiation is extremely important to the child's development. When a 6-month-old offers you the rattle in his hand and you take it, saying "Oh, pretty!" before giving it back, you have acknowledged his action and interest. You have joined in his pleasure. The child will use this behavior over and over. The interaction with you will be a clear memory for him. In terms of behavior management, reflecting positive behaviors that children perform on their own will give them feelings of mastery. Your approval will reinforce their sense of power and their feelings of competence. Behaviors that you reinforce will become their habits. Your expressions of approval are turned inward and help the child to feel that his choice of action was an effective one. "You ate your peas; you should feel good about it." "Thank you for the book; you picked it out by yourself."

Teaching helping behaviors motivates children. Having toddlers help with adult tasks such as carrying pictures for the bulletin board or passing the crackers motivates them. Because they feel pride in being connected to others in this way, they will be stimulated to continue using behaviors that help others. Toddlers seem to like feeling "grown up." They will clamor for the helping tasks in the classroom.

If you respond to children when they ask for help from you, then they will internalize the "helper" model. When a child says, "Book, that book?" or "Mine, blue plate, blue plate," a responsive caregiver can point out that the caregiver will help. The caregiver points out that she is a helper for the child. The child's success in asking for help will influence the child's desire to give help. This success will reinforce a positive behavioral model in the child's mind. When children learn to command the attention they need through positive actions, they do not need to garner attention through negative behaviors and emotions.

Key Concept Three
Responsive Caregivers Anticipate Behavior Problems

Certain situations predictably lead to behavior problems. There are predictable situations that can lead to behavior problems. Many of these can be anticipated. With an understanding of emotion regulation, internal motivations, and learned behavior patterns, you can be prepared for the child's disequilibrium and avoid the need for discipline.

Structure for Success

As caregivers, we can structure the environment, the activities, and work with the staff to avoid situations that we know cause anxieties for children. In this way, you will be helping the child succeed at performing tasks or integrating into the group. For example, when children first enter group care, there will be predictable caution and separation anxiety. Fussy, fearful, uncooperative behavior is expected. This anxiety in the child and the parent will provide the caregiver with an opportunity to establish a trust relationship with both. Designing a structure within the center for this trust to grow will help the new child make a smoother transition. Consider the challenges in the following scenario.

> Maria (9 months old) has just been dropped off at child care. She is crying. Trudy is to be her primary caregiver. She picks up Maria and carries her as she greets other parents and children coming to school. Every time Trudy tries to put Maria down, Maria cries. Trudy finds Maria's bottle and begins to feed her as she organizes others in her group. Maria dozes off as she sucks but jerks awake as Trudy moves about. She begins to cry. Other children also need Trudy, and other duties need to be done this morning.

How might Trudy anticipate and structure this situation for success? Knowing that this child has been assigned to her as a primary caregiver, she might enlist staff support to manage the other children so that she could have a quiet place and extra time to establish a bond with Maria. Trudy also can anticipate that a new child may be used to a different schedule such as a morning nap. This new schedule causes a feeling of disequilibrium. If Trudy is able to give Maria a sense of safety and protection, Maria will then look to her for emotion regulation and physical equilibrium in the future. She will also look to Trudy for guidance in behavior management.

The toddler who has just entered group care may expect to have a caregiver's attention quickly and often. Children who have not previously experienced group care may seem demanding at first because they may be used to one-on-one attention. You can expect unstable behavior from them. Anticipate spending extra time for orientation with these children. The toddler who has been indulged in other settings may expect to influence you through intense displays of anger or sadness. By respecting and understanding that his expectations have been set by prior experience, you can set limits in a quiet, firm manner. Be calm, clear, and consistent in establishing new expectations.

The child who has been in day care for some time may be more compliant and more group-oriented. The routines and rules will be part of her habits. She knows where her coat goes and what activity will start the day. This child can show others how to behave and what to expect and will probably enjoy showing off her mastery to the new children. You can structure for success by directing and monitoring the competent child as your helper. She will be learning new behaviors that communicate and establish friendships. This child-to-child interaction helps the new child to also feel accepted. If you anticipate and plan, you can organize activities for the self-sufficient children in your group that will allow you more time with the needy children.

Children who are "center wise" may be overconfident and overassertive in their behavior. Caregivers can anticipate that the child who knows the routines of the center may be eager to show off his knowledge or to gain the advantage by jumping into the next expected activity before the class is ready. The following scenario gives us an opportunity to consider how to guide this kind of child.

> Michael has run out the door to the slide. As other children come to play, Michael is finishing his first trip down the slide. Michael pushes a child aside because he is ready to slide again. He zips down the slide, landing on a little girl who has fallen at the bottom, and runs around to climb the slide again.

Michael was focused on a skill with which he is confident; he was internally motivated. He knew that the class was preparing to go to the playground, and he beat them to be first on the slide. He was absorbed in practicing and enjoying his mastery. He was not aware of others in his way, but his behavior was unsafe and had to be stopped. How might you "discipline" Michael?

> Michael's caregiver picks up Michael and holds him. She shows him the others who are waiting and talks to him about taking turns and

safety. Then she gives him a turn and meets him at the bottom of the slide. She goes with him to the ladder where they wait in line for others to take a turn.

This caregiver understood Michael's motivation. She helped him regulate his drive and focused him to think about others.

When the environment or the routines change, even confident, internally directed children might become unsure. If more children enter the play or an additional challenge is presented, they will look for their caregiver to guide their behavior. This person will be the one who can read their reticence and understand what kind of guidance they need and how much to give them. This caregiver will be able to judge what is developmentally appropriate and will understand their particular temperaments and backgrounds.

Teach the Dos

Teaching the dos is a wonderful way to structure behavior for success. When we show children what we want them to do, they are proud to show us that they can do it. By demonstrating what you want and by giving children the necessary space, materials, and guidance, they will try to copy your model. They will show you that they can be like you. This modeling becomes a mastery task for the child and is far more effective for learning than telling a child what we do not want. Teaching the dos works with the internal motivations of the child rather than interrupting or frustrating these motivations with censure.

Particular dos are important for caregivers to remember. Do keep expectations developmentally appropriate. Do use the word *we* as often as possible. Do be clear and calm with your limits. Do turn don'ts into dos. Do ignore the behaviors that bother you, as long as they are not dangerous or harmful. Do commend children for good behavior.

How does a caregiver model the dos? When a new task is presented, the caregiver needs to make sure that he shares in the doing. "Look what *we* can do with this curved block, Alicia. Here's another; you try it." When a child enters a new play area, the adult needs to be there to regulate and monitor the transition. "This is Tad. He would like to help *us* with the blocks. Can you show him how you make a tower, Alicia? Good. See, Tad, it's easy. Shall *we* try?"

As you integrate each child into new activities or situations, select a task that the child can do easily, one that is well within her developmental ability. When you select tasks from lower on the developmental ladder, you are structuring for confidence. With this confidence, the child will then be more able to move forward to new challenges.

Establish Routines, Schedules, and Rules

Routines and schedules shape behavior, a fact that is true in the home, at the child-care center, and throughout life. Routines create expectations that regulate our behavior. Think about your Sunday morning routine. Some households are hustling to get dressed and off to church, where everyone is expected to be quiet and follow the actions of the leaders. In other households, Sunday may be a day to stay in bed late, allowing the kids to join parents to cuddle and play or read the funnies out loud. Still other families may expect to cook a big breakfast together, with everybody sharing in the meal preparation. Although families may have different behavioral expectations, the various family routines contribute to shaping how the children in each situation will learn to regulate their behavior.

Routines establish pathways for thinking and planning. Our habits have been established from the patterns that were practiced early in our lives. These can be habits that give us feelings of accomplishment and pride, like taking a run in the morning before breakfast. They can be habits that enhance efficiency, like knowing the car keys are always on the hook. They can be habits that enrich our learning, like reading a book in the evenings. If you were taught to put the cap on the toothpaste at age 3, you probably still do it. At age 3, it was a mastery task. You were proud to do it, and your parents mirrored your pride. Now, it is part of your routine as a busy adult. You do not even think about doing it, but your inner voice mirrors pride. ("That was good; I never have to go back to clean up an oozing mess of toothpaste.") Your inner voice says, "I'm okay."

> *Many routines, such as hanging up coats and cleaning up, that are established in child care become lasting, internalized patterns for children.*

Many routines, such as hanging up coats and cleaning up, that are established in child care become lasting, internalized patterns for children. When the child-care staff members plan routines for the center, they are making a major contribution toward the self-regulation within children.

Routines can be an oasis for some children. Today, many children are overstimulated. They come from households where routines are lacking. Children are surrounded by a myriad of intense stimuli and inconsistent demands. Think of early morning in a household. The news radio blares; breakfast is a hustle; conversation is clipped; parents show anxiety as they rush past the baby and then return, swoosh, to pick up the baby and dash to the car. What is a baby to do? With so much happening at once, this baby is unable to organize these stimuli; the baby rapidly becomes overstimulated. When the baby gets to child care, she may be fussy and disorganized. Toddlers also can experience this sort of overstimulation. Toddlers become anxious, whiny, or angry when the stimulation around them is too intense or too varied and when the situation has no structure or expectations.

The child-care center can represent an oasis where routines are consistent and children know what will happen soon after they arrive. The anxious child enters the center and can say, "Now, I know what to do. I know what is going to happen next. I am safe and confident. I can calm down." Many children look forward to the consistent expectations and routines of the center that help them self-regulate and find emotional equilibrium.

Rules define behavior. Rules give us clear limits on everyone's behavior. They establish what behaviors are not acceptable, but they also establish the dos of behavior management. When the rules of the center are clear, group members help one another regulate behavior. Have you seen children shush one another as they sit down for story time? They express a sense of mastery in conforming and joining with the group. The rules of group behavior help temper the child's individual assertiveness and keep it in balance.

By setting rules ahead of time and sharing these expectations with the children, you will be helping them develop the ability to think into the future and organize their behavior. Often, they will come to the center excited to demonstrate their knowledge of the rules. They are learning to self-regulate. Rules can give children feelings of safety and continuity as well as help them to succeed.

Some families have few rules. Their family patterns inhibit thinking and problem solving. Consider the household whose family members often leave a job half done or leave the mess until later. The children in the families internalize these patterns, and as adults, they will struggle with procrastination, unfinished projects, and overwhelming messes—which can lead to feelings of guilt rather than mastery. For children raised in households with few routines or rules, switching from the laissez-faire expectations at home to the rules of the center may present a great frustration for the child. "Am I good or bad?" "What can I do that is okay?" "How do I belong in each group?" These are big questions for a toddler. Children from these families have trouble with rules; they will be easily distracted and need constant regulation and reengagement. They may be oppositional and independent in their behavior. Slowly, with responsive caregivers and the consistent routines of the center, these children will come to understand how to negotiate both of their environments. Be patient, and give these children support rather than sanction.

Rules are usually made for the good of a group. Rules help groups get jobs done efficiently. Rules make it easier for several people to function together smoothly. By giving clear instructions or rules for doing tasks, you will be helping many children be successful in mastering their behavior. Like a recipe, the rules for taking turns or sitting at the table to eat make it easier for children to know what is expected of them.

The shared regulation that rules demand will create patterns of affiliation and relationships. Expectations are set for the whole group about where they should be, how to use their voices, whose turn will be next. For example, consider the following scenario in which a group is working with clay.

> Their caregiver says, "Remember the rules. We must wear smocks and we must stay at our places. We may talk and have fun, but don't throw the clay. You can make anything you want with your clay, but don't touch another person's work."

These rules allow the group to share a fun experience together but also limit problem behaviors. There is shared regulation. The children follow the rules because they enjoy the activity and the camaraderie. As a caregiver, you will find these child-to-child relationships helpful for behavior management. You have perhaps experienced your own motivation to conform when there is group pressure. Do you ever call a friend to ask, "What are you wearing?" Group regulation, child-to-child regulation, and child-to-adult regulation are valuable forces in establishing internal self-management.

Follow the rules you set. When you follow the rules, children will model your behavior. "I have my smock on. Do you?" If you do not follow your own rules, children will question or forget the rule and model your behavior. When you help children realize that the rules are helpful for their success, they will demonstrate little opposition.

Key Concept Four
Extreme Behaviors Demand Action

Children's extreme misbehaviors, such as pushing, biting, hitting, and kicking, demand immediate action. These behaviors are quickly added to a child's repertoire because they work in gaining dominance. Caregivers need to have strategies for stopping these behaviors immediately and then teaching alternatives to the child.

Setting Limits Is Crucial to Psychological and Emotional Development

Self-management and self-control keep us healthy, active, and engaged as adults. Self-management skills contribute to success on the job and in relationships with other adults. In the first 3 years of life, children are trying to understand the conflict they feel between their impulses and others' expectations. The internal systems for linking emotions and cognitive skills are just being formed. One-to-one guidance is necessary. Rules, routines, and group activities help, but young children act impulsively. Their emotions overwhelm them. Limits must be defined; consequences, enacted; and repair, available. The next scenario highlights an example of this impulsive behavior.

> Donnell is rocking the baby doll in the housekeeping area. Sue-Ann, a bigger girl, comes in and says, "My doll." Donnell shakes her head and holds tight to the doll. Sue-Ann jerks the doll away. Donnell watches as Sue-Ann begins to pack the doll into the buggy. Then Donnell jumps up and bites Sue-Ann.

Biting, hitting, kicking, pushing, and throwing things are common behaviors in the second and third years. They are part of a natural behavioral repertoire for displaying impulsive reactions to anger. These antisocial behaviors are powerful because they bring results. The biter is rewarded by an immediate emotional display from the victim and an opportunity to snatch back the doll. These extreme behaviors erupt spontaneously out of a volatile and frustrated 2-year-old.

These behaviors demand immediate action. These are behaviors that can injure others, but the child quickly adopts them because they work. They allow the child to attain goals and gain dominance over other children. Caregivers need to have strategies for stopping these behaviors and then teaching alternatives to the child.

Quick Actions Must Be Taken to Change Antisocial Behaviors

Firm limits must be established with respect to antisocial behaviors. Changing extreme behavior is not an easy task because violent actions often get toddlers what they want. If a child comes to the center having experienced these behaviors as being successful for her in the past, this pattern will persist. For the safety of other children, the child-care center will need to devote extra staff time to constant monitoring and mentoring of these children. A behavior such as biting requires immediate attention from the caregiver. Donnell must stop using one of her most effective power tools. As the scenario continues, we can see how one caregiver begins to respond to Donnell's extreme behavior.

> The caregiver responds immediately to Sue-Ann's screams. She kneels down and takes Sue-Ann into her arms to quiet her but also grasps Donnell's hand as she is retreating to the back of the housekeeping area. She sits Donnell down beside her while she comforts Sue-Ann. Then she asks the girls, "What happened? Why did you bite?" Donnell

reaches toward the doll and glowers at Sue-Ann. The caregiver looks into the face of each child and interprets the problem, "Sue-Ann wanted the doll, and she took it away from Donnell." Sue-Ann nods. "Donnell was feeling angry."

Repair Is Essential

The caregiver in the scenario started to repair the situation by reviewing with the children what happened. She made sure that she defined each child's goals. She also gave empathy to each child by describing the two girls' feelings. Listening to children and connecting with their hurt or angry feelings are crucial in behavior regulation. The process continues as the scenario unfolds.

> The caregiver then turns to Donnell, looks into her eyes, and says, "Donnell, you must not bite. Biting is bad behavior. You must come to me for help if someone takes your doll. Don't bite!" Then she turns to Sue-Ann and says, "You must not grab things away from others. It makes them angry." She waits for the children to take in this information. "Now, we need to find something else to do. Both of you come with me."

This caregiver knew that both children were in the wrong. She made sure that they both heard her explain the problem behaviors and sanction them. She also listened and reflected each child's feelings and goals that led to the problem. This attention and feedback will lead to shared understanding among all parties. She will stay with the two girls until they are each focused again on a positive activity. At this point, they will have completed the process of repair.

Did Donnell receive enough sanction for biting another child? Yes, she did in this initial incident. Remember, she was attacked also. However, now she will be carefully monitored. She will have a shadow, and she will know why. Any further attempt to bite will quickly be stopped. Box 6.1 summarizes the process to change extreme behavior at the time of the event.

Responses Need to Separate the Worthiness of the Child From the Unworthiness of the Behavior

Rarely do we find "problem children" in early child care, but problem behaviors are common. Discipline and sanction should be directed toward the bad behavior, not toward the child. Reviewing and reframing the problem helps the caregiver to maintain his own equilibrium while deciding how to support the child. The child will learn best when a caregiver is there to explain alternatives to her and to share and readjust feelings as well as behaviors.

Box 6.1
Changing Extreme Behavior at the Time of the Event

1. Respond immediately.

2. Stop the behavior quickly, firmly, and simply.

3. Comfort the hurt child in the presence of the aggressor.

4. Involve the aggressor in looking at and helping the hurt child.

5. Review and explain what happened.
   a. Ask each child, "Why?" (if children are old enough).
   b. Define the feelings each child showed on his or her face and with his or her actions.
   c. Define what behaviors were wrong or unsafe.

6. Describe alternative solutions for the children (e.g., seeking adult help, negotiating for a turn, or offering a substitute toy).

7. Guide both children to repair (i.e., a positive play situation).

8. Closely monitor the child who uses extreme behaviors. This supervision will help the child realize that he or she must find alternative behaviors. Reward the child's good choices.

9. Use positive shared emotions and positive behavior strategies to repair the child's sense of value.

Sometimes children have been made to feel that they are unworthy when they overpower another child or exhibit problem behavior. Anger and blame are not useful learning tools for children. They can be detrimental. Children who have experienced these reactions use impulsive actions and anger themselves. They often feel powerless in life and have few skills for working with others. When this condition is apparent, the caregiver has an essential role: to repair a child's internal sense of worth and to provide the child with new skills for obtaining a goal and interacting with others.

Caregivers will need to monitor their own emotions. Sometimes, when children attack one another, our natural tendency is to lash out angrily in response to their antisocial behaviors. Our anger must be tempered so that we can remain emotionally available to all of the children involved. If you use negative emotions, you will be reinforcing the internal model already in the child's mind. This child will progress in learning behavior management or self-control when you are both the model and the mediator. Box 6.2 provides a long-term action plan for managing persistent extreme behaviors.

Box 6.2
Long-Term Action Plan for Managing Persistent Extreme Behaviors

1. Involve other caregivers in watching out for the particular behavior.

2. Review the situation just before the aggressive act: the time of day, the activity or event that triggered the act, with whom the child was interacting before or during the act.

3. Keep notes on each incident, including this information.

4. Ask yourself, "Why is this child acting this way? What is he or she telling us?"

5. Get input from parents about possible stress or changes in the child's life.

6. Work with parents to relieve the child of stress or to help the child understand family changes.

7. As the primary caregiver, stay responsive to and supportive of the child's feelings and needs.

8. Plan special one-on-one time to teach this child alternatives for meeting his or her goals.

9. Take precautions. Select a staff person to shadow the child when you cannot, especially during times or events when the aggressive act has occurred previously.

10. Move quickly to intercede when an event triggers aggression in the child.

11. Use firm statements with neutral emotion. State the limits, and guide alternate behavior (e.g., "No biting. Ask for help instead.").

12. Talk to the children (if they are old enough to understand) about alternative behaviors for aggression or actions they can take if attacked.

13. Alert parents of the classroom situation. Inform them of the steps you are taking. Try to keep confidential the name of the child who demonstrates extreme behavior. (Note, however, that maintaining confidentiality may be impossible.)

14. Know that this behavior will also pass. The child who gets help will develop and move on.

Extreme behaviors are a call for help. Knowing that the child's misbehavior is probably the result of some emotional pain or hurt, the caregiver tries to figure out what motivated the action. Why did this child act this way? What happened just before the child erupted? As a neutral judge, you can teach both children who are involved. Both children will need close monitoring. The child who is biting must be intercepted before he does it again. This kind of monitoring is also necessary for the child who overpowers and intimidates others. These children will need extra support from you in sharing the positives and in learning alternatives to negotiating their wants.

Tantrums Can Be Disarming for the Adult

The extreme high emotion of a tantrum alerts everyone. When children collapse and cry furiously, many adults want to turn their energies to fixing the problem. Most tantrums are natural impulsive responses to states of disequilibrium. Children may be overwhelmed, overstimulated, frustrated, or faced with doing the impossible for their developmental level. These kinds of tantrums can be fixed. Tantrums also serve to relieve pent-up emotions that the child does not fully understand. Often, the best reactions to these tantrums are first ensuring that a child is in a safe place and then allowing the child some time to ventilate her frustrations.

When children discover that these extreme displays of emotion are ways of winning, tantrums can become manipulative. This realization increases the child's power over others. Such tantrums can be ignored. Soon, the child will seek out more acceptable behaviors to get the attention of a caregiver. Caregivers must assess the situation and determine what type of tantrum is occurring. Repair will be offered when the tantrum quiets.

Keep the child and other children safe during a tantrum. If the tantrum is manipulative, do not respond to the child's needs until the child has had some time alone to release those pent-up emotions. When these tantrums are ignored, most children will quickly self-quiet. A caregiver should stay nearby to respond with calm guidance when the child stops screaming.

If children are hungry or overwhelmed, they may not be able to self-quiet. They may have a genuine problem that you, as caregiver, can assess and mediate. Temperament plays a strong role when children cannot stop crying. Most tantrum behavior occurs during the ages of strong autonomy, at about 12 months and then again at about 18–30 months. When infants or older children become truly hysterical, caregivers need to intervene.

When the child has returned to a calm state, the caregiver can talk about what angered the child. He can explain the rules or limits on the child's behavior and help the child reenter the activities of the center. Repairing the effects of anger is extremely important for development. When children experience anger in others or within themselves, they need positive shared emotions and positive strategies for future success. For example, the child who always wants the toy that is being used by someone else can be taught how to look for a duplicate on the shelf or ask an adult for help.

Chapter Summary

Discipline is about mediating internal disequilibrium. When we are physically or emotionally off balance or when we are consumed by our personal mastery goals, problem behaviors tend to occur. Adults can manage the causes of disequilibrium in the child and help the child begin to develop some self-control. Through mutual regulation, children learn to modulate their exploding emotions and to make positive behavior choices.

For infants and toddlers, this process follows a developmental sequence. From infancy, children learn state regulation. They learn to trust adults and to accept them as models. Soon, they learn to interact and realize that their actions affect others. Toddlers want desperately to fit in or belong with the group. They enjoy group activities and are easily regulated by the rules and routines of the center. But they are also motivated to be independent and to strive for their own goals. A major hurdle in development is learning to negotiate these two strong and conflicting motivations.

What are the implications of this developmental window for caregivers? First, caregivers must learn to understand the reasons for problem behaviors. Then, they need to be aware of temperaments, preferences, and needs of the children in their care. Prevention is an important part of behavior management. The caregiver's role is to guide behavior toward positive learning experiences. Caregivers must anticipate problems and structure for success. These tasks include scaffolding, sharing positive emotions, and teaching the dos. Caregivers model the actions and words that children will need to effectively ask for help or to successfully negotiate on their own. This teaching process involves establishing rules and routines and then setting limits. Finally, caregivers must intercede quickly, firmly, and compassionately when children become overwhelmed or frustrated. When the preventive steps in behavior management (regulation, modeling, guidance, and limits) become an integral part of caregiving, then the need for sanctions is greatly reduced.

Resources

Bronson, M. B. (2000). Recognizing and supporting the development of self-regulation in young children. *Young Children, 55*(2), 32–37.

Brownell, C. A., & Carriger, M. (1990). Changes in cooperation and self-other differentiation during the second year. *Child Development, 59*(3), 675–685.

Butterfield, P. M., Pagano, B., & Dolezol, S. (1997). *Playing is learning.* Denver, CO: How to Read Your Baby.

Eaton, M. (1997). Positive discipline: Fostering the self-esteem of young children. *Young Children, 52*(6), 43–46.

Egeland, B., Kalkoske, M., Gottesman, N., & Erickson, M. (1990). Preschool behavior problems: Stability and factors accounting for change. *Journal of Child Psychology and Psychiatry, 31,* 891–909.

Gatrell, D. (1997). Beyond discipline to guidance. *Young Children, 52*(6), 34–42.

Greenberg, P. (1991). *Character development: Encouraging self-esteem and self-discipline in infants, toddlers, and two-year-olds.* Washington, DC: National Association for the Education of Young Children.

Gunnar, M. R., Tout, K., deHann, M., Pierce, S., & Stansbury, K. (1997). Temperament, social competence, and adrenocortical activity in preschoolers. *Developmental Psychobiology, 31*(1), 65–85.

Howes, C. (2000). Social-emotional classroom climate in childcare, child-teacher relationships and children's second grade peer relations. *Social Development, 9*(2), 191–205.

Howes, C., & Stewart, P. (1987). Child's play with adults, toys, peers: Evaluation of family and childcare influences. *Developmental Psychology, 23,* 423–430.

Kaiser, B., & Rasminsky, J. S. (1999). *Meeting the challenge: Effective strategies for challenging behavior in early childhood environments.* Ottawa, Ontario, Canada: Canadian Child Care Federation.

Lewis, M. (1993). Self-conscious emotions: Embarrassment, pride, shame, and guilt. In M. Lewis & J. M. Haviland (Eds.), *Handbook of emotions* (pp. 563–573). New York: Guilford.

MacTurk, R. H., & Morgan, G. A. (Eds.). (1995). *Mastery motivation: Origins, conceptualizations, and applications.* Westport, CT: Ablex.

Nahum, J. P. (2000). An overview of Louis Sander's contribution to the field of mental health. *Infant Mental Health Journal, 21*(1–2), 29–41.

Reinsberg, J. (1999). Understanding your children's behavior. *Young Children, 54*(4), 54–57.

Rutter, M., Giller, H., & Hagel, A. (1998). *Antisocial behavior by young people.* Cambridge, England: Cambridge University Press.

Schreiber, M. E. (1999). Time-outs for toddlers: Is our goal punishment or education? *Young Children, 54*(4), 22–25.

Sroufe, L. A. (1996). *Emotional development: The organization of emotional life in the early years.* Cambridge, England: Cambridge University Press.

Stone, J. G. (1983). *A guide to discipline.* Washington, DC: National Association for the Education of Young Children.

Tronick, E. (1989). Emotions and emotional communication in infants. *American Psychologist, 44,* 112–119.

Webster-Stratton, C. (1990). Long-term follow-up of families with young conduct problem children: From preschool to grade school. *Journal of Clinical Child Psychology, 19*(2), 144–149.

Zahn-Waxler, C., & Radke-Yarrow, M. (1990). The origins of empathic concern. *Motivation and Emotion, 14,* 107–130.

Chapter 7

Responsive Relationships Promote Learning and Cognition

In recent years, much attention has been focused on the cognitive capacities of infants. Cognition refers to one's ability to perceive, to process, and to evaluate information and experiences. Cognition includes judgment and choices of action, as well as the ability to store and access knowledge from memory. Although it is good to recognize that babies are thinking creatures from birth, their brains are just beginning to develop. The experiences and relationships surrounding infants and toddlers will sculpt their cognitive abilities.

Some of the new information about brain development has been misinterpreted. The result has been an emphasis on specialized programs that are highly stimulating and information based. These programs have as their goal "creating a smarter baby." In the first 3 years of life, learning is different from in the preschool years. The ability to store knowledge is immature; most memories are about sensory and affective experiences. Efforts to immerse young children in new information fails to consider the fact that first learning is about initiating neural pathways, not about storing knowledge. The key elements for advancing intellectual growth in the first 3 years are affect sharing and affect regulation. These elements will influence neurochemical messengers that provide the medium for neural pathways to expand. Relationships with caregivers guide the formation of early brain structure and will shape the child's ability to think.

Goals of Chapter 7

▦ Examine the cognitive abilities, motivations, and early learning that are characteristic of infants and toddlers.

▦ Understand how children learn by experiencing the world around them.

▦ Understand the role that emotion regulation and shared positive emotion play in early brain development.

▦ Learn that the caregiver fosters cognition and learning by observing and responding to the child's signals.

▦ Discuss the development of imitation and pretend play as milestones in and pathways to cognitive development.

▦ Explore examples of how caregivers can use everyday experiences to introduce cognitive concepts (e.g., object permanence, cause and effect, problem solving) and demonstrate how understanding and skills grow within the child.

▦ Consider how the physical environment and the daily schedule can support cognitive growth.

Key Concept One
Responsive Caregivers Scaffold Cognitive Development

Humans are born ready to learn. Infants and toddlers are internally motivated to explore and master the world around them. They are active agents in their own learning, persisting in the face of challenge and deriving pleasure from mastery. As their brains begin to develop, infants actively seek new things to learn. By 3 months old, they are able to focus their attention and maintain an interaction with an adult. They can anticipate a familiar event, and as neural pathways expand, their ability to remember experiences expands. By the time a baby can sit steadily, she can also repeat an action, influence others, recognize familiar toys, and expect certain people and routines to be part of her day. Infants learn that they can grab, kick, reach, and pound. They begin to imitate the actions and sounds of others around them.

Cognition and Learning Expand Rapidly

In the first year of life, children's emotions lead their learning. They receive sensory stimulation both internally (e.g., hunger) and externally (e.g., touch, sound). In response to this sensory input, children experience an emotional reaction of pleasure or displeasure. They may also experience a physical reaction; for example, infants startle to a loud noise or a firm touch. These emotional and physical responses initiate learning pathways, a process that rapidly expands cognition and learning. The following scenario provides a small example of a process that occurs in many ways throughout a baby's day.

> In the infant room, Danielle (4 months old) lies in an infant seat, gazing at the toys hanging from a mobile in front of her. Her caregiver gently taps the mobile, and the images sway. In response to this movement, Danielle begins kicking and moving her arms. She is excited and accidentally kicks one of the images, an action that moves the mobile again. She stops momentarily to gaze at the movement and then repeats her kicking and arm waving. The mobile moves faster. A smile appears on Danielle's face as she begins to make the connection between her actions and the moving mobile. She turns to her caregiver, who returns the smile and says, "Whee! See, Danielle!" Danielle waits a moment and then kicks at the mobile again, repeating the game she has discovered.

As we see in the scenario, Danielle's delight in the moving mobile began with a reflexive action that became purposeful. Danielle repeated her kicking when she observed its effects. This experience created neural connections that were strengthened with repetition and stored in memory. Her understanding of the physical world and her ability to affect it were expanded. In the future, Danielle will know that she can choose to kick the mobile and cause it to move. This understanding—"My actions affect my world"—is a vital step in early learning.

Relationships Initiate and Support Early Learning Experiences

In the scenario about Danielle, her caregiver played an important role. First, the caregiver was responsive to Danielle's cues. She noticed that Danielle was staring at the mobile and increased Danielle's interest by slightly altering the sensory experience. A light tap on the mobile invested Danielle in a learning situation. Second, the caregiver did not overstimulate or intervene; rather, she watched and waited as Danielle experienced her own excitement. Danielle expanded her own learning by voluntarily repeating her kicking, purposefully moving the mobile. If she had not had success with moving the mobile herself, the caregiver might have moved the mobile again or showed Danielle that her feet could touch it. Instead, the caregiver waited for the baby to experience and understand her own actions and then shared Danielle's joy by returning her smile.

Research on cognitive development suggests that early attentional capacities predict later learning success. Infants demonstrate individual differences in their abilities to focus selectively on stimuli and engage in goal-directed behavior. Caregivers can support early learning by being attuned to each child's developmental capacities and by helping infants develop their abilities to focus and attend. In the scenario, the mobile (an object) took on more importance because of the caregiver's involvement. The caregiver helped focus the child's attention by sensitively altering the stimulation, which led to the child's goal-directed response.

As infants' brains develop, they become able to remember their experiences and their actions. By 4–8 months old, they can anticipate the effects of their actions. They make sounds and watch for their effects on others. They begin to remember patterns and to expect similarities of schedule and relationships. This memory ability is evident in the 9-month-old who screams when his mother leaves, demands to drink from "his" cup, and wants to have "his" bear at all times. These actions show that repeated patterns of experience have organized a child's cognitive abilities. Toward the end of the first year, babies' actions will be more goal directed. Danielle will become an active problem solver as she tries to secure a favorite toy or move to an area of the room where something interesting is happening. Box 7.1 highlights milestones in cognitive development during the first year.

Box 7.1
Highlights of Cognitive Development in Year 1

1–4 months old
— Produces simple, self-directed motor actions and vocalizations
— Begins to imitate
— Makes initial playful actions
— Gives simple emotional cues

4–8 months old
— Acts to repeat interesting effects
— Anticipates patterns and routines
— Recognizes familiar faces, voices, and touches
— Spontaneously imitates simple behaviors
— Expands emotional signals
— Becomes aware of the power and value of emotional signals

8–12 months old
— Initiates goal-directed action
— Demonstrates some spatial and causal reasoning
— Remembers events and retrieves useful information
— Playfully exercises means-end sequences
— Acquires new behaviors from watching a model
— Purposefully uses emotional communication
— Babbles and imitates sounds

As the Child Matures, Relationships Offer Different Types of Support

During the second year, memory expands and pathways for more complex thought are established. This growth is evident when toddlers attempt to build a block tower or try to fit shapes into a form board. To do these activities, they must link previous bits of knowledge into a series of coordinated actions. For example, placing shapes in a form board requires reaching, grasping, and visually inspecting a shape, then deciding on a proper action and releasing the shape to place it in the board. These are isolated skills that must be linked for the child to achieve her goal. Similarly, the toddler who is trying to create a block tower is combining objects and actions that have previously existed as separate entities. In the process, he is also learning about gravity, balance, and design. Through experience with this task, the toddler soon becomes aware of his choices and his control over how the tower looks or how long it remains standing. This task involves focusing attention, problem-solving (i.e., choosing between alternatives, correcting

---

Box 7.2
Cognitive Milestones in Year 2

12–18 months old
— Explores objects and experiments with novel uses
— Remembers location of toys and possessions
— Refines manual dexterity
— Plays turn-taking and problem-solving games
— Categorizes and solves simple problems
— Demonstrates an early understanding of symbols
— Expands conceptual memory
— Links previous information in a coordinated action
— Makes choices
— Asserts self
— Uses full range of extreme emotions to communicate
— Begins to understand simple words and act on them
— Uses simple sounds and words to communicate

18–24 months old
— Solicits interactive play
— Understands intentionality
— Matches and classifies objects
— Predicts events and matches actions
— Anticipates patterns and routines
— Participates in pretend play and in taking the role of another
— Communicates with words and expands vocabulary
— Shows extreme, uncontrolled emotional swings
— Shows some social responsibility as helper and fixer
— Enjoys some social interaction
— Participates in some group routines

---

errors, predicting outcomes), physical dexterity, and conceptual as well as sensory motor memory. Box 7.2 highlights milestones in cognitive development during the second year.

Children in relationship-based programs learn how to think. During the second and third years, children are beginning to gather a store of knowledge. They are learning some words, naming people and things, learning colors, and so forth. This kind of learning is rote learning. It involves learning the "right" answers from another person and acquiring knowledge to be stored and accessed when needed. In contrast to rote learning, complex learning requires reasoning. Relationship-based programs provide opportu-

---

Box 7.3
Cognitive Milestones in Year 3

24–36 months old
— Understands the difference between intentional and accidental behavior
— Distinguishes right from wrong
— Shows empathy
— Takes the perspective of another
— Enjoys and seeks the social group
— Prefers predictability, rules, and patterns
— Can engage in numerical reasoning
— Uses language to communicate thought
— Demonstrates emotional and behavioral control

---

nities to develop complex thinking processes. Responsive caregivers add structure and meaning to the experiences the child is having. They ask questions, model and demonstrate, encourage autonomy, review memories, and use these memories to further understanding. They present choices and reinforce the child's positive actions with emotional signals. Box 7.3 highlights milestones in cognitive development during the third year.

Children need to be active agents in their own learning. Academic instruction (i.e., copying letters, coloring in the lines) has no place in the infant-toddler center because it ignores this basic premise. Mastery requires experimentation and exploration. Early learners need to play with ideas and concepts, to try eating and pounding sand, to try pouring through spouts and open buckets, to enjoy coloring the whole page red. Learning does not emerge through repetition or exploration alone. Rather, learning is organized in meaningful ways through relationships. Caregivers who understand this concept plan interesting activities that are developmentally appropriate. They allow the children some time to explore the task on their own, staying mindful of when they can enter a child's world and enrich or expand learning. These caregivers are continually involved in the child's thinking process. They use shared emotions to invest children in a task and then allow the children the autonomy to master it at their learning level.

Caregivers Can Use Specific Techniques for Supporting Cognition and Learning

As we learned in chapter 1, observation is a key to understanding and supporting young children. Observation is also important for supporting cognitive development. When we watch a child strive to climb the stairs or open the door, that child feels our attention and is more motivated to accomplish the task. But watching, waiting, and listening also allow a caregiver to evaluate the child's state, goals, and skill level. Can she climb the stairs or will the child need help? Is he focused and energetic or tired and distracted? By observing for a few minutes, we can enter the child's world and offer the appropriate level of support. Box 7.4 lists specific techniques for supporting early learning.

Cognitive skills are advanced when a caregiver follows the child's lead. All of the skills of relationship building that you have learned will serve you well as you support the child's developing ability to think and to process experiences. A caring teacher looks at problems through the eyes of the child, accepting her motives and intentions rather than focusing on a pre-scribed learning task. Respecting and attending to the child's interests requires knowing the child's developmental age, abilities, temperament, and emotional stability. The teacher must be committed more to drawing the child into a thinking process than to focusing on a specific outcome. The following scenario shows how this commitment translates to a class-room activity.

> In the toddler room, Anna sets up the rice table, hoping to give the children in her care some scooping and dumping experiences. Soon, Joe approaches the table and begins filling a cup with rice. He uses a small spoon and then tries a larger scoop. He dumps the cup as soon as it is full and laughs gleefully as he pours the rice back into the tub. Joe repeats this process using different containers. Eventually, he has collected and filled every available container. "Look!" he calls to Anna. She exclaims, "Joe, you filled all those containers." He smiles and begins dumping out each container, calling to Anna, "Look, look!" with each pour.
>
> Anna notices that Jolene is ignoring the scoops and containers. Rather, she concentrates on burying her hands in the rice and then wiggling them free. She does this maneuver repeatedly and shares her mock surprise with Anna. "Where are your hands?" asks Anna. They both laugh as Anna exclaims, "There they are!" Later, Anna notices that Jolene is using her hand to pound on the rice piles, forcing them to change shape. Anna hands her a shovel and shows her how to flatten and smooth the rice using the back of the shovel. Jolene seems delighted and becomes absorbed in scooping and flattening mounds of rice.

Anna was correct in assuming that toddlers would enjoy scooping and shoveling. She also knew that this activity would help advance their knowledge and their fine motor skills. Joe's behavior was what she had envisioned when she planned this activity. She skillfully observed his play and connected with his emotion.

Box 7.4
Techniques for Supporting Early Learning

▨ **Observing**—Watch, wait, and listen. Caregivers assess the child's state of arousal, focus of attention, affect, and the actions or goals. Assessing these four *As* (arousal, attention, affect, and actions) is important in meeting the match between the motivation to learn and the guidance and materials that will expand knowledge. Consideration of the four *As* is important in defining the teachable moments and the need for mutual regulation that enhances learning.

▨ **Following the child's lead**—Being child directed during these early years is the most effective way to enhance development and learning. Infants and toddlers learn at their own paces and are internally motivated to seek their next cognitive challenge. They are not ready to amass knowledge or participate in competitive learning. Caregivers present opportunities, expand thinking, keep learning safe, and model skills.

▨ **Entering the child's world**—Joining the child in play is a powerful way to support learning. The savvy caregiver learns how to join the child without disrupting that child's interest in the task. The caregiver asks to join in. He takes a turn and shares the interest and joy of the child. The caregiver then can model an extension of the task and expand the learning.

▨ **Interacting through turn taking**—The ability to act, inhibit actions, wait for a partner's response, and act again is a complex sequence. Even if a child participates in only one exchange of give-and-take, progress is made in her understanding of a shared communication. Turn taking gives confidence to the child. The adult is imitating the child, but the adult can also change the task a bit during her turn and thus stimulate the learning process.

▨ **Scaffolding**—The caregiver and child together create a shared understanding; meaning is added a bit at a time as the child's mind is ready to process it. By first allowing the child to experiment and experience, then gently extending, reinforcing, and regulating the child, the caregiver will effectively nurture cognition and learning.

▨ **Allowing time to experience and enjoy**—Allow time for the child to experience each object and experiment with it. Much is learned by trying to put a round block into a square hole. The sensitive caregiver allows time to enjoy a victory. Often, toddlers quietly cherish their accomplishments, and they need the opportunity to internalize their feelings of satisfaction. The caregiver should wait for the child to seek his approval.

▨ **Offering quiet, specific praise**—When the child masters a cognitive task, she may want to share her feeling of accomplishment with her caregiver. The caregiver can support the child by offering specific feedback on her success (e.g., "You stacked six blocks." "You figured out where the circle goes."). Using words that focus the child on her own actions will motivate her to continue learning.

Although Jolene's self-initiated actions were not anticipated, Anna entered the child's world and joined in her discovery. The "hidden hands" game reinforced Jolene's understanding of object permanence and offered pure sensory experience. Anna allowed her to learn at her own developmental level and did not demand that she scoop, fill, and pour. Jolene changed the activity on her own, pounding and flattening the piles of rice. As the shape of the rice mounds changed, Jolene experienced cause-effect learning. She gained a new understanding of the relationship between her actions and the rice. When Jolene began pounding the rice with her hands, her caregiver, using minimal intervention, offered her the shovel and some guidance. Anna was careful not to extend the task beyond Jolene's abilities and interests. The child must be able to experiment and learn from an activity, not become frustrated by it. Anna realized the value of these unstructured activities and adjusted her support according to each child.

A child must be able to experiment and learn from an activity, not become frustrated by it.

As we learned in chapter 4, when we allow children to feel mastery, they become engaged in tasks and willing to take on challenges. Their curiosity and drive can be guided by the caregiver toward positive learning experiences. Cognition is enhanced when we allow children to struggle with a problem and experiment with their actions. Anna allowed Jolene autonomy in her play at the rice table. Jolene set her own pace, followed her own interests, and tried out her own ideas. She also learned.

Turn taking also advances cognitive skills. Turn taking has social and cognitive components. The ability to act, inhibit actions, wait for a partner's response, and act again in response to that partner's action is a complex cognitive sequence. Turn taking can begin as early as 4–5 months old, with cooing games or with passing a rattle or spoon back and forth. Turn taking is taking place when a 12-month-old holds a favorite toy out for the caregiver to see, waits for the caregiver's reaction, and then takes the toy back to reexamine it. One-on-one turn taking will be refined during the first year, but group turn taking does not emerge until children are between 2 and 3 years old. Toddlers can begin to follow the rules of simple games (e.g., "Ring Around the Rosey") or action songs (e.g., "The Wheels on the Bus"). The joint sharing of turn taking and the social experience of group activities are strong motivators for learning. Also, the structure of group activities can lead toddlers to try cognitive skills that they might not try on their own. The repetition of group activities and games within the child-care center tends to reinforce learning and memory for the child.

Responsive caregivers scaffold cognitive development. As the previous examples illustrate, the caregiver supports and expands the child's learning experience. By using the scaffolding techniques, the caregiver and the child together create a shared understanding and a shared space that nurtures intellectual growth. As children mature, the adults in their lives have unique opportunities to enrich their abilities to process information and knowledge.

Caregivers must allow children time to experience, time to process, and time to enjoy. When infants and toddlers are building neurological pathways and expanding memory, they often take time after each step to reflect on and appreciate their actions. This reflection is important to cognitive development. Caregivers who choose a slow pace for activities with a lot of "open space" for children to pause and think are supporting cognition and learning.

Key Concept Two
Imitation and Pretend Play Are Important in Early Learning

Imitation is an inborn mechanism for learning. Babies seem programmed to learn from watching the actions of others. Simple imitative actions can be elicited from a child as young as 2 months old. When the caregiver smacks his or her lips, the baby does also. When the caregiver croons, the baby often coos in response. In most mammals, the adult serves as a model for the young. Infants and toddlers learn how to behave and how to think about experiences from copying the actions, attitudes, and behaviors of their caregivers. When an adult responds to a baby's imitations by showing pleasure, then imitating becomes a mastery skill for the child. The baby will try to repeat the positive interaction. Simple imitation becomes an expected interaction pattern, giving the caregiver a powerful teaching tool.

Learning Is Enhanced When Adults Imitate and Serve as Models for Children

Responsive caregivers also imitate children. When they imitate in this way, a different kind of learning pathway is organized. This action is similar to reflective praise. When you imitate a child's action, you are showing approval. The child will repeat the action to gain your attention and your praise. Imitating the child is an important technique for enhancing learning.

By 6 months old, children are copying the adults around them and beginning to respond to imitation games. Waving bye-bye, clapping hands for joy, and pointing to body parts are actions that will become part of the

1-year-old's repertoire. Children no longer have to wait to make a random connection between their actions and the world around them. The fact that children can now copy an action they observe means that other people, especially caregivers, provide constant models for new learning. Much of our learning, even as adults, happens from copying models. We often request a model when we have a letter to write or a computer task to learn. Similarly, when toddlers observe other people hugging dolls and pushing toy cars, they attempt to reproduce these actions. Consider the following scenario.

> The caregiver, Albert, sits down in the block area, where four toddlers are playing. Albert and the children begin building separate block towers. They are good at this task because they have done it before. There is much laughter and confidence in the group. They begin to knock over their towers. Then Albert says, "I'm going to make a choo-choo." The children look at him. Slowly and carefully he puts four blocks in a straight row end to end and then adds one to the top of the first block. "Choo choo choo," Albert calls as he drives his train past the children.
>
> Jose gathers some blocks close to him. Then he begins to put them end to end, looking carefully at Albert's blocks. Soon there are two trains. The others begin reaching for blocks. Ahmed copies the train and then adds blocks at each end to make twin towers. Albert says, "Ahmed, you made something new. I like it. Jose, tell me about what you made."
>
> Sarah is just sitting and watching. Albert goes to her side and squats next to her. "Sarah, do you want to make a train?" Sarah shakes her head no. Albert says, "Okay, make another tower." Sarah smiles and begins.

By building block structures together, the group will be motivated to copy one another's models. Knowing that children like to copy, Albert extended their learning. They discovered that blocks could become many different things and that blocks could symbolize something that was not there, the train. Sarah was not ready for this complicated task. She was still struggling with the motor skills of putting one block on top of another and she wanted to keep mastering that skill. Albert knew her developmental level and honored her with his support.

At first, imitation takes time. Several repetitions of an action bring a delayed response from the baby. The more imitation is encouraged through caregiver-child interactions, the more these copied behaviors will be used in other ways by the child. For example, you may see Johnny waving bye-bye as other parents leave the room or wave to his favorite truck as he goes home.

This behavior shows that a pattern that was initially an imitation game has become part of the child's knowledge base and is linked with leaving.

Deferred Imitation Is a Cognitive Milestone

Deferred imitation—the ability to imitate an action that was observed previously—is a more advanced cognitive skill. It requires the young child to store information in memory and retrieve it at a later time. For example, the toddler sitting in his high chair may observe a peer throwing a beanbag into a tub. After nap time, this toddler may head straight for the beanbags in an effort to try a new action that he has held in memory. The ability to think in this more advanced way emerges with age. It depends on brain maturity and experience.

When a child takes a pattern of behavior that she has learned through imitation into a different situation, for example, asking for a hug from a new friend, the responses she receives will extend the child's knowledge. That child will learn, for instance, that some people are happy to hug her, but others are not. The child's cognitive learning is extended and modified by her interactions with others. The responsive caregiver will notice when a child is trying a behavior in a different context, and that caregiver will scaffold the child's success.

Toddlers are just beginning to show deferred imitation. This ability allows them to pretend. Pretend play is important for learning to plan ahead, to relate to others, to gain control, and to foster identity. Children practice, rehearse, and reinforce learning through pretend play. Caregivers have many opportunities to nurture pretend play. The following scenario describes just one example.

> Shirley, a caregiver, proposes a teddy bear picnic. She gets out the toy dishes and asks Chella and Sally to bring the bears to the blanket that is spread on the floor. The girls sit down with the bears, and Shirley gives each a plate and a cup. She pours an imaginary drink from the pitcher into the cups and puts imaginary food onto each plate. Chella and Sally begin to feed their bears and help them drink. When Shirley leaves the girls alone to check on another child, they continue to replenish the cups and plates for their bears.

Pretend Play Is Important for Cognitive Development

Pretend play involves symbolic representation, and it is an important way to integrate cognitive learning. Concepts and patterns of behavior that the child has observed can be practiced with dolls or cars to reinforce them in memory. The ability to believe that one object can represent or symbolize another is a major difference between the way humans and animals function. This kind of symbolic thinking leads us to accept words or numbers as representations of objects or thoughts. This kind of thinking gives us the ability to conceptualize objects we have not yet built and share ideas that give us hope.

Initially, pretend play is reality based (e.g., pretending to pour milk from the pitcher), but it becomes more make-believe as the child's cognitive capacities grow. When Caleb is pretending to be a dog who picks up the playground toys, we realize that he is creating a role that he has never observed. This pretending requires going beyond the concrete and imagining a new combination of ideas. This experimentation is important to learning. By trying out ideas and solutions in many different ways, the child is able to settle on the one that fits a familiar model—for example, turning a book upside down or sideways and then preferring it upright because it looks like it does when the caregiver reads it to him.

Pretend play also stimulates new brain pathways for creative and innovative thinking. When children try playing many roles—for example, being the mother, then the child, then the dog—they are learning about empathy and relationship. In this way, children rehearse or relive their feelings and plan their experiences with others. They also affirm their preferences about their identity (Who do I like to be?).

Caregivers can structure and model pretend play. The same principles that formed the basis of relationship building are critical to supporting pretend play. First, the caregiver must be a good observer, attending to and interpreting the child's initial attempts to pretend. Second, the caregiver must be a willing partner who follows the child's lead. Rather than take over and direct the pretend themes, the caregiver can expand on what the child says and describe what the child is doing. The caregiver might also take on a role that meshes with the one the child has assumed. For example, if Ted says, "I'm going to put gas in the car," the caregiver might reply, "Thank you, sir. Could you also wash the windows?" Your comments and participation indicate that you value the child's idea and the child's play.

Your additions to pretend play can teach language, social skills, and safety. Pretend is an excellent way to get toddlers to remember safety rules such as stopping and looking before crossing the street. For example, when 2-year-old Kayla is teaching what she has learned to the stuffed doggie ("Fido, stop and look"), she will be more apt to remember it for herself.

Often, children prefer to pretend by themselves. Caregivers can support and extend their play even without joining in. When you see Joanna taking on the mother's role in the housekeeping area, you know she has made a cognitive leap by pretending to be another person. As she feeds the baby, washes the dishes, or dons a fancy hat, you realize that she is stepping outside herself and using advanced cognitive skills to create this role. As a responsive caregiver, you do not interrupt or try to join in Joanna's play, but you might bring more housekeeping or baby-care objects into the area to extend Joanna's learning.

A caregiver should stay in touch and monitor private play because it can turn angry or sad. If the child is reenacting violent behaviors, such as beating on dolls or desperately trying to comfort a bunny in distress, then the caregiver may join in and talk about these emotions. Through the pretend situation, she can ask questions that help the child put these hurtful feelings in perspective. These moments of high emotion are salient opportunities to connect with the child on an emotion-sharing level and help the child understand the experiences in his life that were eliciting these feelings in pretend.

Imitation and pretend play give children practice in logical thinking and problem solving. In their pretend roles, they try out solutions and talk through possibilities. Many children work through their fears and uncertainties in the pretend arena. If Megan is afraid of thunder, you might find her comforting her doll when it rains. If Alex has been trying to work up enough courage to use the slide, you might find him with an action figure, walking and talking the doll through the motions of using the slide. As children take control of their feelings in a pretend role, they feel power and mastery over their anxieties.

Key Concept Three
Learning Is Enhanced by Planning a Child-Focused Curriculum

Our knowledge of cognitive development informs our decisions about curriculum and environment. Infants and toddlers need to be active agents in their own learning. They need to have predictable responses from their social and physical environments. They need objects to manipulate, spaces to explore, and people to be available as guides and models. The caregiver must think about the physical space as well as the distractions and the safety of the learning environment. She or he must also consider the availability of caregivers to scaffold learning. Caregivers must plan the center's materials, routines, daily schedule, and interactions with the child's cognitive and emotional development in mind. Box 7.5 lists characteristics of environments that nurture and protect.

A simple, orderly space will help young children process and learn from their experiences. When we learned about mastery motivation, we became aware of the toddler's need to explore. When a toddler seems to be "just wandering," she is also experiencing. This child needs an uncluttered space to wander and to decide on the next area of interest or exploration. To sup-

---

Box 7.5
Characteristics of Environments That Nurture and Protect

- Safety
- Freedom to explore
- Quiet space to focus
- Caregiver availability

- Minimal distractions
- Place to share group activities
- Defined activity centers

---

port children's development, the caregiver needs to plan environments that are safe for all children—for the explorer, for the group entrenched in floor play, and for the solitary puzzle solver.

Having time to experience one or two objects alone or with a special caregiver expands learning more than quick exposure to many objects. Especially for infants, a limited number of toys that are rotated regularly will maintain interest. Playing with a rattle or mirror for several days in a row can be beneficial repetition, but soon, the child habituates or masters the object and will need a new stimulus to continue learning. When toys are rotated, the same toy that appears a week or two later seems like a new toy or a familiar friend. Open-ended materials—blocks, cars and trucks, water, sand, and other sensory materials—invite experimentation and discovery.

Keeping similar toys in certain places helps the child learn about grouping and categories. They will benefit from having an expectation of where to find these toys. Children like to know that the pull toys are in a certain place and the balls in another. The center should provide places for outside toys and places for quiet toys. Structure helps children begin to plan ahead and focus their actions. "Today I want a pull toy. I'm going straight there."

Provide toys to fit the interest of your group. Caregivers can expand the availability of materials in an interest area to fit the changing interests of their group. For example, when the main interest of Terry's group of 2-year-olds seemed to be holding big dolls and putting them to bed, he expanded the housekeeping toys to include more big dolls and more beds. He made the beds from cardboard boxes. At another time, these children became fascinated with the large blocks, so Terry doubled the space where they could build and brought out more blocks from the storage cupboard. The materials and the spaces in the curriculum were adapted to be responsive to the changing interests of the children.

If a caregiver realizes that a child is particularly motivated by an activity, he can respond by manipulating the environment in a way that extends the child's involvement. This manipulation may involve removing a barrier, making a task slightly less challenging, or offering support that ensures success. For example, consider the following scenario.

> Alice, a caregiver, noticed that Luke was trying to load blocks onto the flatbed truck and transport them. They kept falling, which frustrated Luke. The next day, Alice brought a strawberry basket from home and tied it to the flatbed of the truck. Luke was delighted and successful in transporting his blocks.

Alice provided changes within the environment that would allow Luke's learning to grow. She enhanced his motivation to practice filling and transporting by making a small change in the truck. Alice nurtured Luke's understanding about the function of sides on a truck. She can begin to teach him about "inside and outside," concepts within his experience. This scenario also illustrates how children's play situations give them opportunities to practice symbolic representation. Luke's thinking is being stretched to allow one object (a strawberry basket) to represent another (a truck bed).

Preparing an environment that is conducive to pretend play is also important. For infants, a few familiar adult items can encourage imitation. Realistic items such as hats, doll families, dishes, cars, and animals will prompt the child to copy actions that they have observed in adults. As children move into toddlerhood, they benefit from an area designed for dramatic play. This space should be outfitted with theme-based items, such as a housekeeping corner, a doctor's office, and a fire station. Here is an opportunity to represent the cultural mix of the center by having some clothing and household items that reflect cultural differences.

> *Routines will shape the children's ability to think, to focus, and to become self-directed.*

The daily schedule must speak to children's developing cognitive abilities. Times must be planned for children to explore, to practice, to experiment, and to feel in charge. Yet, children also need to experience patterns within the schedule of the day. Routines will shape the children's ability to think, to focus, and to become self-directed. Expecting or anticipating events by time (lunchtime, nap time, morning, afternoon) or sequence (before snack, after a walk) is helpful to the developing brain. Also, scheduling group activities where a patterned activity takes place is beneficial because children learn by watching one another for behavior cues and through the shared emotions that motivate the activity.

"Teachable moments" are unplanned teaching opportunities. Children benefit from the learning that occurs in everyday interactions and routines.

Caregiving routines—diapering, feeding, putting on coats—are examples of everyday activities during which adults can focus attention and expand learning. For example, if a caregiver notices that Rosemary is touching her image in the mirror while she lies on the changing table, the caregiver can imitate the touch and talk about the image. Rather than rushing through the diaper change, the responsive caregiver uses this time to follow the child's lead. Similarly, when dressing children for outdoor play, caregivers can talk about warm and cold, body parts, types of clothing, colors, and textures. If we are good observers and good listeners, then we can capitalize on the unplanned sights and sounds that occur during a morning walk or the child's interest in a photo that he has brought from home. Every day, children present us with teachable moments. The responsive caregiver will capitalize on these unplanned opportunities in ways that enhance both learning and relationships.

The responsive caregiver will capitalize on unplanned opportunities in ways that enhance both learning and relationships.

Carefully planned activities also must remain flexible. Caregivers who are responsive to maturational changes in children may realize this necessity during an interaction. For example, a caregiver had planned to play outside with the wagons and tricycles. She asked Jessica to pull the wagon. When they approached Charlie, he did not want to leave the blocks. Although the caregiver was ready to go, she responded to Charlie's needs. She asked Jessica whether Charlie could put his blocks into the wagon to take outside. These children merged their interests, and a new activity, initiated by a responsive caregiver, was suddenly underway.

The curriculum must be individualized and child focused. The responsive caregiver knows each child's interests and capabilities. Because of her knowledge of the child's temperament and learning style, the caregiver can gauge the pace and intensity of the curriculum. Because she is attentive to developmental changes, the caregiver anticipates how individual children will connect with various activities. A child-focused curriculum changes constantly because the children change.

The caregiver continually thinks about matching his response to an individual child. When Samantha brings a clutch ball to her caregiver, Kyle, he uses an understanding of Samantha's temperament to decide how to respond. Kyle could examine the ball and the pictures printed on it with the child, he could hand it back and say "ball," he could calmly roll the ball across the floor, or he could provide excitement with a swift roll saying, "Run! Chase after the ball." Kyle uses his knowledge of Samantha's current skill level and motivation to help determine how he should focus or expand the learning that the child suggested.

Curriculum decisions are based on careful observations of children's interests and abilities. The caregivers in the following scenario are engaged in this process.

> Terry, one of the caregivers in the toddler room, sees Evan (15 months old) watching the water go down the sink drain. Evan tries to stop the water with his small hand. Terry smiles but must leave to help another child. Evan stuffs a paper towel into the sink. Terry returns to see the sink filling up with water. "Ooooh, Evan, it's going to run over!" Terry helps Evan to remove the towel and to let the water run down the drain. Evan fusses when they have to leave the bathroom.
>
> Terry shares his observation of Evan with Sharon, the other care-giver in the toddler room. "Let's do funnels and pouring this afternoon so that Evan can get experience with water going down the drain. He is really interested in water and how it moves." Sharon adds, "Karen and Michael seem to have that same curiosity. That would be great for all of them. They can even help unplug the water table when it is time to clean up!" Terry says, "Why not? They are learning about what happens with water. Let's make the afternoon activity all about water. We could also put water into the short hoses and see it come out the other end. I think Julie and Sally are ready to try splashing and pouring."

Here, curriculum plans emerged from one child's curiosity. As this new interest unfolds, water activities may be repeated or modified to extend the learning. Because children of different developmental levels can participate in the same activities, caregivers must individualize their scaffolding to the learning level of each child. For example, if a caregiver is planning a tactile experience using play dough, she must consider individual needs. If the caregiver knows that Toby does not like to get his fingers messy, she might add more flour to make the dough less sticky. Also, she might decide to have rollers and cutters on hand to structure the activity for Donna, a child who is excitable and easily distracted.

Chapter Summary

First learning is about sculpting and expanding neural structures. Relation-ships initiate, guide, and interpret first learning. As infants and toddlers explore their worlds, caregivers shape the children's learning experiences. Through responsive relationships, caregivers connect with children and sen-sitively move them to the next developmental challenge. Responsive relationships help children to associate stimulation with meaning, to process their experiences, to evaluate, to problem solve, and to access pertinent information from their memories. Through relationships, children experience the joy and excitement of learning. When we plan programs that give children opportunities to build on their inborn readiness to discover and master cognitive skills, their minds develop in remarkable ways.

Resources

Bornstein, M. H., & Sigman, M. D. (1986). Continuity in mental development from infancy. *Child Development, 57,* 251–274.

Bredekamp, S., & Copple, C. (1997). *Developmentally appropriate practice in early childhood programs.* Washington, DC: National Association for the Education of Young Children.

Bronson, M. B. (1995). *The right stuff for children birth to eight: Selecting play materials to support development.* Washington, DC: National Association for the Education of Young Children.

Bronson, M. B. (2000). *Self-regulation in early childhood: Nature and nurture.* New York: Guilford Press.

Dombro, A. L., Colker, L. J., & Dodge, D. T. (1997). *The creative curriculum for infants and toddlers.* Washington, DC: Teaching Strategies.

Dunn, L., & Kontos, S. (1997). What have we learned about developmentally appropriate practices? *Young Children, 52*(5), 4–13.

Gonzalez-Mena, J., & Eyer, D. W. (2001). *Infants, toddlers and caregivers* (5th ed.). Mountain View, CA: Mayfield Publishing.

Goodrow, M. E. (2000). The teachable moment. *Young Children, 55*(3), 42–43.

Meltzoff, A. N. (1999). Born to learn: What infants learn from watching us. In N. A. Fox, L. A. Leavitt, & J. G. Warhol (Eds.), *The role of early experience in infant development* (pp. 145–164). Skillman, NJ: Johnson & Johnson Pediatric Institute.

Videos

Curriculum for Infants and Toddlers: Child-Centered Curriculum. (2002). Barrington, IL: Magna Systems, Inc. (29 min.).

Curriculum for Infants and Toddlers: Exploring and Learning. (2002). Barrington, IL: Magna Systems, Inc. (29 min.).

Discoveries of Infancy: Cognitive Development and Learning. (1992). Sacramento, CA: Far West Laboratories. (32 min.).

Infancy: Beginnings in Cognition and Language. (2003). Barrington, IL: Magna Systems, Inc. (29 min.).

The Next Step: Including the Infant in the Curriculum. (1992). Sacramento, CA: Far West Laboratories. (22 min.).

Chapter 8

Relationships Promote Language and Literacy

In chapter 7, we described ways in which responsive relationships support early learning and cognition. Now we turn our attention to how relationships support the development of language and communication.

Humans are the only mammals that develop spoken language. Throughout history, we find evidence of humans using written symbols for communication. Language is the verbal form of symbolic representation. Our minds are able to accept a verbal symbol such as the word *kitty* as representing the real being or object. The human brain is able to copy verbal models with some precision (e.g., the model "I am here" or "You are here") and to record patterns of sound into permanent memory (e.g., "Buenos dias. Que pasa?" or "Hasta la vista"). Our ability to use language emerges without direct instruction, but it requires a social context. We must hear words and be around others who are using word patterns to develop language skills effectively. The language environments that children experience in their first 3 years will differentiate their future language abilities. In this chapter, we will examine how language skills develop and the role that caregivers play in enhancing these skills.

Key Concept One
Caregivers Foster Communication

Infants are predisposed to communicate. Infants can hear the spoken word before they are born. From birth, they tune into the sounds, rhythms, voices, and music that surround them. They also connect with their caregivers through nonverbal cues, which signal their needs. Responsive

---

Goals of Chapter 8

■ Review how young children are predisposed to engage in coordinated exchanges with adults using first nonverbal and then verbal communication.

■ Examine how early communication with responsive caregivers determines the later language ability of the child.

■ Understand the ways in which adults model and reinforce language and literacy.

■ Discuss the use of language for self-regulation.

■ Become acquainted with the use of books, songs, and fingerplays as vehicles for supporting language development and relationship themes.

caregivers are adept at reading these cues. They know when their babies are pleased or distressed—and why. When the baby's needs are met, the first communication links are made. Similarly, infants understand and respond to their caregivers' facial expressions, touch, and verbal tones. This relationship between infant and caregiver establishes the interaction patterns and expectations of human communication.

Infants also communicate with vocalizations (e.g., cries, whimpers, coos, laughter, squeaks, and squeals) to tell us their feelings. These sounds often bring an immediate response from caregivers. For example, when a baby coos, the caregiver smiles and coos back. When a baby coughs, caregivers jump up to attend. Babies soon learn that their voice has meaning and that their verbal signals are powerful. They begin to experiment with sounds. Soon, they are practicing a range of sounds such as trills, clacks, gargles, hisses, and raspberries. At 4 to 6 months old, babies speak a universal language; they make sounds found in every language in the world. By imitating the sounds of others, babies begin to form strings of sound with intonation similar to the conversation they hear around them. By the end of the first year, the voice tones, speech rhythms, and words that a baby imitates and practices are those of her native tongue.

When a caregiver uses words such as "juice," "more," and "dog" as he responds to his baby's cues, his baby will connect that same word with the intended object or action. At about 12 to 15 months old, toddlers will try using some of these sounds to indicate their intentions. When caregivers respond to their attempts ("up," "mo," "dog") not only verbally but also with an action ("Want up? Come up," "More? Here is more," "Yes, pat the doggy"), toddlers will use their words again. These first words connect toddlers to a wonderful world of mastery. They realize, "My words give me power." When toddlers discover that words can command attention or fill their needs, their vocabulary expands rapidly.

Language Development Is Similar for All Children

In all cultures, the developmental progression of utterances is the same: crying, cooing, babbling, single words, then combined words. The language models that children hear and the responses they evoke from others with their verbalizations will shape the language skills that they develop. Box 8.1 shows this full developmental progression.

Language development does not unfold in equal measure for everyone. Although most people speak and understand words, their use of language is variable. Perception, memory, and motor capacities are important factors that influence language development. However, communication capabilities differ primarily because of the relationships and the language environment that infants experience. Infants and toddlers who are in a

---

Box 8.1
Language Development

▓ All babies vocalize.

▓ In all cultures, babies develop the same first sounds.

▓ In all cultures, toddlers learn language.

▓ Language acquisition progresses in the following developmental pattern:
  — Crying
  — Cooing
  — Babbling
  — Saying single words
  — Comprehending words
  — Combining words
  — Forming simple sentences (subject-verb-object)
  — Expressing complete thoughts

---

language-rich environment, where caregivers are not only talking to them but also listening and responding to their cues, develop a much broader vocabulary. Some toddlers have a 200-word vocabulary by their second birthday, whereas in a language-poor environment, toddlers know fewer than 50 words by the same age. The size of a toddler's vocabulary at age 3 is a good predictor of the child's future competence in reading, writing, and school performance.

Language comprehension precedes language production. Initially, before they understand words, infants understand nonverbal communication and shared emotions. Then, with experience and repetition, toddlers come to understand what a caregiver is saying (e.g., "Sally, sit down," "James, bring me the cup," or "Let's get our coats now") before they are able to use the words themselves. Even when toddlers are using only a few simple words to express themselves, they are understanding more complex messages. The more infants and toddlers hear language and are rewarded for responding to words, the more they will expand their use of language to communicate their wants, needs, and intentions.

Caregivers Consciously and Unconsciously Scaffold Language Development

Caregivers nurture language development in many ways. The caregiver's response makes the connection between a sound and its meaning. When a caregiver responds to the child's early cries, he or she is teaching the child that the child's message has been received. When caregivers take time for quiet interactions with infants (e.g., smiling in response to a baby's coos), the value of sound is reinforced. When caregivers imitate the sounds a baby is making, the baby feels a sense of mastery in being acknowledged and is motivated to continue trying to communicate with his or her voice. When a child realizes that expressions such as "W'zat" or "Lov-ou" have meaning, they start a remarkable learning adventure toward amassing vocabulary. Both the responsiveness and the emotional expression of the caregiver provide the emotional stability necessary for learning. For language to develop, both affect and meaning must be shared by child and caregiver.

> *Both the responsiveness and the emotional expression of the caregiver provide the emotional stability necessary for learning.*

Responsive caregivers adjust their speech to the child's level of understanding. Child-directed speech is attuned to the child's perceptual system. This adjusting (i.e., a short, simple sentence spoken slowly in higher-pitched tones) is a naturally occurring phenomenon that helps children differentiate sounds. Most adults do this adjusting automatically when they talk to a child. Without realizing it, they enhance the contrasts among sounds and thereby simplify the child's task of figuring out words. Adults also naturally use simple language, adding and emphasizing a new word that matches the developmental changes in the child. For the 1-year-old, we hear caregivers say, "Bird. See *bird.*" When the child has learned the word *bird*, the caregiver naturally moves on saying, "*Pretty* bird. See the *pretty* bird." The tonal emphasis is on the new word or a new use for word combinations that the child already knows. As the child matures, caregivers expand vocabulary into action words and concepts that the child will understand from her own experience. "Bird is *eating*, yum, yum." "Pretty bird, *fly away*, bye-bye."

Caregivers create the language environment. When caregivers describe what they are doing, what is going to happen next, or how they feel, they are establishing a language environment. This running commentary from the caregiver serves several functions. First, it gives the child a sense of emotional sharing and can provide mutual regulation. Second, it pulls the child into the shared activity and gives him a sense of focus and expectation. Third, it provides a model for language sounds and rhythms that the child internalizes. Caregivers should share verbal explanations and descriptions of their actions (e.g., "Is it time to change your diaper now? Here is the washcloth. Now I will dry you all off."). When babies hear words that are

---

Box 8.2
Characteristics of a Good Language Environment

1. The environment is not too noisy.

2. The child hears normal conversation sounds.

3. Caregivers interact verbally with baby.

4. Positive emotion is shared in language and music.

5. Caregivers talk to baby about baby's interests.

6. Words are appropriate for baby's development.

7. Caregivers imitate baby's sounds.

8. Caregivers listen to baby and provide contingent responses.

9. Caregivers act on baby's verbal requests.

10. Simple words and phrases are repeated.

11. Caregivers share music and rhythm games.

12. Caregivers share books and pictures with baby.

---

directed toward them or paired with activities they are experiencing, neural pathways for language are created and reinforced. Box 8.2 lists the characteristics of a good language environment. Can you think of two examples for each characteristic?

Caregivers can simplify and focus sound input. Background noise, even wonderful music, must be monitored so that it does not interfere with the child's efforts to extract meaning from the auditory environment. A people-filled space that contains lots of talking and other sounds might seem enriching, but it is *not* conducive to helping children determine the meaning and function of single words. It is important not to overwhelm the child with continuous sound. Rather, the adult should talk to the child, then stop and wait to give the child a chance to process, react, and respond to what has been said. A responsive caregiver is aware of the sounds in the environment (including their volume and complexity) and their effect on each child.

Caregivers must be good conversation partners. Children whose caregivers have talked to them and have responded to their signals or words throughout the day develop larger vocabularies than those whose caregivers have not. Engaging in conversations about daily activities that have captured the children's attention is an important activity. Children develop vocabulary more quickly when caregivers converse with them. The number of words a child acquires depends on the relationships they experience.

When these relationships are positive, responsive, and verbally rich, children use up to four times more words by the end of their second year than children whose parents and caregivers do not talk to them.

Caregivers model grammar and pronunciation. They are giving children speech structure and rules of grammar just by talking to them and with them throughout the day. Early speech models are powerful because children copy the language they hear. The structure of sentences and conjugations of verbs are difficult and boring to learn in an academic setting, but they come naturally through the modeling of speech from adult to toddler. When the child says, "Purdy bird," the caregiver might respond with, "Pretty bird, pri-tee, pri-tee." If a toddler says, "I comin'," the caregiver should model, "Okay, I am coming, too." No correction of the toddler is necessary. When caregivers respond to the child's meaning, reinforce her efforts to communicate, and model proper grammar, the amazing mind of the toddler will correctly reproduce the word or language pattern. The language environment of the first 3 years provides models of grammar and pronunciation that are deeply engrained and hard to change.

Contingent responses are also important. Children learn from meaningful exchanges, not language lessons. A good conversation partner speaks, waits for the child's response, and then connects with that response by addressing the message. As adults, we expect a child to listen to what we have to say and then respond appropriately. Toddlers can learn this process only if we do the same for them. When a child attempts to use a word, a contingent response will affirm and reinforce the meaning of that word for the child. How often have you watched a toddler say, "Moe, moe" and hold up a cup only to be ignored by a caregiver? A contingent response of, "More? More juice?" could have solidified the word and the communication for the child. Responses to verbal signals are strong motivators for the development of speech. Consider the following scenario.

> Lettie says, "It's time to go outside now." Chong Sun says, "No. Cold."
> Lettie says, "Everyone get your coats. It's nice out. Come along, Chong Sun."

Did Lettie connect with Chong Sun? Was her response contingent to the child's attempts at speech? Did she address the child's message (his worry about the cold)? How might Lettie's communication have been different?

Language Development Is Supported Through Specific Techniques

Language can be nurtured quite effectively by using simple techniques such as responding, labeling, and singing. Box 8.3 provides an extensive list of techniques that caregivers can use to support language development. We will discuss these approaches in a bit more detail in this section.

Box 8.3
Techniques for Nurturing Language Development

- Responding
- Labeling
- Imitating
- Providing choices
- Expanding

- Questioning
- Turn taking
- Encouraging verbal games
- Encouraging rhythm games
- Singing

In addition to responding, which we have discussed earlier, caregivers label objects that are meaningful to the baby (e.g., "bottle," "doggie," "ball," "Teddy"). If a caregiver names an object when he gives it to a baby or when the baby points to it, then that caregiver is helping the child to pair the object and the word in the child's mind. The word becomes the symbol for the object. The caregiver can also extend the word-symbol by using it in other situations. "See the doggie in the picture." "Duffy is your doggie." "Look outside. It's a doggie."

Responsive caregivers talk about the child's interests. They notice what the baby is gazing at, and they talk about it. They let toddlers direct the topic of a conversation, expanding on their utterances and valuing their message. Responsive caregivers answer questions about the child's interests or feelings. "Yes, that bug goes fast." "You are sad because you miss Lydia." They also ask questions of the child, expecting and waiting for a response. "Maria, what is this?" "Where is your spoon?" "Who just came in the door?"

Repetition and expansion foster language learning. As children mature, memory expands. By repeating words that children have tried to use or words that you want them to learn, you will help them attune their ear to patterns and sounds of speech as well as connect to the meaning of the words. Almost unconsciously, caregivers expand a child's social language by combining words they use to greet other children or parents and words they use to initiate games or play situations (e.g., "Hi, how are you?" "Bye-bye, have a good day"). These patterns are learned as if they were a single word. The whole sentence carries one meaning. We see toddlers picking up often-repeated phrases or jingles from other adults in a household or from television (e.g., "Good Morning, America," "Are you ready for some football?"). Some four-letter words may come to child care from a language environment in which the children may hear them repeatedly in adult conversation.

Encourage children to make choices with words and gestures. "Danny, do you want an apple or a banana?" As Danny points to his choice, name it again for him. "A banana. Here is your banana." Soon he may ask for a "nana" on his own. When Danny says "nana" and the caregiver produces and names the banana, Danny has learned that he can use a single word and be understood. He will be highly motivated to continue using this word and then try other words to obtain his goals.

Verbal activities foster language and listening skills. Children are drawn to the sound of voices and enjoy making their own joyful noises. Fingerplays link verbal and nonverbal communication as well as provide the repetition on which infants and toddlers thrive. For example, in the "Itsy Bitsy Spider" song, the actions for "down came the rain and washed the spider out" give the words meaning. The visual image plays out in the child's mind as she says the words. "Call-and-response" games establish temporal structures for interaction. Turn taking and imitation in verbal games set the stage for the exchange of conversation. When the group joins together to say "round and round" in the song "The Wheels on the Bus" or "all fall down" in "Ring-Around-the-Rosey," they not only are having fun together but they are also putting meaning to words that have a broader meaning. In addition, when children are saying words in unison or rhythm, they must sharpen their listening skills to respond in sync with the group.

> *When children are saying words in unison or rhythm, they must sharpen their listening skills to respond in sync with the group*

In a child-care center, group activities can stimulate toddlers to express themselves. Within the social group, children learn songs, phrases, and patterned speech that can give them courage to try words on their own. Song phrases such as "up we go" or "Ho, ho, ho" or commonly heard cheers such as "Go, team!" carry meaning and feelings of connection. Because these words are linked with fun and feelings of belonging, they encourage the child to repeat them and to experiment with other words.

Music fosters language and shared enjoyment. Music is a natural way to express the sounds and meaning of language. Infants attend to rhythms, are attracted by music, and perceive the repetition in lyrics. Fingerplays and songs with movement provide an active way to learn language and offer immediate feedback by connecting words and actions. Singing to and with children encourages them to use words. Young children feel the beat of music in their bodies and respond with movement. Parents can contribute music to the classroom by audiotaping songs that they sing at home with their children. This sharing a bit of home with classmates not only can foster language development but also can help the young child bridge the separation gap between home and school.

Children from non-English-speaking families require special caregiver attention. At the child-care center, the child may be asked to learn English, a new symbol system. The caregiver may need help to be responsive and connect with the toddler who has established word meaning in a different language. For example, does the child use the word *la cama* or *charpoy* to refer to a bed? Getting language information from the parents and learning a few words (e.g., greetings, common objects) that are used in the child's home language will serve two functions. First, this knowledge will help the caregiver understand the child's attempts to communicate through words or culture-specific gestures, and second, it allows the caregiver to respond and reinforce appropriately. In addition, this simple gesture will enhance the relationship that the caregiver shares with the child and family because it shows that the caregiver values them and their culture. Although this suggestion requires extra effort, it can be an important component in relationship building and language development. Even though the task of learning two languages at the same time may seem to slow the process initially, it also establishes multiple language pathways, which serve the child well in the future. The child who learns that an object can have several labels has a cognitive advantage.

Human connection is the strongest force in promoting early language development. Relationships stimulate, model, and enrich language development. Speech gives children a new way to communicate; thus, the 2–3-year-old child will be using more and more words in his interactions with caregivers. When caregivers offer children choices, play word games, and ask questions, they are expanding the child's cognitive and communicative skills. However, as children become talkers and use language more often, caregivers must remember that words are not the child's primary communication path. Even after the child seems to be using words, her motivations, needs, and feelings will continue to be expressed through nonverbal cues.

Key Concept Two
Language Can Be Used to Regulate Emotion

Learning words will help to give the child feelings of control. The child who knows the word for what he wants is more likely to use that word instead of an emotional display to achieve the intended goal. Imagine Alyson, who says "bunny" to her caregiver. The responsive caregiver knows that the bunny is Alyson's favorite beanbag toy and hands it to the child, smiling. The caregiver—by being there to hear Alyson's request, knowing the context of the situation, and being connected to the child's likes and dislikes—is able to respond effectively with action and emotion. This person pairs Alyson's word with her goal and also reinforces Alyson's confidence in the use of language. Alyson is in control with one word. She does not have to reach and whine for the beanbag. Her success in this situation will prompt her to try using other words she knows and to learn new words.

The task of connecting feelings with words is an important one for caregivers. Using emotion words and talking about feelings is at the core of relationships and behavior regulation. Achieving emotional balance requires us to identify our feelings, yet many people avoid putting their feelings into words. Child care may be the first place where children learn to use emotion words. Because responsive caregivers know how to read and interpret emotion cues, they can help children find the words that will communicate their feelings to others, for example, "I'm tired," "I'm frightened," or "I'm angry." By teaching children how to identify and talk about their feelings, we help these children learn to self-regulate. When you say, "Sarie, that must have hurt. Do you feel sad?" you are comforting Sarie and helping her define what she is feeling. If Sarie uses her own words to say, "I feel sad," she will feel better and will be willing to talk about her feelings and to think of ways to solve her dilemmas.

> *Using emotion words and talking about feelings is at the core of relationships and behavior regulation.*

The tone of one's voice communicates and regulates emotion. Calm voice tones tend to soothe an overstimulated child. When caregivers model these tones by singing a lullaby or cooing "There, there," the child not only is calmed but also begins to learn to self-comfort and self-regulate. In other situations, happy, excited, or surprised voice tones tend to orient and focus a child. However, the tone of a voice can also disregulate children. We tend to talk about behavior that annoys us in an angry tone of voice. Adults commonly use harsh speech when they want to modify "naughty" behavior. Yet, we have learned that anger dampens learning. Expressing our frustrated feelings to the child with an angry voice is usually unproductive. Children who are subjected to harsh adult voices often respond with fear, anger, or withdrawal. Toddlers may scream, "No, no, no" and run from the speaker. Even worse, they may try these voice tones themselves in a pretend situation or when playing with another child. A neutral tone, used with clear words that are paired with actions, will express your meaning best to the child, especially for messages that are meant to limit or redirect. The emotion cues associated with your voice tone will not only express your feelings but also regulate or arouse feelings in others.

Voice tone should match the meaning of the words used by an adult. The tone that accompanies words affects whether or not the message is understood and remembered. For example, saying, "Okay. It is time for the picnic" in a bored or gruff voice will be confusing for the child who may have thought that *picnic* was a fun word but now is unsure. In the same way, saying "No, no, children. Don't touch" in a friendly, happy voice will not bring the results you hoped for. The children will not have a clear understanding of the meaning of these words.

Actions give words meaning. The caregiver's use of words to inhibit or change behavior should be guided by the fact that words alone are not meaningful for the infant and toddler. A firm, neutral voice that is followed by action will give meaning to your sanctions. If "Sit down" is followed by the caregiver gently helping the child to sit, the word begins to define an action. When you use simple words (e.g., "No," "Stop," or "Sit down") followed by calm, clear actions, the child begins to pair the words you used with what happened and then understands what you want. The child learns that words express actions and ideas as well as represent objects. If the caregiver says, "No" and, after that, produces an action such as putting away the ball or taking the plate to the kitchen, then the child will begin to honor the meaning of the word *no* and will change a behavior at the caregiver's request before any action occurs. However, if *no* is a word that adults often use with scary voice tones but after which nothing happens, then it becomes a word without meaning that is fun to imitate.

Toddlers experiment with words to test their meaning and their power. They experiment with the words, saying them over and over in search of their meaning. Because adults seem to use the word *no* often and with high emotion, toddlers realize that the word has power. They begin to say, "No" to everything. "More juice?" "No." "All done?" "No." "Want a cookie?" "No." During this kind of experimenting, the responsive caregiver may choose to ignore the "No" expressions that seem meaningless. Instead, this

> *Actions give words meaning. A firm, neutral voice that is followed by action will give meaning to your sanctions*

caregiver might determine when to honor the "No" that has a valid choice attached to it. She might respond to the examples above in different ways. "No juice? Okay." "Oh, yes. *We* are all done." "No cookie? Yes cookie? Ah, yes, baby wants one." When children realize that they can make choices and negotiate their wants with a simple word such as *yes* or *no*, the power of language becomes evident.

Words set to rhythm can be used to regulate emotions as well as guide transitions and routines. A song can be a signal for activity to quiet and cleanup to begin. A lullaby can be a cue for nap time. Rhythms organize thought patterns and focus children. Caregivers often make up short songs or rhythmic speech to accompany caregiving tasks or classroom activities. For example, while changing Geri's diaper, a caregiver might sing, "Geri, Geri, happy as can be. Geri, Geri, I love thee." If Geri listens to these words, she might not squirm during the diaper change. Similarly, when Marco is trying to master a puzzle, his teacher can scaffold his learning by chanting, "You can turn it and twist it. Turn it and twist it. And it will fit."

Children Use Language to Self-Regulate

Infants engage in crib talk to release their feelings and integrate their thoughts. They coo and babble to the patterns on the wall or to toys in their cribs. Toddlers self-regulate by talking aloud about what they are doing or about what they remember. Children use this private speech to scaffold themselves as they undertake new and challenging tasks. They use private speech when they are pretending or when they are involved in a difficult cognitive activity such as gluing or coloring. Eventually, this verbalized private speech becomes internalized private speech that guides actions and activities. "Self-talk" is an important regulator. We all use it, but not always out loud. Self-talk can be a rehearsal for a future event or a pep talk for a job well done. Children and adults benefit from self-talk. Caregivers should not join into a child's self-talk because this verbalizing is a form of private speech.

Key Concept Three
Literacy Activities Can Build Relationships, Language Skills, and Problem-Solving Abilities

Pictures and marks are symbols for objects. They are another form of symbolic representation, similar to imitation and pretend. For the child, developing literacy is a cognitive process that is different from learning spoken words because it involves visual symbols instead of auditory ones. Pictures of objects help children accept these visual symbols. As children's cognitive processes mature, those children who have seen a printed word in conjunction with a picture begin to pair these symbols. They begin to accept the marks on the page and the patterns they form as visual symbols for words in much the same way that they accept the picture as a symbol for an object. More maturity is needed to build the cognitive processes that allow for written word recognition. Some 2–3-year-olds can recognize certain letters or words that are repeated often in their books. Some parents are able to teach a toddler to recognize his written name through repeated exposures.

Literacy, like language, should be introduced in the first year. One enhances the other. Reading books to an infant gives the baby pleasure through your voice tones and the patterns of your speech. Reading aloud to a 9-month-old enhances the caregiver–child relationship and can focus the active child. Reading aloud to the class expands children's cognition and learning. As the caregiver reads the words in a book, a new idea can begin to take root or a wonderful imaginary world can unfold in a child's mind. Activities that foster literacy and language development include having books available, reading aloud, talking about books, reciting fingerplays, singing songs, and modeling a love of books.

Books Enhance Relationships

When a caregiver nestles a child in her lap and focuses the child's attention on the visual images displayed in a book, two important phenomena are happening. First, the child is in a warm, comfortable setting with a special adult. This relationship connection makes what is being shared more meaningful for the child. Second, the child is learning a new skill. As the caregiver points to pictures, describes what is happening, asks the child questions, and turns pages, the child begins to see books as sources of discovery and fun. Eventually, we may notice a toddler sitting alone, holding a book, turning pages, and pretending to read by babbling expressively, and we know that the foundations for literacy have been established.

Books offer a shared focus. Reading is a tool that caregivers can use to expand language and explore new cognitive concepts. When a caregiver points to familiar pictures in a book and asks, "What's this?" the child must pair the image with something in memory. When the teacher says, "We have one of these in our room. Where is it?" The caregiver is expanding cognitive pathways beyond the book and into the life space of the child.

The responsive caregiver will match the child's developmental level when planning a reading activity. Young infants will be mesmerized by the sound of the reader's voice and the pictures in the book. Toward the end of the first year, babies will begin to turn pages. They are eager to move quickly from image to image. They want the caregiver to turn pages more than read. Young toddlers will have favorite books, anticipate familiar characters, and use words or sounds to label illustrations. They will want to read more slowly so that they can interact and show you that they recognize the images. Older toddlers will have a better understanding of a character's feelings and will be more interested in following a story line. Box 8.4 shows the progression of a child's steps toward reading. Books become a wonderful new way to explore. With each page, something familiar or novel appears. Books provide a whole new world of mastery for a child.

Box 8.4
Developmental Steps to Reading

Early reading (3–9 months old): Likes the sound of the caregiver's voice and being close to the caregiver. Likes pictures with color and patterns (including magazines). Wants to listen to the caregiver and be held.

First books (9–12 months old): Is learning to turn pages and needs washable, durable books. Likes simple pictures (single images), touch-and-feel books, rhyming books, and animal books. Wants the caregiver to turn pages quickly and read many books.

Picture books (12–18 months old): Has favorite books and likes to see familiar objects in books. Will look for hidden pictures and will anticipate the next page. Makes sounds for pictures and answers questions about characters or familiar stories. Wants the caregiver to personify characters, to talk about the pictures, to express feelings related to the story, and to read the same book over and over.

Simple words (18–24 months old): Still prefers simple story lines. Likes more complex illustrations. Will anticipate and hunt for objects and characters in pictures. Is interested in books about feelings and categories, books with rhyming and repeating words, and vocabulary-building books. Wants the caregiver to match pictures with objects, to ask questions, to describe feelings, and to use character voices.

Storybooks (24–36 months old): More interested in the story line and may memorize parts of it. Expresses empathy for the characters and learns from morals. Likes jokes and adventure stories. Can accept new words and new ideas. Begins to recognize letters and numbers. Enjoys group reading and pretends to read. Wants the caregiver to read the story and then ask questions.

Reading to children should be an interactive process. The story is less important than the process of talking about the characters' feelings (e.g., "Miss Mouse is so happy") and asking questions about what is happening or is about to happen (e.g., "Why do you think she is happy?"). In addition, the caregiver will be advancing a child's cognitive growth when he asks the child to discover details in the pictures (e.g., "Where is the ladybug?") and to extend the story with dramatic play (e.g., "We have a hat like that in our basket. You could be like Miss Mouse"). Many toddler books explore relationship themes and provide opportunities for a caregiver to talk about the emotions and values that connect people (e.g., "Miss Mouse helped

Mr. Mole when she brought the food. How do you think he was feeling? Would you ever do something like that?"). Books provide us opportunities to understand the characters' feelings, take on their roles, and explore their emotions.

Group reading for toddlers is an important shared experience. In this activity, we are creating positive associations between books and feelings of connection with peers and caregivers. Many books for toddlers use predictable patterns and repetitious sounds that encourage group participation. As the toddlers shout out anticipated words, the shared pleasure strengthens neural pathways. Caregivers can talk with the group about the problems and lessons that the book presents (e.g., "Was Baby Bear frightened to be lost? Did he let the hedgehog help him? Did he find his way home? Is he happy now?"). Group problem solving reinforces learning. When caregivers engage in group reading activities, they must accommodate toddlers' short attention spans and understand that individual children may not sit still during the activity. However, the wandering toddler can also be listening to the story.

Books Are Vehicles for Strengthening Language Development

Books connect images with words. Young children enjoy picture books about familiar objects and events. The caregiver can extend a word's meaning for the children by using that word in other contexts (e.g., "Look, Kassie Kat has shoes. I have shoes too. Where are your shoes?"). When a caregiver names a familiar object in a picture and then points to the object in the room, children make connections. The word becomes meaningful and useful. After this kind of reading activity, the toddler may start using the word (e.g., "See, shoe," "Hi, big bear"). Many children's books are written for this purpose. For example, when the book is about color, the responsive caregiver may find something else in the room or on the child in the same color. This matching activity provides a way of helping the child understand that a word can represent the visual image of a color anywhere. It also personalizes the word for a child to use (e.g., "My shirt, blue," "My blue blankie," "My blue socks").

Children enjoy repetition and predictability, which extend also to their selecting books. As an infant-toddler caregiver, you will be reading the same books over and over again. These books become "old friends" and are associated with positive feelings. This repetition is also a stimulus for vocabulary building. Often, children will know these books well enough to anticipate a picture and the words that go with it. Rereading a familiar book invites interaction. For example, children may say the words that they remember either with you or before you. Caregivers can ask children to join in with the words in the next repeated phrase (e.g., "but the old cow always said, '____'"). This activity becomes great fun for them and reinforces their verbal expression, even when they do not understand the meaning. You may even hear them repeating these phrases by themselves when they are "reading" the book alone.

When the book is familiar, you will be able to ask the child questions about where something is (e.g., "Where is the ladybug?") and teach action words such as *hiding, falling down,* and *jumping over.* The pictures in children's books offer ample opportunities to introduce concepts that are used in daily experience, for example, *on top, under,* or *inside.* Reading also teaches about dangers such as those connected with roads, storms, and wandering away. Books can reduce fear by illustrating how to solve problems. They open the way for caregivers to discuss how a child might avoid these same dangers.

> *The pictures in children's books offer ample opportunities to introduce concepts that are used in daily experience.*

Be aware, however, that books can induce or reinforce fear. Images of growling animals are a major source of bad dreams in toddlers. Some of the images, which seem benign to you in a children's book, represent real objects or animals for the toddler, just as the picture of a shoe or cup does. Reality and fantasy are not separated in a toddler's mind. The responsive caregiver who knows that certain images are frightening for a toddler can defuse them by talking about stories being pretend, not real. Often, television images will combine with images in books to magnify a child's fears. Small children will identify with the baby bear who got lost or the bunny who was captured. They become distressed. When the caregiver talks about the message of a story and focuses children on sharing in the solution rather then in the fear, toddlers begin to separate themselves a bit from the emotion of the characters and identify with the problem-solving experience. It is important for toddlers to realize that the stories both in books and on television are pretend.

Caregivers Can Use the Power of Books to Reinforce a Child's Identity

Having children create "A Book About Me" is a good activity for enhancing each child's sense of self or emotional connection to family. Ask parents to bring photos of the child and the special people in the child's life. As children page through their books and see images of themselves and their loved ones, they recall the positive emotions associated with family life. Similarly, a book tailored to the group can include photos of children and caregivers at the center with captions describing the activities they have shared. These books provide a vehicle for enhancing shared memories and for talking about relationship themes. They also tie a child's experiences to the images that represent them. In this way, the child realizes that books can be about real things and pretend things.

Chapter Summary

Caregivers create the language environment for children in their care. Language skills grow out of early interactive experiences with caregivers. Responsive caregivers help children learn to connect sounds with meaning, they establish patterns and rhythms of interaction, and they model speech sounds. Responsive caregivers connect with a child's attempts at verbal communication, imitating and refining the child's first sounds and words. They expand the child's vocabulary through natural conversation, adding new words to the ones the child already is using. Caregivers repeat words for the child, encourage verbal games, and plan music activities, all of which expand word meaning and word usage. Caregivers use language to mutually regulate children. Using an appropriate tone of voice, labeling feelings, and teaching feeling words are all ways to advance language development and emotional growth.

Pictures and simple word books foster both language and literacy. Books help link pictures with words and expand a child's sense of reality and of pretend. Caregivers provide the printed images that initiate pathways for reading. It is through relationships that children listen to their first stories, explore and discuss new ideas, or are asked to think in new and different ways. Books allow children to imagine themselves in another place or time. Caregivers are able to merge the fantasy and the lesson in the child's mind. Caregivers introduce the magic of first books and thereby open the door to a new world of reading and of lifelong learning.

Resources

Barclay, K., Benelli, C., & Curtis, A. (1995). Literacy begins at birth: What caregivers can learn from parents of children who read early. *Young Children, 50*(4), 24–28.

Bates, C., & Bates, R. (1999). Mother and daughter set out to promote literacy in a family child care home and a child care center. *Young Children, 54*(1), 12–15.

Baumwell, L., Tamis-LeMonda, C. S., & Bornstein, M. H. (1997). Maternal verbal sensitivity and child language comprehension. *Infant Behavior and Development, 20*, 247–258.

Dombro, A. L., Colker, L. J., & Dodge, D. T. (1997). *The creative curriculum for infants and toddlers.* Washington, DC: Teaching Strategies.

Gonzalez-Mena, J., & Eyer, D. W. (2001). *Infants, toddlers and caregivers* (5th ed.). Mountain View, CA: Mayfield Publishing.

Hart, B., & Risley, T. R. (1995). *Meaningful differences in the everyday experience of young American children.* Baltimore: Brookes Publishing.

Hart, B., & Risley, T. R. (1999). *The social world of children learning to talk.* Baltimore: Brookes Publishing.

Hoff-Ginsburg, E. (1986). Function and structure in maternal speech: Their relation to the child's development of syntax. *Developmental Psychology, 22,* 155–163.

Huttenlocher, J. (1999). Language input and language growth. In N. A. Fox, L. A. Leavitt, & J. G. Warhol (Eds.), *The role of early experience in infant development* (pp. 69–82). Skillman, NJ: Johnson & Johnson Pediatric Institute.

Jalongo, M. R. (1996). Teaching children to become better listeners. *Young Children, 51*(2), 21–26.

Kuhl, P. K. (1999). The role of experience in early language development: Linguistic experience alters the perception and production of speech. In N. A. Fox, L. A. Leavitt, & J. G. Warhol (Eds.), *The role of early experience in infant development* (pp. 101–125), Skillman, NJ: Johnson & Johnson Pediatric Institute.

McMullen, M. B. (1998). Thinking before doing: A giant step on the road to literacy. *Young Children, 53*(3), 65–70.

Murray, A. D., Johnson, J., & Peters, J. (1990). Fine-tuning utterance length to preverbal infants: Effects on later language development. *Journal of Child Language, 17,* 511–525.

Roskos, K., & Christie, J. (2001). On not pushing too hard: A few cautionary remarks about linking literacy and play. *Young Children, 56*(3), 64–66.

Walker, D., Greenwood, C., Hart, B., & Carta, J. (1994). Prediction of school outcomes based on early language production and socioeconomic factors. *Child Development, 65,* 606–621.

Zero to Three. *Brain wonders: Helping babies and toddlers grow and develop.* Retrieved June 10, 2003, from http://www.zerotothree.org/brainworks

Videos

Beginning Language Connections. (1995). First Steps: Supporting Early Language Development. Beaverton, OR: Educational Productions. (20 min.).

Building Conversations. (1995). First Steps: Supporting Early Language Development. Beaverton, OR: Educational Productions. (20 min.).

Curriculum for Infants and Toddlers: Language and Literacy. (2003). Barrington, IL: Magna Systems, Inc. (29 min.).

Talking With Young Children. (1995). First Steps: Supporting Early Language Development. Beaverton, OR: Educational Productions. (20 min.).

Chapter 9

Relationships
With Families

PHOTO: COMSTOCK

When infants and toddlers enter into our care, we begin a partnership with their families. We will be sharing in the care of these children and in their developmental milestones. To best support the early development of each child, we should connect with each family in a trusting relationship. Although this alliance may develop slowly over time, it will be a support for the child, for her parents, and for us as caregivers. Our knowledge of the value of emotion-sharing relationships for child development will serve us well as we work with families.

Parents often struggle with their feelings about entrusting someone outside of the family with the care of their children. Consequently, parents may be anxious when they come into a child-care setting. For parents to feel comfortable leaving their children in our care, we must establish trust with them. In our interactions with parents, we will be modeling our relationship-building skills. Parents will be watching us as we interact with their children, listening to what we say and reading our body language. We will be establishing an adult-to-adult relationship at the same time that we are establishing an adult-to-child relationship. This process requires that we respect parents and listen to their beliefs and concerns.

Key Concept One
Building Relationships With Parents Is Important

Parents and caregivers bring unique perspectives to the child-care setting. The parent is an expert on his own child, including the child's tempera-

---

Goals of Chapter 9

- Identify and discuss the normal, often intense, and complicated feelings of caregivers and parents who are sharing the care of a child.

- Explore continuity issues between child care and home.

- Discuss potential differences between family values and center values.

- Identify ways to support parenting and validate cultural differences.

- Give caregivers and teachers language to communicate with families and to explain the goals of the center.

- Identify aspects of programs that promote responsive relationships between parents and caregivers.

- Describe the skills that enable caregivers to listen and relate to parents in everyday interactions, group meetings, and individual conferences.

ment. The infant-toddler caregiver brings expertise about the developmental needs of young children, including how to plan an appropriate program to meet those needs. By sharing information and observations, the parents and child-care provider support each child's individual needs.

Even parents who distrust "experts" may appreciate your ideas presented in the context of a loving relationship for the child. Parents commonly rely on family and friends for advice, modeling, and emotional support. Caregivers can become a part of this informal support network. As we join with parents to form a respectful partnership, we will have an opportunity to engage in relevant discussions about their children's growth and development. Unlike parenting books or news briefs, the information we share is individualized and pertains to their children at the appropriate time, not to "the typical 1-year-old." The following two scenarios illustrate this point.

> Dr. Evans, parent of Aaron (10 months old), tells his son's caregivers how much he relies on them to answer his questions on parenting issues. "You have helped us so much in figuring out the feeding problems Aaron experienced. We also feel so relieved to learn from you that his inability to crawl at this age is normal. Because Aaron is our first child, we have so many questions, so many expectations."

> Kyle (28 months old) begins running wildly around the room when his mother arrives. His mother appears extremely frustrated and tries to control him by being angry and demanding. The teacher, Jennie, suggests that the mother's arrival at the end of the day might remind Kyle of their morning separation. She explains that Kyle's behavior could be a reaction to being left each morning. "Kyle may be acting out his excitement at seeing his mother. It is a way of showing his love and attachment for you," adds Jennie. "Whew! Deep down, I was really feeling that he did not love me any more and that you had replaced me," Mrs. Murray shares. "Let's talk for a few more minutes and let Kyle wind down," says Jennie. " I think he will be coming to you shortly."

Children are capable of forming secondary attachments. Although parents generally accept children's attachments to grandparents and other relatives, they may be less comfortable with attachments that occur outside the family. However, infants and toddlers will become attached to their child-care providers. These secondary attachments give emotional continuity and emotional equilibrium to children. Parents often misunderstand and do not realize that these emotional connections do not threaten the child's primary attachment to the parents.

Be aware that the emotional bonds we form with children in our care evoke a range of feelings in their parents. Some parents may come to the center with strong opinions about the hazards of their child forming attachments to non-family members. At one extreme are parents who believe that the child's relationship with the caregiver threatens the child's love for mother or father. Although they are looking to us for child-care assistance, they may experience feelings of jealousy, guilt, or anger when they observe the child's affection for us. At the other extreme are parents who believe that the more caregivers the child has, the more adaptable she will be in the future. They may feel that a primary caregiver limits the child's development. Although neither of these viewpoints is supported by research, both can exert a powerful influence on our efforts to establish an emotionally connected relationship with the child and his family.

> *Be aware that the emotional bonds we form with children in our care evoke a range of feelings in their parents.*

No evidence indicates that the parent–child bond is weakened when infants and toddlers develop a secondary attachment to a caregiver at the child-care center. The parent remains the primary attachment figure, the one whom the infant prefers (especially when stressed). Communicating this information to parents is crucial. When a child-care setting is committed to a staffing pattern that is centered around primary caregivers, the advantages of relationship-based care must be communicated to families. If parents understand the stability that a consistent, emotionally connected relationship gives to their child, they usually accept the partnership, and their confidence in the caregiver grows.

A spirit of open communication can be established when the family first visits the child-care setting. Our willingness to listen to the visiting parents, to find out their goals for the child, and to give thoughtful responses to the parents' questions will pave the way for connection. During the intake process, directors and caregivers have an opportunity to explain their relationship-based philosophy. At this time, we can explain how we individualize caregiving within the context of the group. It is a good time to begin establishing the caregiver-family alliance and to enlist parents' support for using a primary caregiver staffing pattern.

Often, however, the intake interview and the initial parent tour are done by staff members other than the primary caregiver. Parent–caregiver alliances are not established during this process. Later, when a new child is assigned to a caregiver, the caregiver should make time to meet with the child's parents and begin building the partnership that will best serve this individual child.

Caregivers Communicate With and Support Parents in Many Ways

Caregivers use many techniques to communicate with parents. These include shared positive emotions, reflective listening, speaking through the child, modeling baby watching, and affirming parents' child-rearing efforts. Remember that, as a caregiver, you will be using the same skills in building a relationship with parents that you have used with children.

Begin by greeting parents as partners. Ask how their day is going. Share professional information about yourself. At first, both caregivers and parents may hold back because they worry about being judged and seeming inadequate. Encourage questions and present yourself as a fellow human with strengths, weaknesses, likes, dislikes, and a range of emotions. Defensiveness can thwart the tone of emotional availability and the openness that you are trying to create. Parents and caregivers alike need support from each other and must be able to accept imperfection in each other.

Shared positive emotions. Emotion sharing is an important factor in all relationships. Shared positive emotions will be the strongest link in building a relationship with parents. They are the basis for cooperation and partnership. As caregivers, we are the ones to initiate and project the positive. Smiles, laughter, and funny stories will exemplify your love for the children in your care. When parents see this positiveness in you, then your efforts to establish the parent–caregiver alliance will be well underway.

Reflective listening. Make a special effort to use reflective listening. When parents discuss their concerns, first state what you hear them saying. Include a statement about the emotional tone you have heard. Consider the example in the following scenario:

> A parent arrives in the morning and says, "Why does Ramon come home with paint on his clothes every day?" The caregiver, using reflective listening, says, "You seem upset that Ramon's clothes have paint on them." The parent responds, "Yes, I can't afford new clothes every week."

In this scenario, reflective listening enabled the caregiver to hear the reason for the mother's concern. Using this dialogue as a starting point, parent and caregiver can engage in joint problem solving. If they agree that some valuable activities are also messy, then it will be easier to agree that the child needs to be appropriately dressed for these activities. The solution might be for the mother to leave a set of old clothes in the child's cubby or arrange for the center to provide a smock for a small fee.

Speaking through the child. Caregivers can connect with parents by using the child's perspective to identify the positive ways parents are supporting early development. For example, if a mother comes to child care with a book, the caregiver might say, "Stefan, your Mommy knows that you like the pictures in this book. You want to share it with us." This statement will open the door for also using the child's "voice" to introduce problems in child care. "Your baby seems to be saying that he is still hungry after lunch. 'I'm growing—I need more.' Could you bring extra food for him tomorrow?" By using the voice of the child, we give parents another window for understanding the child's feelings and development. This technique provides a constructive way to help parents understand their children's dilemmas and relate to their children's feelings.

Modeling baby watching. Be a model for baby watching and thoughtful reflection. "He is so focused on pouring the sand into different-sized containers. He is ignoring everything else that's going on around him. It's almost as if he's trying to figure out why it fits in some and overflows in others." This comment may draw the parent's attention to a child behavior in a specific way. Sharing these observations is a way to sharpen parents' baby-watching skills and focus them on the developmental status of their children. Through our observations, we show that we value these everyday occurrences, and we model a way of seeing the children and interpreting their actions that will enrich parent-child interactions. As we think out loud about what we are observing, parents may begin to join our reflection and use these ideas at home.

Affirming parents and supporting their child-rearing efforts. It may be helpful to remember that parents are doing the best they can to care for their children. For the most part, their emotions and behaviors are motivated by their love for the child. However, parenting in today's world can be difficult. Balancing family needs with the demands of work or training can be stressful for parents. Sometimes these stresses compromise parents' best intentions.

Avoid comments that elevate a parent's uncertainty, anxiety, or frustration (for example, "Sarah takes so long to settle down. Do you rush her in the mornings?"). Instead, focus on the positive connections between parental actions and child outcomes. "She really brightens up when you walk in the room." Speak through the child about what the parent is doing to support early development, rather than focusing on what may be going wrong. Blaming parents is not a productive way to help a child. Acknowledging the demands and stress that parents are experiencing will lead you to problem-solving ideas that will enable child care to support a parent or help a child.

Caregivers Strengthen Trust With Parents Through Specific Techniques

Part of the process in building a relationship is establishing trust. Caregivers can strengthen trust with parents by attentively using specific techniques, including asking questions, taking the parent's perspective, monitoring their own perspectives, and being sensitive to ethnic and cultural differences.

Asking questions. Ask questions that empower parents. For example, "I wonder why her mood changes when it's time to leave for the day? I know it's frustrating for you. Why do you think she becomes so uncooperative when you are trying to get out the door?" These questions encourage parent participation in problem solving. They indicate that we are not the experts with all the answers. We are empowering the parent to join us in interpreting the child's emotional cues, and we are showing respect for parents' ideas. Also, share some of the problems of the caregiving staff. "I have school-age children at my house, so it is important that I get home in time to greet them. Can you make alternative arrangements if you are going to be late picking up your baby?"

Taking the parent's perspective. To gain new insights into a problem or situation, try taking the parent's perspective. For example, we may be puzzled when a parent expresses concern about his toddler having a tantrum because we view this event in the context of normal development. However, tantrums have more of an emotional effect on parents. A parent's attachment to the child and his feelings of responsibility for the child's behavior can result in embarrassment, anger, or disappointment when his child is "making a fuss." Our role is to empathize and label his real feelings while focusing his attention on the normalcy of the child's behavior.

Our ability to observe parents' emotional signals will help us connect with their interests, enthusiasms, and concerns. Some parents experience jealousy when they watch their children engaging with a caregiver. Although their rational thinking tells them that the child is happy and nurtured, they may feel emotionally displaced.

Monitoring our own perspectives. Our own perspectives can create barriers to relationships. Caregivers create barriers when they are judgmental about parental practices or when they become possessive of a child in their care. For example, if the child arrives at the center hungry or underdressed, the caregiver may immediately blame the parent and say, "Doesn't Jimmy have a warm coat?" Another common occurrence is when caregivers observe a parent's harsh discipline tactics. They may react impulsively in a way that will strain the parent–caregiver relationship. Some child-care providers unconsciously resent parents. Working for low wages in a field that has not always been valued by society, caregivers may feel taken for granted and unappreciated, especially if large discrepancies exist between the incomes of parents and providers. We must be aware of our own emotions and how they can interfere with relationship building.

Being sensitive to ethnic and cultural differences. Ethnic and cultural differences can be obstacles to building partnerships with parents. When caregivers and families do not share similar backgrounds, extra effort must be exerted to find common ground. Ultimately, the goal of caring about the child is what unites parents and providers in a common cause, supporting the child as she adapts to two cultures. For some families, the child-care setting provides a bridge between these two worlds.

It may be challenging for a caregiver to support a family's values while maintaining a commitment to the center's goals. For example, if a parent considers the child's autonomy as a threat to his authority, he may feel that you should restrict mastery attempts. If the parents value interdependence over independence, they may question how we handle routines. Some cultures believe that food is sacred, and parents from these cultures do not want children feeding themselves until they can treat the food with respect. Other parents consider the way they dress the child as an outward manifestation of their love. These parents are troubled when the caregiver fails to keep the child's clothes clean. When the caregiver fails to honor the parent's perspective or treats a parent's different belief as inferior, the relationship suffers. Although our child-care settings must meet the needs of the group, caregivers can also incorporate the parents' goals and values into the program whenever possible. In the words of one perceptive caregiver, "When I try to incorporate what the parents want into the care that I provide for their children, it is amazing how much that helps build their trust in me."

Separation Issues Bring Emotions to the Surface for Parents, Children, and Caregivers

Leaving a child at the center is an emotional experience for parents. Caregivers who focus on the child's adjustment might unconsciously overlook the fears, sadness, and anxiety of the parents. Even when parents believe that they have chosen the best possible environment away from home for their child, nagging doubts and a sense of loss are common. Parents are concerned about what they might miss in the child's development and are worried that the child will feel abandoned. These feelings are legitimate.

Caregivers must acknowledge the emotional challenges that the parents are experiencing and must create a supportive environment for helping parents come to terms with their feelings. Parents will appreciate our sensitivity when we empathize with their feelings and pace our responses to match their moods. Your emotional connection with the parent will not go unnoticed by the child. The child will look to the parent for reassurance that the caregiver is someone to be trusted. When parents trust us, the child will mirror this trust.

Because caregivers repeatedly witness the separation of many parent-child dyads, they might begin to underestimate the emotions surrounding this routine transition. Parents react to their own feelings in different ways, and caregivers must remain aware of the parent who is struggling. In an effort to distance themselves emotionally, some parents walk away without saying good-bye to the child. At the other end of the spectrum are those who cling to the child and are too emotionally distraught to leave. The separation routine described in chapter 5 will help parents deal with their ambivalence. It is important for the caregiver to find a way to be available to a parent when she presents a concern. A few minutes of listening will often end the anxiety and solve the problem. Our understanding of these emotional dynamics will allow us to intercede in a sensitive way when parents need support.

Key Concept Two
Children Can Experience Continuity and Discontinuity Between Home and Child Care

Children enrolled in child-care centers experience two different worlds, home and center. Although both settings may be nurturing environments, they are not identical. Each setting can present different schedules, stimulation, expectations, and opportunities for personal attention. Part of our job is to help the children and parents we serve bridge the gap between these two worlds.

Most infants and toddlers learn to adapt to minor differences in routines and caregivers. However, even when a good relationship between family and caregiver has been forged, discontinuity can present difficulty for parents. When expectations at home are completely different from those at the center, the gap may seem to grow as the child matures or spends more time at the center. These differences become unsettling for the family and difficult to negotiate. For example, if self-feeding is encouraged in the child-care setting but is discouraged at home, toddlers may be confused or make mistakes at home. Often, the parents do not express their frustrations or concerns to the caregiver, but instead, uncertainty about the child-care situation grows into misplaced resentment of the caregiver.

Discontinuity Can Lead to Conflict

Discontinuity in values, beliefs, or practices can lead to conflict between parents and caregivers. Disagreements about toilet training, discipline practices, or schedules may be unsettling for both parties. Rather than merely stating the center's policy, the responsive caregiver will examine his own feelings and consider the parent's perspective. He may reflect on a range of questions. For example, Why am I so upset when a parent insists that I should begin toilet training her 18-month-old? What is motivating the parent to make these demands? Should I dispute the parent's request by describing the signals from the child that tell me to do otherwise? How would my disagreeing make the parent feel? How does this situation affect the parent–child relationship?

If we have established an alliance with the child's parents and a regular communication pattern, then caregiver and parent will have a foundation for joint problem solving when conflicts arise. When a parent or a caregiver identifies a concern, either person must feel free to approach the other party. Then, parent and caregiver must make time to talk about their feelings and discuss possible solutions. Consider the following scenario:

> It is a brisk fall day, and Jason (18 months old) arrives at the center with his mother. Elana, his caregiver, notices that he is not wearing a jacket but is being kept warm by his mother's embrace. This observation concerns Elana because, for the past 3 days, she has asked Jason's mother to bring warm clothing for outdoor play. Elana is frustrated and wonders to herself, "Doesn't this mother care about her child?" As they go through their drop-off routine, Elana says, "We'll probably be playing outside this morning, Mrs. C. Does Jason have a jacket in his cubby? Mrs. C. replies, "Oh, I don't think so. But that's okay because it's too cold for Jason to be outside today." Elana hears her concern about the cooler temperatures and says, "It sounds like you don't want Jason to go outside in cool weather." Mrs. C. answers right away, "That's right. I'm not going to let my baby get cold. If he gets sick, it's bad for him and me." Elana says, "You're right. You want to make sure that he's protected. I don't want Jason to get cold or sick either. The other toddlers really enjoy our playground, and we feel that the exercise and fresh air helps them be healthy. But I hate leaving Jason behind when we go out. He seems so lonely. He could play outside with the other children if he were dressed warmly."

Both caregiver and parent can become judgmental if they do not address the feelings surrounding a problem. Without communication, the intentions of each party may be misconstrued and tensions can intensify. By reserving judgment and by listening to the parent, Elana learned that this mother had not responded to the requests for outdoor clothing because she does not believe her child should be subjected to cool temperatures.

When we use reflective listening to hear the parent's concerns and beliefs, the parent feels valued. This interaction allowed Mrs. C. to hear the caregiver's concern for her child and to think about the potential benefits of outdoor play for Jason. Elana included the parent in the problem solving. As Elana and Mrs. C. work together to resolve their differences, they might compromise by establishing a time limit that the child will be outside when the temperature is below 40 degrees and by agreeing that the parent will provide a coat for the child.

> *When we use reflective listening to hear the parent's concerns and beliefs, the parent feels valued.*

Sometimes, families and caregivers can agree to live with their differences. When confronted with challenges from parents or when frustrated by family practices that seem to be at odds with the caregiver's, caregivers must step back from the situation and determine how important the issue is. If I give in to the parent's request, will the child be harmed? Is the demand irritating but not really a threat to the goals of our child-care program? Try to see the issue from the parent's perspective. On some issues, parents and caregivers can agree to disagree without compromising developmentally appropriate practice.

Children can adapt to and learn from minor differences among different settings. They are not always harmed when parents and caregivers have different approaches to similar problems. However, children feel anxious if they sense a smoldering tension between two people who are important to them. Disagreements can be an opportunity for parents and caregivers to learn more about each other and renew their commitment to the shared goal of supporting the child.

In rare instances, it may be appropriate to counsel a family out of the child-care program. When efforts to resolve the conflict have failed over a period of time or when a center's caregiving goals risk being severely compromised, caregivers can offer to help parents find another provider. These instances are not common; they often involve discipline methods, particularly spanking. When parent beliefs are clearly at odds with developmentally appropriate practice, caregivers may feel that a middle ground is not viable because the stakes are too high. For example, if a parent insists that the child be punished and isolated when he wets his pants, then a responsive caregiver would be hard pressed to respect or follow these instructions.

Although we may feel disappointed, frustrated, or angry when we cannot collaborate with parents, we should not lose sight of our values and goals. We do not need to feel inadequate when a child leaves the center because of a conflict. Family belief systems are slow to change, but a family's brief experience with your child care may have opened some new thoughts and options for those parents. As caregivers in a relationship-based program, we seek to provide emotional stability for young children when they are with us. This experience will be meaningful to the child, even if it is for only a short time. Conflicts between a caregiver and a parent may affect a parent's interactions with his or her child. Ending the relationship and helping parents move on can be viewed as being responsive to the child and the family.

Key Concept Three
Caregivers Need to Maintain Their Connections With Families

For the caregiver–family alliance to be successful, the child-care setting must be organized in a way that promotes open communication. To form positive relationships with parents, caregivers must have opportunities to listen to parents' concerns and to share their observations with parents. Caregivers must respect parents as equal partners, welcome their insights, and keep them informed and emotionally connected. Because no two families are alike, caregivers must have multiple strategies for connecting with families. The goal is to meet the match for the diverse families that the child-care center serves.

Caregivers Use Particular Techniques, Routines, and Time Frames to Enhance Connections With Parents

During the intake interview, parents will be asked about the child's sleeping patterns, eating preferences, temperament, likes, and dislikes. Caregivers need to know who the important people in the child's life are, be they parents, siblings, stepparents, grandparents, or neighbors. Some parents will volunteer this information, whereas others will be more hesitant. Caregivers must balance the need to gain a fuller understanding of the child with a respect for the family's beliefs about privacy. Over time, as trust is established, parents may feel more comfortable divulging family information, thereby giving the caregiver another window for understanding the child.

Some centers try to arrange home visits for the primary caregiver. These visits are often scheduled before the child's first day or soon after enrollment. Caregivers value the opportunity to see parent and child in their natural setting and can come away from the visit with more ideas for relating to the child. However, in some cases, the caregiver may want to wait until after he has established a relationship with the child and has been able to identify key questions. Many parents are impressed by a caregiver's commitment when he takes the time to meet with family members on their own turf, but all families may not welcome this effort. Many families feel strongly about keeping their home environment private. Keep in mind that home visits may be difficult to schedule given the time constraints of parents and caregivers.

> *Connections with families are easier to maintain when rules and expectations are defined clearly.*

Connections with families are easier to maintain when rules and expectations are defined clearly. When a child is enrolled in a child-care setting, parents and caregivers agree to take on specific responsibilities. For example, parents may be required to provide diapers and formula for their baby, and caregivers may be responsible for putting a note in the child's cubby when the supplies are low. Similarly, the center may promise specific adult–child ratios, and families agree to pick up their children at specified times. Providers who clearly explain these responsibilities at the outset can reduce potential misunderstandings later.

Printed materials that outline the center's philosophy and policies should supplement these initial conversations between parents and staff members. Parents can refer to these materials when they are at home and have additional questions. The center's phone number should be included so that parents can clarify concerns and contact caregivers. The usefulness of written documents will depend on the literacy levels and language capabilities of the families served. Translating materials into families' home languages may be helpful in some settings.

Daily communication with parents is accomplished in many ways. First, the primary caregiver can have direct contact with the family at drop-off and pick-up time. Although these transition times can be hectic because the children need the caregiver's personal attention to feel welcomed and make a smooth transition, the parent often has genuine concerns or important information to share. By hiring an aide or parent volunteer to engage the children at these times, the primary caregiver will be able to maximize the encounter with the parents, giving them full attention, making eye contact, and being emotionally available to receive their cues and their comments.

Second, drop-off and pick-up times can be important occasions for caregivers and parents to exchange information that helps them share the care. For example, a mother might comment casually that Sasha did not eat much for breakfast, or a caregiver might report that Ted seems to be enjoying the riding toys on the playground. Some days, this transition from home to center will follow the established routine; at other times, the child or the parents will come to the center with different needs that will require more of the caregiver's time. For example, if a sibling has suddenly taken ill, the child may sense tension in the parents. The child may be fussy and clingy during separation or throughout the day. The parent may be exhausted and impatient with the child. When the caregiver is sensitive to these cues and takes extra time to listen to what is happening in the family, she can put the atypical transition in context. The attuned caregiver can offer the parent emotional support and be more available to the child throughout the day.

Some child-care settings provide a communication notebook in which parents can write down special instructions or information that will help caregivers meet the child's needs that day, for example, "Tomas did not sleep well last night," "We're missing Julia's red jacket. Has anyone seen it?" or "I'll be picking Ellie up at 1:00 p.m. today for a doctor's appointment, so please don't put her down for a nap. Thanks!" When staff members read these messages, the family will be better served because continuity of care will more likely occur.

Bulletin boards chronicle daily activities. Parents feel connected when they see group activities chronicled on the bulletin board with notes and photos. Some caregivers write brief daily messages about individual children, which they accomplish by carrying index cards in a pocket and jotting down observations as they occur. Some caregivers streamline this process with preprinted forms that target specific routines (e.g., diaper changes, napping times, favorite activities). Positive information can also be communicated to parents by means of occasional phone calls. These messages bridge the two worlds for parents, keeping them connected to the people and activities of the center by providing insights into the child's expanding world. However, although memos and electronic messages are convenient, personal contact is the best link between family and day care.

Some child-care settings provide a communication notebook in which parents can write down special instructions or information.

Some centers use periodic newsletters to communicate with parents. The content of these publications might include descriptions of recent classroom activities (e.g., the toddlers' trip to the zoo), announcements of upcoming events (e.g., parent meetings), reminders of important dates (e.g., deadline for updating health information), and staff member profiles or professional development activities of various teachers. Newsletters can also be vehicles for disseminating child development information (e.g., handling tantrums in toddlers) and explaining the rationale underlying various center policies (e.g., the philosophy about primary caregivers). Again, the usefulness of these publications will depend on the literacy levels and preferences of the families served. Remember, the goal is to meet the match for the families who are served.

Scheduling parent–caregiver conferences offers a different opportunity for communication. Ideally, conferences provide uninterrupted time to share information, set goals, and solve problems. The scheduling of conferences must be done with care. Given the busy lives that parents lead, it is important to pick convenient times when the parent is free to focus and when child care can be arranged.

After the conference has been scheduled, ask parents to think ahead about what they would like to discuss. Some centers distribute a simple form that allows parents to write down their questions and comments and drop them off at the center some time before the meeting. Caregivers can then give some thought to these topics before the conference. Caregivers need to be organized and positive in their comments about the child. Comments should begin with something wonderful that the caregiver has observed about the child. The schedule should allow enough time to hear parent concerns and process unanticipated issues. Two-way communication is important. Caregivers may do as much listening as talking during these conferences. The effective caregiver will pay attention to parents' words, body language, and affect and, above all, will remain open to the ideas of others. In addition, he will take notes and follow up on issues that demand further attention.

> *The effective caregiver will pay attention to parents' words, body language, and affect and will remain open to the ideas of others.*

The use of parent volunteers and parent drop-in visits are encouraged by some centers. Although parents might want to participate in the daily program, the reality is that most children are in child care because their parents have other commitments. If a child-care setting is near the work place, some parents may be able to drop in for visits or join the group for lunch. For the most part, children have positive feelings about these visits; however, if these visits are not consistent events, children may be anxious and confused about their parents leaving again without them. Caregivers can talk with parents about the need to set expectations for their visits and review with the child the fact that her parent will be leaving again for a short time. If a definite ritual for a midday visit can be established, many caregivers find that these connections are helpful rather than disruptive. With advance notice, a parent might arrange to accompany children on a field trip. When the parent shares time with the child at the center, he creates an overlap between the child's two worlds, which strengthens the alliance.

Busy parents are hard to engage. In the evolving world of child care, children are coming to group care earlier in life and staying for longer hours when they come. Participating in activities at the child-care setting may be difficult for parents who are already stressed for time. Finding alternative ways to keep them connected and collaborative is crucial. Some programs plan social events to bring families together informally. Potluck dinners at the center or in a neighborhood park give adults a chance to meet their children's playmates, spend time with other parents, and connect with caregivers. Children enjoy seeing the important people in their lives—parents, caregivers, peers—sharing time, space, and laughter. These events also give caregivers an opportunity to observe the child in another context. The shared emotion of a fun-filled evening can foster feelings of connection among families and caregivers.

Caregivers may also bring families together to discuss specific issues related to children and parenting. Parents with same-age children often have similar concerns. They seek out information related to developmental issues such as toilet training, sibling relations, and discipline. The center might survey parents to determine their areas of interest or might decide on a topic based on parent questions or caregiver observations. Program staff members or community resource people could address these issues at evening meetings. These forums can be used to promote a better understanding of the center's relationship-based philosophy and to strengthen the caregiver-family alliance.

Chapter Summary

As child-care providers, our job is to support young children and their families. The relationships we develop with parents will help us understand them and be more responsive to their children. Connecting with the beliefs and goals of parents fosters mutual respect and a shared sense of purpose. Establishing open patterns of communication with families and using relationship-based techniques for supporting them will help us manage conflicts and bridge the gap between home and child care.

Resources

Adler, J. (1999, June 14). Stress. *Newsweek, 133*(24), 56–63 (table credited to Sheldon Cohen).

Bromer, J. (1999). Cultural variations in child care: Values and actions. *Young Children, 54*(6), 72–77.

Daniel, J. E. (1999). A modern mother's place is wherever her children are: Facilitating infant and toddler mothers' transitions in child care. *Young Children, 54*(6), 4–12.

Dombro, A. L., & Bryan, P. (1991). *Sharing the caring: How to find the right child care and make it work for you and your child.* New York: Simon & Schuster.

Dombro, A. L., Colker, L. J., & Dodge, D. T. (1997). *The creative curriculum for infants and toddlers.* Washington, DC: Teaching Strategies, Inc.

Gonzalez-Mena, J. (1992). Taking a culturally sensitive approach in infant-toddler programs. *Young Children, 47*(2), 4–9.

Gonzalez-Mena, J. (1997). *Multicultural issues in child care* (2nd ed.). Mountain View, CA: Mayfield Publishing.

Huntsinger, C. S., Huntsinger, P. R., Ching, W., & Lee, C. (2000). Understanding cultural contexts fosters sensitive caregiving of Chinese American children. *Young Children, 55*(6), 7–15.

Kaiser, B., & Rasminsky, J. S. (2003). Opening the culture door. *Young Children, 58*(4), 53–56.

Koch, P. K., & McDonough, M. (1999). Improving parent-teacher conferences through collaborative conversations. *Young Children, 54*(2), 11–15.

Lally, J. R., Griffin, A., Fenichel, E., Segal, M., Szanton, E., & Weissbourd, B. (1995). *Caring for infants and toddlers in groups: Developmentally appropriate practice.* Washington, DC: Zero to Three: National Center for Infants, Toddlers, and Families.

Lerner, C., & Dombro, A. L. (2000). *Learning and growing together.* Washington, DC: Zero to Three: National Center for Infants, Toddlers, and Families.

Manning, D., & Schindler, P. J. (1997). Communicating with parents when their children have difficulties. *Young Children, 52*(5), 27–33.

Melmed, M. (1997). Parents speak: Zero to Three's findings from research on parents' views of early childhood development. *Young Children, 52*(5), 46–49.

Melmed, M. (1998). Talking with parents about emotional development. In J. G. Warhol & S. P. Shelov (Eds.), *New perspectives in early emotional development* (pp. 239–264). Skillman, NJ: Johnson & Johnson Pediatric Institute.

Pawl, J. H. (2000). The interpersonal center of the work that we do. *Zero to Three, 20*(4), 5–7.

Pawl, J. H., & St. John, M. (1998). *How you are is as important as what you do … in making a positive difference for infants, toddlers and their families.* Washington, DC: Zero to Three: National Center for Infants, Toddlers, and Families.

Powell, D. R. (1998). Reweaving parents into the fabric of early childhood programs. *Young Children, 53*(5), 60–67.

Rockwell, R. E., Andre, L. C., & Hawley, M. K. (1996). *Parents and teachers as partners.* Fort Worth, TX: Harcourt Brace.

Sturm, C. (1997). Creating parent-teacher dialogue: Intercultural communication in child care. *Young Children, 52*(5), 34–38.

Weston, D., & Ivins, B. (2001). From testing to talking: Linking assessment and intervention through relationships with parents. *Zero to Three, 21*(4), 47–50.

Wieder, S. (1989). Mediating successful parenting: Guidelines for practitioners. *Zero to Three, 10*(1), 34–36.

Videos

Diversity and Communication. (1996). Barrington, IL: Magna Systems, Inc. (34 min.).

Protective Urges: Working With the Feelings of Parents and Caregivers. (1992). Sacramento, CA: Far West Laboratories. (27 min.).

Chapter 10

Making Responsive Relationships Work in Your Program

A s we begin this final chapter, a quick review will help us focus on the practical aspects of making responsive relationships work. We have learned that consistent and trusting relationships with infants and toddlers are crucial for their strong emotional and cognitive development. First learning involves developing the architecture of the brain. New pathways for learning and processing information are being stimulated with each sensory experience. Caregivers provide these first learning experiences and give them meaning.

First learning is not only about practicing emerging motor skills but also about learning coping skills and social skills. It is about feelings of identity as well as feelings of discovery and mastery. First learning depends on the nurturance of caregivers. Caregivers form emotional connections with children, and this connection guides learning toward patterns of thought and action. Caregivers define experiences as good or bad. They present possibilities and solutions that will begin to give the developing child the ability to think in these ways and to gain confidence in her own inner resources.

In the preceding chapters, we have learned that early relationships affect children's feelings of anxiety and emotion regulation. When children have feelings of stability and connection during the time when their neural struc-

Goals of Chapter 10

▦ Explore the meaning of a relationship-based model of child care.

▦ Elucidate the importance of primary care.

▦ Apply the concept of ongoing primary care to a center situation.

▦ Identify solutions to existing barriers that affect continuity of caregiving.

▦ Understand how to adjust the daily schedule and staffing patterns so that relationship building remains the foremost goal.

▦ Understand how to collaborate in planning environments and materials for young children to enhance relationship building, scaffolding, motivation, and mastery.

▦ Realize how team members can profit from planning curriculum together.

▦ Learn to use empowering language to propose and effect change.

▦ Understand how self-reflection, especially with a supportive staff person, can enhance professional growth.

▦ Envision yourself as a caregiver and a team member who collaborates to carry out quality care through relationship building.

tures are being formed, their ability to control anxiety, to make choices, and to express feelings will be enhanced. Caregivers need to be consistently available and emotionally connected to the children in their care.

In this chapter, we will examine the practical aspects of relationship building within the child-care setting. How can we as child-care providers plan programs and systems that promote and preserve emotional connections as well as provide for consistency in responsive relationships? Workers in each child-care setting face different hurdles. This chapter will examine some of the obstacles that block consistency of care. It will present ideas and strategies that may help you design and support individualized responsive care plans within your work sites.

This chapter also will suggest ways for child-care providers to maintain their own equilibrium. It will explore techniques that will help you to benefit from self-reflection, emotional refueling, and positive affirmation of your needs and beliefs. Relationship building is as important among staff members as it is with children. Positive, responsive relationships among coworkers can lead to solutions that make a child-care center or child-care home a great place for both adults and children.

Key Concept One
A Relationship-Based Model Is Vital

Infants and toddlers flourish when they are emotionally attached to their caregivers. When children spend a significant part of the day in child care, away from their families, they must be able to continue to find an attachment base within the child-care setting. These feelings of stability and safety, which attachment relationships bring, are what most parents are hoping their children will experience when they leave them in child care.

The first goal of the child-care center should be to provide each child with this continuity of attachment, which involves pairing each child with a caregiver who is attuned to the child's emotional cues and who has formed a trust-based relationship with the child. Infants and toddlers rely on their caregivers to know their scheduling needs for naps and food. They rely on their caregivers to know their temperamental triggers of overstimulation or anxiety. They rely on their caregivers to be responsive to their emotional changes, for example, knowing when they need a hug, where they can find their "blanket," or when they need some autonomy. For meaningful development and learning to take place, these infants and toddlers need to feel safe and attached to their caregivers at the center.

The primary-care model provides this attachment figure. In this model, trust-based relationships can be established with one adult, who will remain available to the child. More and more, parents realize that, when their child is at the center or in family child care, the caregiver—more than the facility, toys, or curriculum—will have the most effect on their child's development.

Each child-care site will need to define its goals for attaining relationship-based care. To provide a primary-care model, many changes may need to be made in staffing patterns, routines, and physical space. Ideally, all infants will experience some primary care and will remain with the same caregiver until they reach 3 years old. This continuity of relationship is invaluable, especially at a time when children are beginning to form their sense of identity (Who am I? What is my power? How do I fit in?).

Each time a child has a new caregiver, the child has to focus emotional energy on seeking and forming another trusted relationship. This effort causes anxiety and disequilibrium for the child and interrupts learning. When caregivers change often, children may experience chronic anxiety, even when centers are safe, clean, and well appointed.

Primary Care Does Not Mean Exclusive Care

The approach with which caregivers share the care becomes a viable solution to the reality that caregivers must take breaks, vacations, and sick leave as well as move on to other employment. During these times, other caregivers in the center who are familiar with the children help sustain them through these changes. For example, if a primary provider of infants and toddlers will not be moving with her group into the 2-year-old room, then the teacher of the 2-year-old classroom visits the toddler room and joins the children's lunchtime for several days a week. Later, their own teacher takes them to visit the 2-year-old room for brief periods. Ideally, when the children change to their new classroom, their own teacher moves with them for a few days, then gradually decreases his time there, allowing the relationships to grow between the children and their new teacher.

Because some centers are open 12 hours a day, the primary caregiver's working day may not match the children's hours. That caregiver will need to entrust her group of children to other members of the team, just as a parent might depend on a regular baby-sitter. The goal here is to provide consistency of care.

As infants mature, they will be able to relate to more caregivers, but they will need to establish a feeling of safety and trust with each one. Working as a team, caregivers can plan to share some tasks that will help each child feel comfortable with the other team members. If those who are sharing the care are consistently the same people, then toddlers will gradually expand their meaningful relationships.

Sometimes, a child will become so closely attached to one caregiver that he cries when left with another. Caregivers need to pay particular attention to the separation anxiety that this child is expressing. Helping the child adapt to another team member is important. The team's planning for sharing the care will gradually ease the anxiety and tensions a child may feel when transitions must occur.

Barriers to Continuity of Care Will Exist

Relationship-based care may be a center's first priority, but each center will encounter different problems in carrying out the model. Working though the barriers requires dedication among the staff members to the relationship-based model. It also requires time and patience. For some centers, developing a plan for continuity of care is a process that evolves over time. The pros and cons of each decision must be heard and discussed by all caregivers to ensure that most of them feel committed to the joint goal. Even if primary care is not currently an option for some centers, relationship building is possible. Each caregiver must work to connect at a shared emotional level with each child who is entrusted to her care. The following sections describe some typical barriers to continuity of care.

Resistance to change will be one barrier that will need to be overcome. Including staff members in designing creative staffing patterns that allow for responsive care can be a way to combat resistance to change. One center may plan mixed-age groupings, giving each caregiver a range of ages, as in a family or family-care home. Another center may prefer to keep a group of children with their caregivers throughout their time in the center, moving the caregivers with the children as they progress from the infant room to the toddler room. New enrollees would be placed with their age group as vacancies occur.

A third program effectively accomplishes continuity of care by moving one caregiver with his group to merge with another caregiver and her children. The original caregiver remains with the combined groups for a length of time, providing an extra hand, while the children adapt to their new situation. For example, a caregiver might move with a group of infants as they join a toddler group. Then, when the older toddlers in the group graduate to a 2-year-old room, their primary caregiver would move with them to join the 2-year-olds or perhaps he would return to the infant room to enroll another group of babies.

For this kind of change to occur, caregivers must be enthusiastic about making big changes in their schedules and accustomed procedures. Although this model is more interesting and varied in a teaching day, it requires more knowledge and skill from the caregivers to advance across this broad developmental spectrum from 2 months to 2 years.

Teacher–child ratio can be a barrier to primary care. Traditionally, classrooms in child-care settings have been age based to simplify meeting developmental needs. Classroom size and teacher–child ratios are usually defined by state and local regulations. Although these standards are designed to ensure safety, they represent maximum limits. Caregivers may need to be forceful in promoting their commitment to adopting policies that support a relationship-based model with no more than four children per caregiver.

Teachers' beliefs and preferences may be a barrier. For example, in a relationship-based model, a caregiver may be asked to move from a classroom that he feels is "his" teaching home. Some caregivers may be resistant to becoming attached to only one group of children, knowing that these children will eventually move on and that the caregivers will feel a sense of loss. Sometimes, teachers are wary about being asked to become team members with unfamiliar staff members. Other caregivers may feel that they are experts with only one age group of children. Addressing these types of issues in staff meetings where many ideas are brought to bear is a valuable way to move the group toward commitment to a primary-care model.

High staff turnover is a serious impediment to continuity of care. Public policy changes, higher staff salaries, and support from child-care administrators will be needed to mitigate high staff turnover. Maintaining the balance between adequate caregiver salaries and what parents can afford to pay is problematic. Until parents begin to understand the value of primary care and work to implement policy change within our society, centers will struggle with funding the primary-care model. Child-care providers must continually work to educate the public and to find alternative ways to accomplish their primary-care goals.

Key Concept Two
Caregivers Can Influence Change

In your place of employment, you may find that factors such as the schedule, class routines, classroom environments, materials, and curriculum planning do not meet your expectations. If your goal is to provide relationship-based care, you will need to strive toward appropriate changes in these areas. Responsive caregivers do more than just "be available." They plan the when, the who, and the how that a child comes to expect in child care. As you join a center's staff or manage your own child care, you will need skills for effecting change and carrying out new ideas.

Positive Solutions Influence Change

The overriding rule for negotiating change is to remain positive. As a frontline staff member, you can often identify changes that would help you and others be more responsive to the children. When these ideas for change are proposed in a positive light, they may appeal to many others. You will gain allies in your cause. There are specific techniques that can help you present your ideas for change: (a) state your ideas in a positive way, (b) provide a valid rationale for the change, and (c) present viable solutions. The following scenario shows an example of these techniques in action.

> The caregivers for the toddler room saw that their ability to meet as a team at nap time was always interrupted by the few children who were hard to settle down. At a staff meeting, one member of the team reported that, at another center, a staff member from another team would substitute during the nap period so that the team could meet without interruption. This process was repeated throughout the week in different classes so that all teams could use this time for planning.
>
> Because the other teaching teams were also experiencing this problem, they were in favor of trying the proposed plan. Someone suggested that each team could meet in the hall outside the nap room, so that they would be in earshot of their children. The director suggested, "Let's try using our floater, Ms. Locket. She is familiar to the children, and that will be a good use of her time."

In this situation, the director responded quickly to the staff's suggestions. They seemed reasonable and positive to her. Suggestions are not always received so readily, however. Change may not be easy in light of budgets, regulations, and interpersonal staff needs. This team suggested a viable solution that did not extend the budget. If you decide to suggest a change in procedure, you will need to be patient. The process of transforming an idea into a concrete plan of action takes time.

Learn to Disagree Amicably

An important skill to learn is how to disagree in a friendly way. Large families and small communities must master this skill for survival. Discussing and resolving disagreements works best when you can keep a problem separate from your emotions. By keeping the mission or goal for your group foremost in mind, the discussion can remain more focused. Accept the fact that, although you may not get your way, you will have been heard. The following process outlines one formula that you can use to initiate change:

   — *Identify your concerns and frame them clearly in your mind.* When you present your concerns, plan to frame them as a problem for either you or the children in your care. Define how this problem affects responsive caregiving (e.g., "I am concerned about ...," "It is hard for our team to ...," "It is difficult for our children when ...").

— *Clarify reasons for change.* Keep the best interests of children as an overriding goal for the group when you present reasons for change. Describe how the change will positively affect the children and their care. Remain focused on one issue at a time. Do not present your entire wish list.

— *Present one or more solutions to the problem.* Propose change in a way that is practical for the center situation. How will your solution affect other caregivers and staff members? How will it affect the budget? Represent the viewpoints of others, including parents, being sensitive to their needs.

— *Think ahead about what concerns others might raise.* Define a plan that will work. Think of ways that your solutions can be put into effect easily.

— *Restate your idea and find out whether clarification is needed.* If others do not respond to your idea, rephrase your plan. Ask questions and discuss the problem to be sure that it is understood.

— *Listen to others' points of view.* Request alternate solutions from your team or your supervisors. Be open to their suggestions. Others may suggest ways of solving this issue that may also be viable.

— *Focus on resolution.* Ask the meeting chairperson to summarize the discussion in light of the goals of the center. Request or state a possible solution and ask for consensus. Then, summarize what you understand to be the group's thinking and the reasons for the decision.

— *Bring the discussion to a conclusion.* If changes cannot be made at this time, be sure that you ask for a summary explanation of the reasons. This summary will clarify the problem and the resolution for the group. Thank the group for considering your concern, and show your positive resolve to try their solution.

— *Present your idea at a later date.* If your concern was not satisfactorily resolved or your idea not accepted, present it again later. Sometimes, others need a period of time to think through and envision the benefits of change.

Knowing that our concerns have been heard and considered by the group can be emotionally satisfying. We feel a sense of personal value when we are part of making a difference in the functioning of the work place or of changing others' awareness about how to respond to children.

Carrying Out Changes in Time, Space, and Curriculum Is Important

Time management is crucial for responsive care. The routines or schedules of the day will set expectations about relationships for children, parents, and team members. These schedules establish expectations for the child about who will be there and when activities will occur. Adults and children become attached to these routines. They represent comfort zones from which confidence and communication can blossom. Because learning and connection occur within these comfort zones, we must carefully plan and preserve scheduling patterns that allow enough time for meaningful connections to occur.

Each caregiver should have some freedom to design her day so that events flow smoothly. The caregiver must be able to allot time for unhurried one-on-one interactions. She must be able to adapt the schedule quickly to meet the emotional and physical needs of a particular child. Staff collaboration is necessary to schedule sufficient staff members to respond at hectic times such as arrivals and departures, meal times, or late afternoon as children anticipate the arrival of their parents. The following scenario describes a typical hectic scene.

> Carrie comes in early to prepare for her morning shift in the toddler room. Four parents arrive simultaneously at 7:15 a.m. and hurriedly drop off their children. Within just a few minutes, Johnny and Jamie, the new twins (16 months old), are handed into Carrie's arms and begin to cry as their parents depart. Trixie and Delbert (both 22 months old) and Chris (18 months old) run past Carrie, eager to see one another. They begin to play chase around the classroom. Carrie feels frazzled already. She wants time to connect with arriving parents because she feels that morning is the best time to communicate with them. She knows that her supervisor also believes that morning drop-off is a good time to connect with parents. She is anxious to calm the two fussing children in her arms but feels that she must first regulate the three children who are running wildly around the classroom. As her tension builds, the two unhappy children in her arms squirm and cry louder.

The chaos that Carrie feels will also affect the parents and others around her. Carrie can work with her team and supervisor to find alternate ways of bringing a sense of calm to the early morning routine. They can carry out small but important changes in staffing patterns or find other ideas to bring the desired comfort zone back to the morning greeting period.

Floating staff members enhance a relationship-based model. Creative use of floating staff can give caregivers more one-on-one time with children. For example, when the primary caregiver needs to devote her attention to the child who requires special care, a floating staff person can spend time with the rest of the group. Extra staff members might be helpful when a child has special feeding problems or difficulty sleeping. A child who is experiencing difficulty in regulating behavior will also require extra monitoring by staff members. In these instances, the teaching team, along with a consistent extra person, can plan an effective way for one member of the team to devote more time to a single child. It may be best for a child with special needs to establish a relationship with a floating staff member who always feeds him so that the primary caregiver is freed up to be available to the other children.

Responsive caregivers plan routines that follow the needs of children. In the infant room, the daily schedule should be designed to follow each baby's biological rhythms of quiet and active play, eating, diapering, as well as rest and sleep. When these routines are planned and the baby's needs are met, the day flows smoothly for both child and caregiver. When a primary caregiver is responsible for only three infants, she can organize her schedule around these children. The babies will come to trust that she will be attuned to their needs, sensing that, "My caregiver knows when I am getting hungry. She will hold me and talk with me then."

When routines are planned and the baby's needs are met, the day flows smoothly for both child and caregiver.

As children mature, their scheduling needs change. The physical, emotional, and mastery needs of each child will dictate the needed routines. A primary-care model will be the most responsive to these changing needs because primary caregivers will be familiar with the children. As an infant matures, the child-care provider remains aware of the child's body rhythms and physical needs, knowing when the child becomes hungry and how quickly he tires. The caregiver knows how easily the child integrates into a group activity. These are factors that are ever changing as the toddler matures. A primary caregiver can advise other staff members on how to help this child adapt to the group routines or when to expand active learning and social experiences. The primary caregiver observes when the daily routines are not matching a child's needs and then can collaborate with the teaching team to make necessary changes.

At certain times, teaching-team members must go beyond their classrooms to solve issues. To change policy or centerwide routines, team members will need to present their concerns to supervisors. For example, when lunch is scheduled to arrive at noon, some toddlers are overly tired, even falling asleep, with their heads dropping on their plates. Supervisors will be the ones to influence policies that involve centerwide scheduling such as those affecting lunchtime. Similarly, by the end of the afternoon, many of the infants become irritable. Extra staff members can be helpful to hold and calm these babies. Staff members can anticipate possible problem areas and work with the broader staff and supervisors to help children get food when they are hungry, sleep when they are tired, and have more arms to hold them when they seem to need it. Everyone on the staff is your ally, including the kitchen staff, those doing housekeeping, and the bus driver. Collaboration is the key.

Plan environments that are child focused and that allow responsive caregiving. The physical configuration and floor area of child-care center classrooms vary widely. While planning spaces that are responsive to infants and toddlers, the teaching team must be creative. Spaces should maintain continuity of connection. In a relationship-based model, the children will expect to have eye contact with their primary caregivers even when they are happily playing alone. When planning environments that foster responsive relationships, caregivers must remember that visual or physical contact with the caregiver must be available for all children. The floor space or interest areas should be arranged so that children and caregiver can engage in floor play together or so that children playing alone will also feel near their caregivers.

> *When planning environments, caregivers must remember that visual or physical contact with the caregiver must be available for all children.*

Because the needs of young children are different, each classroom environment will be different. Caregivers must constantly rethink the design of space within their classrooms. The best classroom spaces are ones that have multiple uses and are able to be changed easily. Spaces must be flexible because they will need to be shaped and reshaped to meet the changing developmental needs of the children.

In the infant room, space is designed with satellite areas surrounding a central zone. Central carpeted floor space should be large enough for the caregiver to sit and be surrounded by infants who may be lying down, sitting, crawling, and pulling up to cruise. The caregiver becomes the hub, and the children surround her, sometimes near and sometimes at a distance. The caregiver will place the nonmobile baby in a safe space that allows eye contact. Some mobile children will meander farther away, but they will still maintain their visual connection with the caregiver (see Figure 10.1).

In toddler rooms, space is organized into interest areas. The room is arranged so that the mobile child feels secure in wandering around the room, moving freely to different interest areas. The more focused child should have an area and material for playing either alone or one-on-one with a caregiver. In addition, the space should provide areas for children to interact in small-group activities such as constructing block buildings or climbing on the toddler tower, which require a larger space (see Figure 10.2).

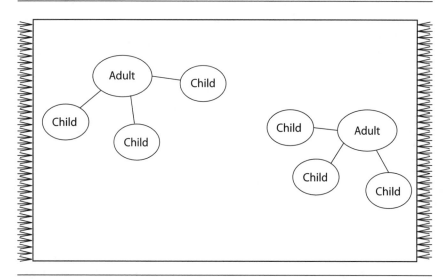

Figure 10.1. Space arrangement for satellite care.

A design that allows the caregiver to be available to all of the children also provides important benefits to toddlers. The caregiver must remain aware of what all children are doing so that he can respond when a child connects with a smile or show of pride as well as when a child withdraws or shows anger. The design should allow the caregiver to connect with children individually to scaffold play or to regulate emotions.

Some children play in an interest area because of the presence of a loved caregiver; others, because of their love of the task. Children will cluster around their caregiver wherever she is. Often, they all choose to do the same activity at the same time. If a caregiver wishes to encourage different activities for the group of children, changing the space configuration can be helpful. Sometimes, team members place themselves at different activity centers, thus giving the children two focal points. If you are particularly interested in focusing an individual child toward a different type of activity, then ask another team member to help by inviting the child to join with another group.

Safe spaces promote mastery. When children are safe, they are more likely to feel confident to explore or expand their learning. The rapid pace and variability of developmental change can demand that caregivers be constantly vigilant about safety issues. Toddlers like to explore and spend most of their time practicing motor skills. They will be climbing, jumping, and running. They need uncluttered areas. In many instances, they try maneuvers that they are not yet competent to manage—such as climbing too high or pulling something heavy off a high shelf. A primary caregiver knows the competencies of each child and can arrange the area to promote both safety and autonomy.

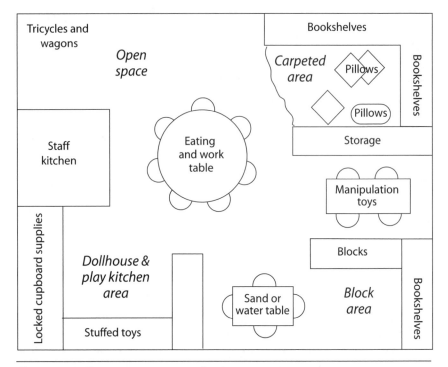

Figure 10.2. Room arrangement using interest areas.

Respond to safety issues immediately. When caregivers notice that one child's activity is impeding another's safety, they respond immediately by redesigning the space to provide safe areas for both children. The mobile infant who is crawling about demands caregiver attention not only for the safety of the crawler but also for the safety of other infants who might be sitting unsteadily or lying close by. The arrangement of furniture, big pillows, and bolsters can provide freedom, flexibility, and structure for the caregiver and the children. Low shelves make movable barriers that the caregiver can quickly rearrange and over which he can see. These changes can bring back the comfort zone for the child and the caregiver. The crawler can continue her motor activity while the nonmobile infant can remain safely on the other side of a bolster or in a soft "play pool" rimmed in pillows.

Teaching-team members should discuss each child's mastery goals so that they can plan spaces that are safe, inviting, and enriching. The teaching team must continually reassess how spaces are being used and discuss creative ways to make the environment more effective for responsive care.

Responsive caregivers affect curriculum decisions. In chapter 7, we learned that curriculum should be child focused. Members of each teaching team must have the flexibility to define and change their curriculum so that it follows the developing interests and needs of their group of children. Some teaching teams are driven to propose using prescribed methods or an academically focused curriculum for toddlers and 2-year-olds. Many parents are pushing for high stimulation programs that urge children to accomplish many structured activities throughout the day. Yet we have learned that children of this age learn most from pursuing their individual interests. Their development is best enhanced when they are provided experiences that follow their motivations and when they are allowed the autonomy to learn at their own speed. A love of learning comes when the caregiver relationship supports a child's feelings of self-mastery.

Key Concept Three
Caregivers Need Emotional Refueling

The multiple roles of caregiving require considerable emotional energy. Although caring for children is a rewarding job, it also is a physically and emotionally demanding job. Caregivers get few moments for breaks, walks, personal space, or collegiality. Replenishing or refueling our emotional energy will be necessary to remain resilient and responsive to others.

To be responsive, we must "be present" in our minds. We need to clear away the "I should have, I ought to, I wish I was" thoughts that can run constantly through our heads. Even in the best of situations, we will have "down days." Some days, the children may seem more demanding. We may have disagreements with team members or with friends that can absorb our thoughts and distract us. At these times, it is easy to become angry with children in our care or with ourselves. Sometimes, we may resent parents who give us orders or who fuss about extra fees or salary changes. The task is complex, with demands from many different people and responsibilities. The following sections describe ways to maintain equilibrium and strengthen yourself in your job.

Self-Reflection Is Important for Emotional Refueling

Self-reflection involves taking time to assess within ourselves the emotions we experience. By paying attention to what emotional events or emotional preoccupations are filling our minds, we can begin to understand what gets in the way of our positive interactions. Small events or comments can loom large in our minds and interfere with our abilities to be emotionally fed by the joys and laughter of the children we serve.

When something frustrates you, ask yourself, as you would ask a child, "What were your goals? What got in the way? What were your alternatives?" Be honest with yourself. Were you angry because you did not get your way?

Was your power threatened or were your goals challenged? Were the actions of another person purposeful or inadvertent?

Through self-reflection, we can explore the possible feelings of the other person and our own underlying feelings. What did the other person do to make us angry or sad? What were his goals? What got in his way? Were we responsive to the other person? This process helps us see reasons for the other person's actions and for our responses. By practicing self-reflection, we will find that we increase our ability to handle similar situations with less intense emotions. We develop skills for moving through a potentially negative situation by keeping our focus on the child.

> *Through self-reflection, we can explore the possible feelings of the other person and our own underlying feelings.*

Self-reflection also includes complimenting ourselves. Each day, we will experience things that go well and that we know we have influenced. Be sure to mark these in your mind. Look in the mirror at night and say, "Good job," or, "Good day." Do not assume that the hugs you give out and the wise thoughts you contribute are not noticed or effective. They are perhaps the most motivating force toward positive change. Consistently being supportive and positive in relationships takes special effort and a special person. Your efforts are valuable contributions to your team and the children in your care. Take a bow!

Ask Others to Help You Reflect

Sharing your feelings is another way to refuel. Asking others to help you reflect on your feelings is another way to find emotional balance. Good practice should provide time for caregivers to share their feelings. This process is part of professional development and professional competence. We have all experienced the same pitfalls and emotional stress that go with being a child-care provider. By sharing experiences with other staff members, we will be continually learning new things and improving our skills.

If staff meetings are not regularly scheduled, you should ask for this kind of sharing support from your coworkers. If possible, some staff meetings should be arranged in which staff members are encouraged to share feelings and frustrations with a person experienced in counseling. These sessions should not be allowed to become gripe sessions. When caregivers assess their feelings by sharing them with others, they also are examining their actions. A teammate or a supervisor can support caregivers by listening and guiding them toward self-reflection and positive resolution. The following scenario, in which Amanda recalls how she assessed a problem with her supervisor during her first year of teaching, presents an example of this process.

> As caregiver in the 2-year-old room, I was intent on showing my team members that I was competent. One fall day, the room was unusually warm. While Steven was getting ready for nap time, I noticed that he had on a long-sleeved shirt and a cardigan sweater that was buttoned up. It seemed that his parent had prepared him in case the day turned cold. After I watched him take off his shoes, I asked, "Do you want to take off your sweater?" "No," Steven answered. "Why don't you take it off?" I said. "It's really warm in here. You will feel better." "No," he said firmly, holding onto the sleeves.
>
> I knew he would be too warm and would have trouble sleeping, so I began pulling the sweater off, saying, "Steven, we need to take this off." "N-no," he stammered, holding onto his sweater tightly with his arms crossed over his stomach. I continued to insist and pulled and tugged at the sweater until it was off. Steven fell on the cot sobbing softly. I laid the sweater on a chair and left him alone. Steven did not go to sleep.
>
> Later, I sought out my supervisor to talk about the situation. She asked me how I was feeling when Steven said no to me. "I was angry," I said. "I wanted to help him feel better, and I thought that, once I got started with my demands, I should not back down." I told her, "I know now that I should not have asked him if he wanted to take off the sweater."
>
> My supervisor listened, then asked, "What was Steven feeling?" I replied, "At first, I thought he was being defiant, but later, I saw that he was expressing his choice of whether or not he would wear the sweater during his nap." My supervisor helped me see the importance of listening to the child. I suddenly changed my thinking. I told her, "Perhaps Steven felt attached to the sweater. Maybe if I had left him with the choice, he later would have felt that he was too hot and would have chosen to take it off himself. He would have been making decisions for himself. Then there would have been no confrontation, and the child would feel confident in his ability to self-regulate." After answering that question, I realized how my feelings changed after looking at this situation from Steven's point of view.

Amanda's discussion with her supervisor helped her work through a situation that was not only bothering her but also overriding her emotions. Her understanding supervisor provided a scaffold for Amanda to gain insight into her experience. The supervisor allowed Amanda to reflect on and assess much of her experience herself by being present as a listener and by focusing Amanda on not only the child's feelings but also her own. This shared reflection will better equip Amanda to monitor herself in the future. Caregivers need to have someone to talk with at any time when strong feelings interfere with their ability to respond to the children in their care. When a caregiver can trust his or her colleagues to listen and give supportive guidance, then he or she will grow as a professional.

Let others be your support system. Team members should observe and respond to one another's emotional signals. They should be available to support a caregiver who is in disequilibrium. If team members inquire about your feelings or offer to listen, accept their concern. Sharing problems is often helpful. Consider the following scenario.

> The eight children in the toddler room know one another well. They all gravitate to the same activity at the same time. Maria is the only caregiver in the room. She walks over to the climbing loft, where the children are swarming over one another. "Jonny and Sarah, come with me. We can play in the sand." The children ignore her. Suddenly she claps her hands and says in a loud, commanding voice, "Stop! Everyone stop. No more free play. I want you to sit down, now!"
>
> Her teammate returns to the classroom as this scene is happening. She goes to Maria and gives her a hug. "I'm back. Thanks for the relief. Shall we put some music on and do a group dance?"

When a team member listens to another caregiver's distress, she will be helping to regulate her colleague's emotions. All of us need to feel that others care about us. If the time seems hectic or if your colleague says, "I'm fine," then you might later ask that person whether he needs a break or wants to talk. This question will be an opening for him to share. When staff members support one another with emotion sharing, they enhance a positive spirit of collaboration. This kind of responsiveness will make your work easier, and your day with the children will be more fun.

Interpersonal problems among staff members are not uncommon. For one caregiver, a situation may pose large problems, yet for another, the same situation may not be a problem. Power struggles or misunderstandings within teams will occur. Building a team takes a great deal of compromise. The team needs to make time to hear and understand one another's feelings and points of view.

When a caregiver experiences interpersonal problems, it often helps for her to understand the role that she played in the negative interaction. Then, she can take the initiative to change the behavior or dynamic involved. Without placing blame on anyone, this caregiver will learn about herself and make personal changes. Negative experiences can be catalysts for self-improvements.

Children are observant. They pick up on the emotional cues of their caregivers. They sense the emotional changes in a caregiver after a confrontation with a colleague, and they feel the caregiver's anger. When caregivers resolve their problems, children will then sense that the negative emotions have changed to positive emotions. Of course, children will be relieved, but they will also benefit from realizing that adults repair their negative feelings through actively solving problems.

Personnel turnover makes relationship building among staff members a continual challenge. With changes in the staff, new relationships must be established. This process will take time and effort. Maintaining collegiality and cooperation is done most effectively when team conferences are scheduled on a regular basis. Frequent meetings allow more time for casual interactions and pleasantries to be exchanged. As interests and feelings are shared in the group, shared understanding increases. Staff members are more apt to solve issues before they escalate. Caregivers should request regularly scheduled meetings that will allow for creative planning and relationship building.

> *Caregivers should request regularly scheduled meetings that will allow for creative planning and relationship building.*

Humor is an excellent tool to defuse tensions. Infants and toddlers are so charming and so unpredictable that many unexpected events happen each day in a child-care center. Caregivers have a warehouse of funny stories to share. If you cultivate the habit of sharing and referring to these stories often, then you will find less staff friction. Also, when tensions arise, rely on your sense of humor to defuse the situation. Take into consideration your tone of voice and facial expressions as you indicate that you are looking for solutions, not a fight. If possible, start talking about your concerns with a story that will invest your listeners and lead them to your point.

Take every opportunity to make work a pleasant place for colleagues and children. Whenever possible, laugh with colleagues. Use nap time to talk about your interests outside of the work place, like movies and magazines. Bring special treats for these adult fun times. Bring cartoons to work. Bring a flower for the classroom or for a coworker. These gestures make a difference.

Reward Yourself: Take Care of You

The most important element in caring for infants and toddlers is you! As a primary caregiver, you provide the ongoing relationship, the emotional connection, the environment, and the curriculum for the children in your care. The children in your care will feed you with their love and laughter, but you will need your own emotional strength to withstand their persistent demands. Remember, your job should allow you to ask for emotional support and to request what you need in the way of materials, supplies, space, and time. When you are not caring for children, you should plan to do the things you love. Think about what refuels you. Make time for yourself to luxuriate in a bubble bath, take a walk in the park, participate in a sport, or curl up with a good book. It is important that you take care of yourself.

As caregivers, our emotional stability will have a positive effect on the children we care for and on our relationship with staff members. When we come to work refreshed and revitalized, we will promote the shared positive emotions so vital for first learning. Shared positive emotions involve an exchange of positive feelings. These feelings go two ways; when we give our love and respect, we will receive replenishment. Relationship-based care depends on our being able to be responsive and positive to the children for whom we provide care.

Chapter Summary

Relationships are catalysts for learning in the first 3 years. Responsive relationships foster healthy emotional development. Responsive relationships also provide experiences and give support that will stimulate cognitive and social growth. The goal of every child-care provider should be to provide relationship-based care. Primary care with four or fewer children per caregiver will help us achieve our goal of being child focused and able to observe and respond to each child.

Primary care involves establishing continuity of care. Collaboration among the team of providers, supervisors, and support staff is vital. Caregivers will need to use negotiating skills in working within a team and in effecting positive change. As caregivers, we will be responsible for planning the schedule, the environment, and the curriculum that will be responsive to each of the children. We must keep lobbying for our needs. Our ability to stay positive will help us overcome the many barriers that we may encounter.

To be a responsive caregiver, we must find ways to refuel our own emotions. Using self-reflection, asserting our needs, seeking help when needed, and treating ourselves to some personal time are effective ways to refuel. Our emotional energy will help us find confidence and joy in our ability to be good relationship builders. The children in our care will reward us with their love and their learning.

Resources

Bernhardt, J. L. (2000). A primary caregiving system for infants and toddlers: Best for everyone involved. *Young Children, 55*(2), 74–80.

Bertacchi, J., & Norman-Murch, T. (1999). Implementing reflective supervision in non-clinical settings: Challenges to practice. *Zero to Three, 20*(1), 18–23.

Brazelton, T. B., & Greenspan, S. (2000). Our window to the future [Your Child Special 2000 Edition]. *Newsweek,* 34–36.

Butterfield, P. M., Dolezal, S., & Knox, R. M. (1995). *Love is layers of sharing.* Denver, CO: How to Read Your Baby.

Feeney, S., Christensen, D., & Moravcik, E. (2000). *Who am I in the lives of young children?* (6th ed.). Columbus, OH: Merrill Prentice Hall.

Field, B. (1992). Toward tenacity of commitment: Understanding and modifying institutional practices and individual responses that impede work with multi-problem families. In E. Fenichel (Ed.), *Learning through supervision and mentorship* (pp. 125–131). Arlington, VA: Zero to Three: National Center for Infants, Toddlers, and Families.

Gilkerson, L., & Young-Holt, C. L. (1992). Supervision and management of programs serving infants, toddlers, and their families. In E. Fenichel (Ed.), *Learning through supervision and mentorship* (pp. 113–119). Arlington, VA: Zero to Three: National Center for Infants, Toddlers, and Families.

Gordon, T. (1974). *Teacher effectiveness training.* New York: David McKay.

Greenman, J. (1988). *Caring spaces, learning places: Children's environments that work.* Redmond, WA: Exchange Press.

Greenman, J., & Stonehouse, A. (1996). *Prime times.* St. Paul, MN: Redleaf Press.

Honig, A. S. (1993). Mental health for babies: What do theory and research teach us? *Young Children, 48*(3), 69–76.

Howes, C. (1998). Continuity of care: The importance of infant, toddler, caregiver relationships. *Zero to Three, 18*(6), 7–11.

Jorde-Bloom, P. (1988). *A great place to work.* Washington, DC: National Association for the Education of Young Children.

McMullen, M. B. (1999). Achieving best practices in infant and toddler care and education. *Young Children, 54*(4), 69–76.

Pekarsky, J. (1992). Scenes from supervision. In E. Fenichel (Ed.), *Learning through supervision and mentorship* (pp. 53–55). Arlington, VA: Zero to Three: National Center for Infants, Toddlers, and Families.

Glossary

associative play   Playing with others, but without sharing common roles and goals (Chapter 5, Key Concept 3).

attunement   Tuning in to a child's physical and emotional needs and focus of interest (Chapter 2, Key Concept 2).

autonomous   Self-directed, independent; pursuing one's own actions (Chapter 4, Key Concept 3).

axon   An extension of the neuron through which messages are sent to other neurons (Chapter 1).

baby watching   Observing detailed behavior and reading emotion cues (Chapter 1, Key Concept 3).

behavior regulation   Changing or controlling behavior through planning, guidance, and emotion sharing, either through relationships or self-control (Chapter 6, Key Concept 1).

biological system   Inborn behaviors and reflexes (Chapter 1, Key Concept 1).

caregiver-family alliance   A working relationship between family and caregiver (Chapter 9, Key Concept 3).

child-directed speech   Changing regular speech patterns and words to attune to a child's level of language comprehension (Chapter 8, Key Concept 1).

cognition   Complex thought, the process of knowing, planning, problem solving, integrating knowledge, and defining resources (Chapter 7, Key Concept 1).

collaborative planning   Planning done by a team of caregivers together (Chapter 10, Key Concept 1).

comfort zone   The emotional balance felt when needs are met (Chapter 10, Key Concept 2).

competent infant   A baby with the inborn ability to connect with caregivers and tune in or tune out stimulation (Chapter 1, Key Concept 1).

complex learning   Thinking processes that involve reasoning and problem solving (Chapter 7, Key Concept 1).

conjugating verbs   Using the pattern or rules for different forms of the same word, such as "I am, she is, we are" as correct forms of the verb "to be" (Chapter 8, Key Concept 1).

continuity   A match; the feeling resulting when actions meet expectations, such as when expectations between home and school are similar (Chapter 9, Key Concept 2).

continuity of care   A situation in which a primary caregiver remains with the same child through age 2 or 3 (Chapter 10, Key Concept 1).

deferred imitation   Copying actions that were observed at another time (Chapter 7, Key Concept 2).

dendrite   An extension of the neuron that receives messages from other neurons (Chapter 1).

discipline   Guiding a child toward a standard of acceptable behavior and self-control. Being able to define the causes of disequilibrium in a child and to repair them (Chapter 6, Key Concept 1).

discontinuity   A mismatch; the feeling resulting when actions do not meet expectations, such as when expectations between home and school are different (Chapter 9, Key Concept 2).

disequilibrium   Out of balance, unsteady, in need (Chapter 6, Key Concept 1).

emotion cues or signals   Feelings and needs communicated through face, voice tones, actions, and body postures (Chapter 1, Key Concept 2).

emotion regulation   A situation in which one person is able to calm or balance another's extreme emotions by sharing their own positive feelings (Chapter 3, Key Concept 3).

emotion sharing   A state in which one person feels the emotion of another, such as another's joy, sadness, or anger (Chapter 3, Key Concept 1).

emotional availability   Ability to connect with a person on an emotional level (Chapter 2, Key Concept 2).

emotional connection   A shared understanding of the feelings of another (Chapter 1, Key Concept 2).

emotional refueling   Changing a negative emotional perspective to a positive perspective, for example, by having fun, sharing problems, or finding hugs (Chapter 10, Key Concept 3).

emotional scaffolding   Supporting and encouraging another's emotions (Chapter 4, Key Concept 3).

equilibrium   Feeling of balance or well-being in emotional, mental, and physical states (Chapter 1, Key Concept 1).

expansion   Adults lengthening a child's phrase by adding a new word to enhance language learning (Chapter 8, Key Concept 1).

extreme behaviors   Behaviors that are dangerous to others or to oneself, such as biting, kicking, throwing, or screaming (Chapter 6, Key Concept 1).

goodness of fit   Compatibility of the child's temperament with that of the caregiver (Chapter 2, Key Concept 1).

grammar   The study of word usage; the functions and preferred placement of words in sentences (Chapter 8, Key Concept 1).

identity   One's belief in oneself as an individual; the identifying characteristics of a person; his or her uniqueness (Chapter 4, Key Concept 1).

imitation   Copying actions of another (Chapter 7, Key Concept 2).

impulsive   Prone to spontaneous actions in response to strong emotions, such as excitement, surprise, anger, or fear (Chapter 6, Key Concept 1).

interest areas   Spaces designed for specific kinds of play in the classroom (Chapter 10, Key Concept 2).

internal motivation   A force or drive within us. These motivations direct our behavior and focus our emotional and physical energy (Chapter 1, Key Concept 1).

internal working model   A set of expectations derived from early experiences that shape future actions and relationships (Chapter 1, Key Concept 2).

internalized feelings   Feelings gained from others that one begins to believe about oneself, such as guilt, shame, or pride (Chapter 4, Key Concept 1).

language comprehension   Understanding the meaning of words as they are heard or read (Chapter 8, Key Concept 1).

language production   The ability to use or produce words in speech (Chapter 8, Key Concept 1).

mastery   Gaining a skill; practicing until one feels confident in one's ability (Chapter 4, Key Concept 2).

meeting the match   The situation in which a caregiver meets a child's temperament needs by reading the child's cues (Chapter 2, Key Concept 2).

mutual regulation   A situation in which each partner in a relationship modifies their feelings or behaviors in response to the other (Chapter 3, Key Concept 3).

nature   The inherent character or constitution of a person or living thing; our unique genetic mix, temperament, biologic motivations, abilities, and connections (Chapter 1, Key Concept 1).

neuron   A nerve cell (Chapter 1).

neurotransmitter   A chemical messenger that bridges the synaptic gaps between neurons (Chapter 1).

nurture   The experiences and relationships that influence and nourish growth and development (Chapter 1, Key Concept 1).

object permanence   Knowing that an object exists when it is no longer in sight (Chapter 7, Key Concept 1).

parallel play   Play focused on one's own goals, but close to and influenced by another (Chapter 5, Key Concept 3).

perception   A mental image, an awareness, a belief (Chapter 8, Key Concept 2).

pretend play   Ability to suspend reality in play and to role-play someone or something different (Chapter 7, Key Concept 2).

primary care   A situation in which one caregiver cares for the same child for two or more years (Chapter 2, Key Concept 1).

primary caregiver   One person who is identified to be consistently available to a child in care (Chapter 2, Key Concept 2).

punishment   A negative result imposed because of misbehavior (Chapter 6, Key Concept 1).

redirection   Changing a child's focus of attention. Redirecting a child's emotions and his or her area of interest from a negative situation to a positive one (Chapter 4, Key Concept 3).

reengagement   Returning to a focus of attention or activity after it has been interrupted by another event (Chapter 6, Key Concept 4).

reflective listening   Repeating statements made by another so that the speaker feels heard (Chapter 9, Key Concept 1).

reflective self-awareness   An instance when a valued person praises someone in the presence of others (Chapter 4, Key Concept 1).

relationship-based care   Child care that focuses on ongoing, emotionally connected relationships for children (Chapter 10, Key Concept 1).

repair   To restore a negative situation to a state of balance or well-being (Chapter 3, Key Concept 2).

repertoire   A list or supply of skills or actions that a person is able to perform (Chapter 7, Key Concept 3).

repetition   Repeating a word or phrase (Chapter 8, Key Concept 1).

resilience   Ability to recover from or adjust easily to change or misfortune (Chapter 3, Key Concept 2).

responsive relationship   A relationship in which interests, feelings, and needs are responded to and shared by two people (Chapter 2, Key Concept 2).

satellite zone   An area of the room in which several children are grouped around one caregiver (Chapter 10, Key Concept 2).

scaffolding   Supporting and expanding learning from within a child's interest area (Chapter 4, Key Concept 3).

secondary attachment   Another adult with whom the child feels an emotional connection, but with less intensity than the primary attachment (Chapter 9, Key Concept 1).

self-reflection   Reviewing one's actions and emotion cues by oneself or with others; becoming aware of one's temperament and emotional preoccupations and needs (Chapter 2, Key Concept 1).

self-talk   Private speech or inner dialogue to process thoughts (Chapter 8, Key Concept 2).

self-worth   Internal feelings of being valued and feeling accomplished (Chapter 4, Key Concept 2).

sensory motor learning   Infants rely on their senses and motor skills to gain an understanding of the world around them (Chapter 1, Key Concept 1).

separation anxiety   Emotional disruption when a child is left by an attachment figure (Chapter 6, Key Concept 3).

shared negative emotions (SNE)   Negative emotions shared between two people, such as fear, anger, or sadness (Chapter 3, Key Concept 2).

shared positive emotions (SPE)   Positive emotions shared between two people, such as interest, excitement, contentment, or joy (Chapter 3, Key Concept 2).

sharing the care   Planning among caregivers to sustain a child through separations from a primary caregiver or a transition to a new teacher (Chapter 10, Key Concept 1).

social norms   Rules that form expected ways of behaving in a society (Chapter 5, Key Concept 1).

social skills   Learned skills for interacting with others (Chapter 5, Key Concept 1).

socialization   Learning the dos and don'ts of human interaction, such as how to cooperate and negotiate with others (Chapter 5, Key Concept 1).

specific feedback   Specific statements that define a child's positive actions or accomplishments (Chapter 4, Key Concept 1).

states of awareness   A person's state of consciousness, such as asleep or alert, including their emotional focus from pleasure to displeasure (Chapter 1, Key Concept 1).

structuring for success   Arranging the environment, choosing objects, and making suggestions or adjustments that allow a child to succeed in a task (Chapter 4, Key Concept 3).

symbolic representation   Use of an object, word, or other symbol to represent another object or person (Chapter 7, Key Concept 2).

synapse   The space between the axon of the sending neuron and the dendrite of the receiving neuron (Chapter 1).

tantrums   A fit of high negative emotion, usually anger; an extreme reaction to a prohibition or action of another. Tantrums are often characterized by screaming, crying, pounding, kicking, throwing, or self-destructive behaviors (Chapter 6, Key Concept 4).

teachable moments   A time when someone is extremely interested and focused on a subject or action; a time when motivation to master is high (Chapter 7, Key Concept 3).

temperament   Inborn responses to internal and external stimulation (Chapter 2, Key Concept 1).

time management   Planning schedules, routines, and obligations so that the most important things get the most time. In this context, planning so that the child and the parents receive responsive attention and feel a relationship with caregivers (Chapter 10, Key Concept 2).

trust   Comfort and security felt when an adult consistently meets a child's needs (Chapter 2, Key Concept 2).

validate   To confirm, make legal, or agree (Chapter 9, Key Concept 1).

verbal activities   Songs, games, or other repeated speech patterns planned by a caregiver to promote the use of language (Chapter 8, Key Concept 1).

About the Authors

Perry M. Butterfield, MA, is retired faculty, University of Colorado Medical School, Department of Psychiatry, where she served as senior research associate to the Program for Early Developmental Studies. Her research focus is emotional development, with particular interest in social referencing of infants and parental interpretation of infant emotion cues, which led to her collaboration with Robert Emde and Joy Osofsky to develop the *IFEEL Picture Test.* She continues to serve as educator and consultant for infant mental health and parenting programs. Perry has collaborated in designing education programs and texts for parents of children with visual or auditory impairments. She has designed home visitation curriculum for parents of low-birth-weight infants and is one of the creators of the *Partners in Parenting Education* (PIPE) curriculum for teenage and high-risk parents. Her degrees are from Smith College, and the University of Colorado, Denver; Internship with Dr. Brazelton, at Boston Children's Hospital.

Carole A. Martin, PhD, has taught undergraduate and graduate courses at Colorado College, Rutgers University, Trenton State College, and the University of Wisconsin–Madison in the departments of psychology, human development, and education. She directed a university laboratory day care center and developed an interdisciplinary graduate training program for infant specialists. Her primary research interests include parent beliefs, assessment issues, and early childhood curriculum. She is a coauthor of the college textbook *Parenting: A Life Span Perspective.* Outside the university, she has worked as a consultant to early intervention programs, neonatal follow-up programs, schools, and foundations. Dr. Martin graduated from Bates College with a degree in psychology and went on to earn an MA from the University of Connecticut in child development and family relations. She received an MS in educational administration and a PhD in child and family studies from the University of Wisconsin–Madison.

Arleen Pratt Prairie, MEd, has taught early childhood education in City Colleges of Chicago for 25 years. In her teaching she has focused on preschool education, infant and toddler care, and brain development in the early years. She has developed a series of videos in infant and toddler care, produced by Magna Systems. Two of these promote quality infant and toddler care and four exemplify appropriate curriculum in center-based and home day care. Also, in conjunction with Magna Systems, she worked on the production of the video course *The Developing Child* and recently has revised eight of the original series. She is currently working on a textbook on science, math, and technology for the young child. She serves on the steering committee to develop an infant-toddler credential in her home state of Illinois. Arleen Prairie earned a BS in child development from Iowa State University, an MEd in early childhood education and, in addition, an infant studies certificate from Erikson Institute.